#YOU KNOW YOU'RE BLACK IN
FRANCE WHEN . . .

#YOU KNOW YOU'RE BLACK IN FRANCE WHEN . . .

THE FACT OF EVERYDAY ANTIBLACKNESS

TRICA KEATON

THE MIT PRESS
CAMBRIDGE, MASSACHUSETTS
LONDON, ENGLAND

The MIT Press would like to thank the anonymous peer reviewers who provided comments on drafts of this book. The generous work of academic experts is essential for establishing the authority and quality of our publications. We acknowledge with gratitude the contributions of these otherwise uncredited readers.

This book was set in Arnhem Pro and Frank New by New Best-set Typesetters Ltd. Printed and bound in the United States of America.

Library of Congress Cataloging-in-Publication Data

Names: Keaton, Trica Danielle, author.
Title: You know you're Black in France when . . . : the fact of everyday antiblackness / Trica Keaton.
Other titles: You know you are Black in France when . . .
Description: Cambridge, Massachusetts : The MIT Press, [2023] | Includes bibliographical references and index.
Identifiers: LCCN 2022011871 (print) | LCCN 2022011872 (ebook) | ISBN 9780262047784 (hardcover) | ISBN 9780262373326 (epub) | ISBN 9780262373319 (pdf)
Subjects: LCSH: Racism against Black people—France. | Black people—France—Social conditions. | France—Race relations
Classification: LCC DC34.5.B55 K43 2023 (print) | LCC DC34.5.B55 (ebook) | DDC 305.896/073044—dc23/eng/20220930
LC record available at https://lccn.loc.gov/2022011871
LC ebook record available at https://lccn.loc.gov/2022011872

10 9 8 7 6 5 4 3 2 1

For Mom, Roy, and my family

For VèVè Clark and Tyler Stovall

CONTENTS

PROLOGUE

I am often asked why I, a Black American woman who was born of racial enslavement and Jim Crow on US shores, decided to write about antiblackness in France rather than "in your own country." The short answer involves a long and ambivalent relationship with *la Métropole*—over more years than I care to divulge—where I have experienced up close its "Black Paris" of expatriate lore, its "Afrique/Antilles-sur-Seine," and its wretched underside where economic precarity and abusive policing inflict immeasurable damage. Then there is my dear mother's wisdom and example that have continually taught me that we must fight "the battle" wherever we are; and so it has been. The longer answer lies in the pages ahead, in the lived experiences of French people racialized-as-black in an officially raceblind France that negates both their existence and the antiblackness suffered in the everyday. Much, then, of what I have witnessed and been subjected to has inspired this book, which is ultimately about violence, making it extremely painful to research and equally painful to write. With that, I am also mindful of vicariously reproducing what I critique in this book—so much so that it often felt like a difficult and delicate balancing act between illustrating very real danger and injuries endured on the ground and adding to that violence in turn. At the same time, I strongly feel that to exclude or "whitewash" my findings or the daily realities that many experience would be to err on the side of the raceblind state. The French state's policy and practices of dismissing and/or camouflaging antiblackness in society powerfully contributes to its perpetuation. Antiblackness is a hydra whose venom is not always most potent in visible or explicit actions. Instead, it often manifests itself in the subtlest of ways due to having been racialized-as-black and treated as less-than on some level in French society. This was memorably illustrated to me and a long-term mentor and friend on a late summer evening in 2014—though it could have happened yesterday, and similar violations are happening as I write.

It was Paris as usual in the Latin Quarter where I lived at the time. The avenues and cafés were teeming with the hustle and bustle of daily life. Street musicians,

Capoeira artists, and rose peddlers vied for attention. Errant tourists and Parisian habitué dashed about the boulevard in search of adventure, libations, or victuals, while Moussa and I soaked it all in over dinner to the serenade of car horns and the occasional cathedral bells tolling in the distance.[1] As often happens, our conversation turned to the topic of this book, and, because Moussa is also a provocateur, it didn't surprise me when he said at one point, "Trica, you know, things are getting better in France." His wry smile, however, suggested otherwise. As I began to cite chapter and verse from my research, our conversation was cut short. Already, it was past midnight, and we were the only two people left in the bistro, save for the waiters who had started their closing ritual of power-stacking chairs and tables that inched ever-closer to where we were seated. On the opposite side of our table stood the unsolicited host with a credit card machine ready in hand. He had that "please go already" look on his face, a not-so-subtle way of saying that we could stay, as the expression goes, but not there. At his recommendation, we decided to continue what had become a debate across the street at the Antoine—or at least that was the plan. The Antoine was perfect because it is one of the few bistros that stays open well past the witching hour, making it a magnet for the after-hours crowd who is unready or unwilling to let Paris sleep.

Cosmetically, Moussa may be right. B/black people[2] in urban metropolitan centers like Paris seem visible everywhere, including in everyday occupations (salespeople, waiters, bank tellers, post office clerks, and so on) that involve direct interaction with the public. A generation ago in the Metropole, people of color were conspicuously absent even in these common jobs, and/or were simply hidden from public view, while overrepresented in kitchens, in backrooms as civil servants, or in offices as after-hours custodial staff. In positions of power and decision-making, from higher education to government to cinema and television to journalism to captains of industry, *on en est loin*. There's still much unfinished work. I confess my own astonishment in 2014 when I saw the first b/Black teller in my bank who, by 2016, had been promoted to a front-office manager in the 6th arrondissement. When I shared my surprise with him, he simply said, "Things have evolved." Still, that the presence of b/Black and non-whitened people is remarkable in public, or their absence unremarkable, only discloses whiteness as the norm, making everything else the exception. This "absent-present" minimal self, as Stuart Hall writes, "is and isn't there," for the blackened body is seen but is racially overdetermined, hence also unseen as a human being whose recognition, as philosopher Katherine McKittrick writes, "can expose domination as a visible spatial project that organizes, names, and sees social differences . . . and determines where social order happens."[3] Later that evening at the Antoine, when the police were called, this fact of antiblackness would be borne out, illustrating McKittrick's pointed observations that "[anti-b]lack matters are [also] spatial matters" in everyday France.[4]

Comfortably seated on the terrace, second row center, facing the boulevard with nothing obstructing our view, I noticed that Moussa and I were the only people visibly of color in the bistro. But then, a man and woman arrived, a couple with whom I had earlier exchanged a head nod of mutual recognition when crossing the street with Moussa on our way to the Antoine. Rather than choosing one of the other prime spots on the terrace, as we had, they opted instead for a back table on its fringes, an area tailor-made for intimacy or a bit of quiet away from the throngs. Later, they would share that they were married, on holiday from Belgium, and, to complicate identity politics, the husband said that he was also Moroccan. However, his dark skin tone, features, and hair texture, like those of his wife, signified blackness as opposed to the customary scripting of someone from Morocco as "Arab," even as these identities are not mutually exclusive, and b/Black people are indigenous to that region.

The ambiance in the bistro reminded me of what a musician friend calls "cool jazz." Unobtrusive melodies played in the background, sweetening the whispers of neighboring voices that fell gently on the ear while alcoholic elixirs of every sort yielded their fruit within the embrace of a temperate August night. As we took it all in, a line from writer Bernard Dadié's satirical novel, *An African in Paris* (*Un nègre à Paris*), captured well that sublime moment, indeed the stuff on which the City of Light's reputation is built: "Yes, my friend, Paris is all that—and more. And no one, absolutely no one, can resist her call." But just as that feeling began to cradle us, it was utterly shattered by the arrival of four loud, white-appearing individuals, three men and one woman, perhaps in their late twenties, who plopped down nearly in front of Moussa and me as if they owned the joint. Their pitched voices, slurred speech, florid faces, red-rimmed eyes, and general demeanor were telltale signs that the evening, for them, was far from young. Impatient to be served, the self-appointed leader headed to the bar, shouting "Beer for everyone," just as the waiter was approaching their table. Once served, they regaled each other with a story about some hapless person from an earlier leg of their evening, which inspired "Monsieur Beer for Everyone" to bolt to the middle of the road in front of the Antoine, where he performed an elaborate Charlie Chaplinesque impersonation, presumably of that hapless person.

For the grand finale, aided no doubt by liquid courage, "Monsieur Beer" then climbed onto a nearby bike, chained to a streetlamp, and, while steadying himself against the post with one hand and the other arm extended, he attempted a pirouette *en pointe* that sent his friends into hysterics but him nearly crashing to the ground. Baby-step style and on wobbly legs, he dismounted from the bike and bowed to shouts of "bravo" and applause that rang out from his friends. However, my thoughts drifted to the unfortunate owner of the bike. I pictured this person sitting unawares on the seat where an inebriated and therefore less attentive "Monsieur Beer" had been standing in shoes that had traversed dog-friendly Parisian sidewalks that are all too frequently streaked by what the French call *les pipis sauvages* ("wild peeing"), or as a friend described it, "males decorating walls and sidewalks," which flows from the corners of buildings used for quick relief. On many a night, I have leaped over this "scourge of urban life, costing millions of dollars for cleaning and the repair of damage to public infrastructure. And, oh, the stench."[5]

By then, the cool jazz ambiance was obliterated, along with any hope of resuming our discussion, so Moussa and I decided to call it a night. But our waiter was already occupied with Monsieur Beer and company who refused to pay their bill, causing the waiter to call in the manager, and from there, things escalated. Slurring his words and apparently speaking for the group, Monsieur Beer attempted to express his displeasure with the quality of the beer that they had nevertheless mostly consumed. Still refusing to settle, the manager then threatened to call the police but was waved off with a dismissive flick of the hand. Then, both the waiter and manager stormed off, making Moussa and me an unwilling captive audience because we couldn't leave until we'd paid our bill, and there was no one to take our money.

Shortly after, an unmarked dark car pulled up in front of the Antoine. Three doors opened quickly. Three white-appearing men in plainclothes exited who, without missing a beat, made a beeline for the Belgium couple. It was unclear at first who the white men were, but all was clarified once the couple pulled out their wallets and presented these men with their "papers." In other words, it was an identity control of people "guilty of blackness," as philosopher Lewis Gordon writes, meaning people for whom racialized blackness is the evidence of their supposed offense.[6] While these law enforcers were inspecting the couple's identification, the waiter rushed to their table, quickly apologized, and escorted them to the actual offenders whose nonchalance betrayed no signs of fear at the arrival of police. Instead, they were arrogant and confident. At that moment, Moussa and I turned toward each other with that "Did you just see what I just saw" look. Then my jaw tightened. Next came that familiar bitter taste, accompanied by a dull pang in the gut where no physical contact is required. The teeth grind. The heart thumps rapidly and audibly in the ear, accompanied by that familiar flavor of blood in the mouth from biting reflexively the tongue or lip, while that age-old feeling of disgust sinks in from the violence of the familiar, from the lived experience of everyday antiblackness.

In seeing only blackened bodies, the law enforcers became perpetrators of a routine violation of another order, one all too common in French and other European societies where race is denied on the grounds of official raceblindness. This fact of antiblackness is sometimes so fugitive and/or implicit that it becomes imperceptible even, at times, to those on the receiving end. Yet, in raceblind contexts, antiblackness renders visible the body racialized-as-black while raceblindness renders invisible the role of race in the assault. Blackened bodies, simultaneously absent and present, necessitate justification in spaces overdetermined by whiteness where they are rendered antithetical "space invaders" vis-à-vis that which has "the ability to pass as the universal human," writes sociologist Nirmal Puwar.[7] Indeed, Frantz Fanon vividly captures the everydayness of this lived experience that reverberates throughout a racialized world:

I am overdetermined from without. I am a slave not to the "idea" that others have of me, but of my own appearance. . . . Already the white gaze, the only legitimate one, is dissecting me. I am *fixed*. Having sharpened their microtome, they objectively cut my reality into pieces. I am betrayed. I feel, I see in those white eyes that it is not a new man entering, but a new type of man. A new species. Why it's a *nègre*![8]

Now facing the actual culprits, the officers asked each of them in quiet tones for their identification, while exchanging a bit of light banter and laughs during this surreally real scene. Empowered by their presence, the manager demanded more forcefully payment for the beer and even drank a gulp of it to attest to its quality. Once more, this group simply shrugged it off. Even as they were told to pay their bill, it was a very light moment of exchanging jokes and smiles. No humiliation, no violence, only conviviality, which stands in stark contrast to what I have known and researched over the years in mainland France. I looked at Moussa who seemed to understand that I was about to raise my voice, but he gestured quietly but firmly with his head "no," realizing that I could be charged with insulting an officer (*outrage*)—a serious charge in France—had I said what was on my mind. With a parting goodbye, the officers departed as quickly as they arrived, not once glancing in the direction of the couple nor offering an apology to *people* who had been "overdetermined from without."

Shortly thereafter, the group of four also left, while the angry manager looked on with contempt. As they hailed a taxi on the other side of the street, we could once more hear their drunken laughter, which seemed to linger in the air as they drove off into the night. At that moment, the manager was not the only one angry, but our reasons differed.

When Moussa and I later spoke with the couple from Belgium, we learned that they were neither shaken nor shocked; it was not the first time they had been unjustly approached by law enforcers in both France and Belgium, nor would it likely be the last. In countries officially blind to race and/as color, the frequency, magnitude, and pattern of such policing remain difficult to measure statistically and go under-reported, leaving a constellation of disconnected and unmapped violations both far and wide. Here, I'm reminded of music scholar William Cheng's prophetic insights that speak to the pitfalls of raceblindness. Replace "we/us" with France. "We like to think that looking past [racialized] identity means we've done right by other people," writes Cheng, as if "such imaginative fictions let us off the hook."[9] Before parting ways, the four of us entertained the proverbial "What if" question that always seems to accompany antiblack attacks of this nature: What if the roles had been reversed? What if Monsieur Beer and friends had been b/Black or some other racially dehumanized people? The experiences of disparate treatment that I document offer little optimism for a similar outcome in a French Republic currently far, very far, from being blind to race or being "off the hook."

However, little did I know on that fateful night that, five months later, Paris; Baga, Nigeria; and my personal life would forever change. The horrifying terrorist massacres in 2015 and 2016 in some ways achieved their end by amplifying hatred, fear, and insecurity amid states of perpetual war seemingly throughout the world. The state of emergency that followed in France, lasting nearly two years, ushered in counterterrorism policing that became a device to justify aggressive tactics, targeting people racialized-as-arab and black who were also victims of that terror. These measures begged the question of whether sacrificing civil liberties was worth the price of a ticket that seemed to offer dubious security gains and perhaps even worsened them. With these tragedies came another: the European refugee crisis that hit with a ferocity the French port city of Calais from January 2015 to October 2016. Situated opposite the English Channel, Calais became the waystation for thousands of migrants, largely from countries in Africa and the Middle East who were desperately fleeing war and/or poverty with the hope of finding relief in the United Kingdom. Instead, families, lone children, and individuals became stranded in a squalid encampment that swelled to over six thousand people. This "Calais jungle," as it was tellingly dubbed by the media, was described by Human Rights Watch as "hell." Still, more convenient enemies could not have been better scripted for anti-immigrant groups and political campaigns that promised a return to supposedly more bucolic, harmonious, and fantastical white-only times, and, for some, 1930s Europe. Parts of the encampment were set ablaze, some say "in retaliation," following the November 2015 Paris terror-murders that claimed 130 lives and left hundreds physically injured with unimaginable emotional costs in a France still reeling from the January 2015 *Charlie Hebdo* attack. By October 2016, authorities evacuated the camp entirely without addressing the cause of their migration. In 2017, a reported thousand more returned, but instead of receiving humanitarian relief, they were met with shock policing, supposedly aimed at preventing another encampment. Human Rights Watch and other humanitarian groups further reported

police abuse of asylum seekers and migrants, their disruption of humanitarian assistance, and their harassment of aid workers . . . by the use of violent force . . . police in Calais, particularly the riot police (*Compagnies républicaines de sécurité*, CRS), routinely use pepper spray on child and adult migrants while they are sleeping or in other circumstances in which they pose no threat; regularly spray or confiscate sleeping bags, blankets, and clothing; and sometimes use pepper spray on migrants' food and water. Police also disrupt the delivery of humanitarian assistance. Police abuses have a negative impact on access to child services and migrants' desire and ability to apply for asylum.[10]

Impacting, indeed eliminating, that desire is precisely the point, as seen along the US southern border in detention centers where children have been separated from their parents and caged in inhumane, deadly conditions. And who could forget the grim images of Haitian asylum seekers on the US/Mexico borders in 2021? The brutality and whipping of b/Black human beings by horse-mounted border police not only echo slave patrols but also demonstrated how the past is prologue. Along the southern borders of some European countries, lifeless bodies and scattered possessions wash ashore, as Manthia Diawara depicts in his poignant film, *Opera of the World*.[11] And it continues. A desensitized public sees mere debris to be hauled away without ever asking who and what set people flowing, to borrow from Farah Griffin's classic work on African American dislocation and migration.

Then, on February 17, 2015, I lost the most important person in my life—my mom—who abruptly and unexpectedly died, an amazing woman who survived the worst that Jane and Jim Crow USA meted out and often thrived against those very conditions. When thinking of my mom and my struggles to breathe life into this book, I am reminded of immortal words attributed to bell hooks: "Sometimes people try to destroy you, precisely because they recognize your power—not because they don't see it, but because they see it and they don't want it to exist."[12] I continue to draw from my mom's example to share with you through these pages the evidence of antiblackness mis-seen.

INTRODUCTION

Setting a Context

France is a country whose roots are Judeo-Christian. There you have it. France is a country of the white race.[1]
—Nadine Morano, member of the European Parliament and *Les Républicains* political party (France), September 26, 2015

I don't exist in France. As a Black French woman, I do not exist.
—Thirty-something interviewee, 2016

There is a very French peculiarity . . . the denial of discrimination, which here takes the form of a belief in the absolute reality of the principle of equality and its real application in practice. This principle has been so strong in the eyes of the French since the French Revolution that many believe it is a social reality which engenders very strong beliefs.
—Slim Ben Achour, attorney and specialist in nondiscrimination law, February 2, 2018[2]

If [people] define situations as real, they are real in their consequences.
—The Thomas theorem—William I. and Dorothy Swain Thomas

SETTING A CONTEXT

To launch its exclusive online screening of Isabelle Boni-Claverie's autobiographical film *Too Black to Be French*, the French daily *Libération* (*Libé*) posed in 2015 a hot-button question to its readers in a France that is officially blind to race and/ as color, arguably since the post–World War II era: "What does it mean to be black in France on a daily basis?"[3] This book offers a response to that question which strikes hard at idealized, cherished French values and constitutional principles of equality, citizenship, and sovereignty upon which the Republic was forged. Put another way, the French state brand messages a seductive ideology of raceblindness under the banner of a dogmatic universalism coupled with indivisibility (*unicité du peuple français*), which tells a story that France is one people and one nation, where equality resides in disappearing ethno-racialized differences.[4] The French revolutionary past legitimizes this myth for people susceptible to it. In France, they are many. However, everyday life is anything but raceblind, as the varied cases documented in this book and findings from a variety of studies on discrimination and racism in France illuminate. For instance, according to the largest survey to date on immigrants and the second generation in France that was also released in 2015, *Trajectories and Origins* (*TeO1*), "the highest incidence of racism suffered is among people from (or whose parents are from) sub-Saharan Africa (53%) or from French overseas departments (51%). The racism experienced by these populations is distinctly related to color racism."[5] Five years earlier, these researchers had reported that the most visible minoritized groups, namely people of "Maghrebin and sub-Saharan origin," also suffer the most discrimination across socioeconomic indicators, and that their risk of unemployment was "20% to 50% higher than the rest of the population with all things being equal."[6] Based on a study of over 5,000 people in 2016, arabianized[7] and blackened young men are twenty times more likely to endure repetitive identity checks by the French police that often initiate acts of police violence that I examine in these pages.[8] As elsewhere, the COVID-19 pandemic and lockdown hit those areas hardest where these issues converged, as in Seine-Saint-Denis, an economically under-resourced department situated northeast of Paris where the inhabitants appear largely of African descent.[9] According to a 2019 study, 87% of its residents reported being discriminated against based on their "origin or skin color," religion (84%), and their neighborhood (83%), within an already racially stigmatized department where respondents between the ages of 18 and 24 years old identified the police and the justice system as primary sources of discriminatory treatment ("88% or 9 out of 10").[10] Fundamentally, what these studies show is that people racialized and politicized as b/Black in France, estimated to be 4 to 5% of the French population, are targets of antiblack discrimination and racism that French raceblindness officially conceals in terms of race.[11]

As they are elsewhere, b/Black people in France are highly diverse, and, as political scientist Audrey Célestine and historian Sarah Fila-Bakabadio remind us, their "trajectories into 'blackness,'" and thereby antiblackness, have been fashioned by a variety of factors (e.g., citizenship status, kinship with origin countries, migration, intermarriage, enslavement, and colonization).[12] These differing experiences have also shaped intergroup solidarities, hostilities, and constructs of "community" in the Metropole between people of African and Caribbean coloniality and migrants from other regions of the Black diaspora, including African Americans. In turn, those lived realities have also conditioned their respective relations and perceptions of France where neither nationality nor those trajectories offer an escape hatch from racialized violence, inequality, and their effects in France or in Europe. What's more, various bodies of the European Union (EU) have loudly sounded alarms about high levels of antiblack discrimination and racism in member states (taken up in the chapter, "The Choice of Ignorance"). Compelling evidence from EU surveys on discrimination and racism echo and buttress findings from *TeO1* and my study, which show that b/Black French people, a distinctive racialized group in French society to which I return ahead, represent an unacknowledged and thus unprotected "national minority," or more aptly a racialized national minoritized group. Meanwhile, antiracists are stripped of the very rhetorical, historical, and political weapons needed to battle racial injustice, including the word and intersectional concepts of race that render coherent disparities and unequal treatment meted out to b/Black people and other racialized as "less-than" groups. Ultimately, by officially turning a blind eye to b/Black life, the French state not only illustrates precisely how structural discrimination and racism operate in a multiracialized society; it also perpetuates them while engendering the very race consciousness or subjectivities that it rejects and that state actors decry and/or attempt to legislate out of existence. As I show in these pages, b/Black people of course not only exist in France, owing to ideologies, laws, and practices of antiblackness, they also know that antiblackness exists in the everyday and other ways.

The ironies and hypocrisy of French universalist raceblind republicanism are not lost in Bon-Claverie's film, which is a scorching critique of France's failure to deliver the raceless inclusion and equality that it promulgates. *Libération* took that critique to an entirely different level by hashtagging and releasing into the Twittersphere a known line in the film: "You know you're Black in France when . . ."[13] On the day of its release, #YouKnowYoureblackInFranceWhen (*#TuSaisQueTesNoirEnFranceQuand*) trended among the highest in France, by some counts ranking at no. 2. Responses ran the gamut of recurring, denigrating (also in the etymological sense) indignities and violence, not apprehended as such, that often played out in the routine of daily life and to which I return in the chapter similarly titled. Judging from the number of likes and retweets in a country that was still cultivating its Twittersphere in 2015, these facts and acts of everyday antiblackness rang all too familiar. For instance, one person tweeted: "You know you're black in France when people make jokes like, 'Oh it's dark; I can't see you anymore!' at least 784494 times in your life," originally retweeted over three hundred times shortly after the hashtag's launch. Others drew attention to socioeconomic disparities and inequalities, such as #YouKnowYoureblackInFranceWhen . . . you see "that all of the kitchen staff in Parisian restaurants are black and all the waiters are white." When citizens are twice demonized as immigrants and by race, it triggers the most common expression of everyday racism and antiblackness, the "where are you *from, from?*" question. A tweeter to *Libé*'s hashtag put it this way: "You know you are black in France when you have to justify your heritage. You're French, but of what origin?" When discussing the hashtag over email in 2015 with an interviewee in her late twenties who self-described as "white," she offered another take on this question of perpetual immigrant status: "People here are 'French' (as you said, we breathe in the Republic) . . . [but] this question ('Where are you from?') is usually suspicious when asked to a black/mixed-race person [lowercase hers] . . . People are not 'happy' when the answer is France, or Normandy, or the Alps, and the real question behind it (here) is, 'Why is your skin not white?'"[14] I discussed the strong reaction to the hashtag not long after its release with a then graduate student interviewee and asked him by email how he would respond. His lucid reply in English also demonstrates the silent, emotional damage and injustice caused by denied antiblackness and specifically racial profiling under the cover of police identity controls:

I know I'm Black [uppercase his] in France when I have to think about not forgetting my ID card every time I leave my house. Even if I leave for only 5 min (or something), I know that it's better for me to have my ID in case the police arbitrarily decide to stop me. If I don't have it with me, I know it would fuck up my entire day because it means that I would spend most of it in the police station. I've become really paranoid about this ID card thing, and unfortunately, I noticed that Black men (especially from the "inner-cities") are like that too. One day, my cousin and I wanted to buy a pizza just ten minutes from where I live, and on the way, he said "shit, I forgot my ID!" Maybe it becomes a reflex for us to have it in our pocket because unconsciously or consciously we know that every time we are in public, we could potentially be questioned about where we're from, so, at any moment, we have to be ready to show proof, especially to the police. So, I know I'm a black [lowercase his] man in France every time I see my ID card or my passport, but paradoxically not "French enough." A white man doesn't need to worry like that, he is just what he is in the world.

While other groups experience racial injustice, what makes these lived experiences antiblack is not their exclusivity to blackened *bodies* but rather that they happen to *people* because they have been racialized-as-black. I revisited this interview excerpt with this person in 2019 to ask again how he would respond. He replied: "I'm getting older now so consequently I am less likely to be checked by the police but the paranoia that racism creates in people like us is still in my mind. I still feel the need to always have my ID with me as a Black [now capitalized] man in French society. So I feel exactly the same way as I did 5 years ago."

As my thirty-something interviewee in the opening epigraph conveys and as historian Pap Ndiaye writes, an added complication, or French twist, obtains for b/Black French citizens, precisely because they are a racialized "social group" who "are not supposed to exist since the French Republic does not officially recognize minorities, nor does it count them" categorically or statistically in its census.[15] In this way, they are also "impossible subjects," in the words of historian Mae Ngai: "persons whose presence is a social reality yet a legal impossibility," that is, diverse people of b/Black African descent who are hidden in plain sight.[16] Similar to kihana miraya ross, by antiblackness I do not mean "just racism against black people" or its outcome in terms of practices and policies, though they are obviously important.[17] Rather, I place the emphasis on racialization-as-black inferiority—the specificity and core of antiblackness—a premodern sociohistorical process honed through European imperialism that has constituted, out of diverse African-descended peoples, an antithetical "blackened race," one that signifies an *a-humanness*, deficiency, and pathology, and thus some*thing* disposable or ignorable in the everyday. The racialized-as-blackened body has been discursively "woven . . . out of a thousand details, anecdotes, and stories," writes Frantz Fanon, onto which all manner of social malignancies have been projected across time and space both to preserve and provide cover for a naturalized and denied white supremacy that seems everywhere and nowhere at the same time in the raceblind French nation-state.[18] On this point, historian Tyler Stovall writes that "the vaunted supremacy of the Western world at the dawn of the twentieth century was in fact white supremacy, symbolized above all by the massive empires that ruled much of Asia and Africa."[19]

Further, Moon-Kie Jung and João Costa Vargas argue in their instructive volume on antiblackness that "the problem lies with the very notions of the Social and the Human underlying these practices" and logics of antiblackness, which, to draw on philosopher Charles Mills, is indicative of a "racial contract" that "requires a certain schedule of structured blindness and opacities in order to establish and maintain the white polity" whose whiteness French raceblind republicanism conceals.[20] Essential to sustaining this system is what Mills calls an "epistemology of ignorance," that is, an inverted logic of unknowing for "successfully" becoming racialized-as-white, "superior," or "more-than" on all levels. This epistemology relies on generating "white misunderstanding, misrepresentation, evasion, and self-deception on matters related to race" with which other racialized groups become complicit.[21] Indeed, this epistemology has been a precondition for making possible race-based enslavement, colonization, and the dismissal of their legacies. And, as a hegemonic ideology, raceblind republicanism necessitates tacit consent, indeed a turning of one's eye away from racial havoc and injustice by seeking refuge in "white innocence," following anthropologist Gloria Wekker. Informed by Mills' concept of an "epistemology of ignorance," Wekker refers to a dynamic of "not knowing and not wanting to know" about the house that race built, especially its interior design, indeed "a disavowal and denial of racism" that creates a social cocoon to preserve racial sameness and the comfort it bestows.[22] Sustaining raceblind republicanism and ignorance/innocence formations operate, then, in the interests of raceblind states, as they disguise an entire system that allows racial injustice, and in this case antiblackness, to persist while attributing disparities and inequalities to putative deficiencies in blackened people. As I show, innocence/ignorance positioning brings to mind the joke about the fish who asks another, "How's the water?" to which the other replies, "What water?" Attempting to show "the fish" its muddied, unbreathable water, that is, the world that racism created through race, activates backlash politics and attempts to suppress and demonize any thought that upends raceblind messaging. We have witnessed this in the United States through campaigns to cancel Critical Race Theory (CRT) and other so-called "divisive ideas," also discussed in the chapter, "The Choice of Ignorance."[23]

ANTIBLACKNESS, RACEBLINDNESS, AND THEIR STAKES

This book is about everyday and other-way antiblackness in contemporary mainland French society from the perspective of b/Black French people whom French universalist raceblind republicanism effectively negates. Invisibilized with them are their lived experience of antiblackness, the *long durée* of black race-making, its future-past continuities, and the underlying racial structure, discussed ahead. Because these problems are typically absorbed into an immigration framework, this focus pushes the needle in the direction of collective rights for minoritized French people, which cut against French republican principles and constitutional law. The issue of everyday antiblackness is woefully understudied and undertheorized in French society, even as a range of activists, scholars, and visual culture on all sides of the Atlantic have long decried and examined antiblack racism and discrimination in the French Republic. None focuses specifically on everyday antiblackness across a spectrum of lived experience from the perspective of the very French people who distinctly lay bare the fallacies of French raceblindness, as I do in this book. While French people racialized-as-black share a stigmata of black color symbolism with noncitizens, such blackness coupled with citizenship status and race negation set b/Black French people apart in the French raceblind landscape, particularly in terms of documenting antiblack discrimination.[24] Eventually, b/Black citizens are folded into the majority population in the French census where racialized origins become undetectable past a certain generation, keeping in mind that French laws prohibit the state from officially collecting data on race. Unlike other racialized and thus homogenized and minoritized French groups (e.g., Arabs, Asians, Jews, Maghrebin, Muslims, and Romani), racialized blackness in France does not connote or represent an ethnicity, organized around norms, institutions, and culture, nor is it associated with geographies, apart from a fabulated "dark continent." Racialized blackness denotes race *explicitly*, and arguably "no other nonwhite group has race been so enduringly constitutive of their identity, so foundational for racial capitalism, and so lastingly central to white racial consciousness and global racial consciousness in general."[25] It is not, then, that external or "foreign" forces have imported into France "divisive ideas"; rather, divisive categories and racialized imaginary have been exported into the world by French and European expansionism, with which we continue to live and battle. As Fatima El-Tayeb writes in her insightful study of the politics of racelessness in Europe, such racelessness "creates a form of racialization that can be defined as specifically European both in its enforced silence and in its explicit categorization as not European of all those who violate Europe's implicit but normative whiteness," arguments also asserted by sociologist Stephen Small.[26] Consequently, state actors and raceblind adherents locate the "race question" from without, as something imposed, not home sown, typically by France's antimodels on all things racial, the United Kingdom and North America.

This point was well illustrated by a Twitter exchange between French Ambassador Gérard Araud and columnist for the *Washington Post* James McAuley during the 2020 Summer of Reckoning in France, ignited by George Floyd's murder and spearheaded by the Truth and Justice for Adama Traoré Committee. McAuley tweets: "As #BlackLivesMatter reverberates around the world, can France still credibly refuse to recognize race? Not if Assa Traoré and #JusticePourAdama have anything to say about it. . . ." Araud's response is classic raceblind republicanism and misdirection that instrumentalizes Black American expatriation to displace the selfsame issues of antiblackness anywhere and everywhere except in France.[27] "No @jameskmcauley," responds Ambassador Araud, "France won't 'recognize race'. Don't project on us an American model. Our history and our historical fabric are different. We'll have to face racism but in our own way. A lot of African-Americans didn't think we are that bad."[28] Because it is ideological and systemic—established societal structures are infused with it—antiblackness becomes an entity of which anyone can partake, as it operates as "a kind of equal-opportunity phenomenon," observes philosopher Linda Martín Alcoff, "infecting all communities of color in both overt and subtle ways."[29] In his classic essay, "Antillean and Africans," Fanon illuminates this aspect among blackened peoples when acknowledging that "often the enemy of the *nègre* is not the white man, but one of his own kind," or presumed to be. In analyzing this "black antiblackness" through Fanonian thought, Lewis Gordon further observes that such a phenomenon is also indicative of how "many blacks have adopted society's attitude toward black life."[30]

Clearly, writings by Charles Mills have informed my thinking, and his lucid meditations continue to illuminate for many of us our explorations of racial contracts and their global implications. The two models that have fundamentally fashioned how I conceptualize antiblackness, however, combine Frantz Fanon's pioneering thought on black racialization, primarily from his classic chapter 5 of *Black Skin, White Masks*, and sociologist Philomena Essed's groundbreaking theories of everyday racism, elaborated in the appendix.[31] This frame elucidates how, in this case, antiblackness and practices of it "infiltrate everyday life and become part of what is seen as 'normal' by the dominant group" and by minoritized people who have internalized and/or become inured to "society's attitude toward black life."[32] Thinking with Fanon, Essed, and others, I further argue that the power and danger of French universalist, raceblind republicanism does not reside solely in its negation of b/Black French life and thereby the existence and magnitude of antiblackness. The danger and power of this hegemonic ideology resides in its capacity to invisibilize *racial* structures that have historically advantaged and individualized whitened people while effacing their racialization of self and others, and thereby the respective accrued benefits and disadvantages.[33] In so doing, France is rendered ignorant and innocent of any responsibility for ever having structured different people's trajectories and opportunities based on race, which conveniently places the blame for racial inequalities and such disparities at the feet of the victims. Ultimately, its perniciousness resides in its wielding (including coercively) by complicit state actors and everyday people who perpetuate antiblackness by denying or/and by camouflaging it with proxies for race (e.g., ethnicity, color, immigrant origins, class, cultural differences and incompatibility), all of which renders French universalist raceblind republicanism *itself* a formidable manifestation of everyday antiblackness. The stakes of negation are therefore enormous, first and foremost being reality itself, and with it France's long-standing ideal of universalism as a model and modality of belonging. In other words, the issue is whether the French state's hegemonic approach to race denial will yield to evidence-based lived reality. What is also at stake clearly extends beyond France with the mainstreaming of white nationalism, extremism, and explicit racism that rely on the power of ideology and propaganda to invalidate historically rooted lived experience, as I note in relation to the debate on "divisive ideas" and the suppression of knowledge on racism in the chapter, "The Choice of Ignorance." And perhaps what is fundamentally and ethically at stake is, as Mills instructs, the fact that the "psychic economy of admitting the magnitude of the wrong done to the human beings represented as n*****s [or *nègres*] for hundreds of years in Western consciousness, might just be too great for whites to bear."[34] Let us pause for a moment to think deeply about that insight and the health implications of antiblackness more broadly. Already, a growing body of scientific research shows how racism and discrimination account for racial/ethnic disparities in mental health and "objective physical health outcomes."[35] Among those noted are life expectancy gaps, higher rates of preterm births, low birthweight, infant mortality, breast cancer, hypertension, asthma, sleep disorders, and other silent killers related to racism's intersectional impact on b/Black, b/Brown, and Indigenous peoples. Beyond a certain generation, raceblind republicanism precludes knowing these outcomes in the French context, which points to needed research in public health.

At the same time, the disavowal of racial structures preserves and fosters a "normative preference for [racial] sameness," to borrow from Essed and David Theo Goldberg's analysis of "cloning culture."[36] As the cases in this book illustrate, this preference for sameness is "predicated on the taken-for-granted desirability of certain types, the often-unconscious tendency to comply with normative standards, the easiness with the familiar and the subsequent rejection of those who are perceived as deviant" or "undesirable" in the discourse of French police violence, as historian Jennifer Boittin further illuminates in *Undesirable: Passionate Mobility and Women's Defiance of French Colonial Policing, 1919–1952*.[37] For its very existence, raceblind republicanism, like cultural cloning, relies upon a normative "unnamed preference for the comfort, safety, familiarity and privilege [or entitlement] associated with [antithetical and normative] whiteness."[38] It is further "reinforced through the very denial of [racial] sameness when racial equality is the formal ideology."[39] Raceblind republicanism, justified in the name of equality, thus becomes a form of national gaslighting on matters of racism's production of race, and those who question this "normalcy" become identified as the racists.[40] Or, as a scholar-activist interviewee put it: "Officially, you do not have the right to say that you are black in France because we don't exist, and if you show that there is a problem of racism against black people . . . it's like a sick person being told that he has a fever and then blaming the doctor for having pointed it out." But nowhere are the failures of raceblind republicanism and its racial structures more evident than in the French outer cities, such as those in Seine-Saint-Denis, that exploded in October 2005, following the horrifying deaths of Bouna Traoré (15 years old) and Zyed Benna (17 years old), who were fleeing a police identity control, to which I return in the chapters on police violence. Those uprisings were a watershed in French race politics because they were understood by many as a *racial* issue, previously inconceivable in the French mainstream. Tasked by President Emmanuel Macron with devising a plan of action for these "sensitive" areas, former Minister of Urban Affairs Jean-Louis Borloo reported in 2018 that these areas were "locked in and isolated" and an "absolute scandal," adding that "the situation is the same as fifteen years ago with the 2005 riots when everything was insidiously deteriorating."[41] He also made plain the dire need for intervention in powder-keg areas where there is "concentrated poverty, mass unemployment, sometimes single-parent families, uprooted youth struggling to find their place (500,000 young people, or more than 50% of outer-city youth)" in areas classified "at risk" in which the number of people so designated are the "the equivalent of the cumulative population of the top 10 cities in France."[42] Although neither racism nor race are overtly stated as factors, Borloo alludes to them through proxies when highlighting the intersections of "social origins" and "color" as contributing factors. "This situation will be untenable," he writes, "if we give up trying to integrate into the French dream 10 million invisible souls, bright youth of color (*colorée*) seeking to participate . . ." in a fictive raceblind republic.[43] Although this book principally covers the period since 2014, the 2005 moment vividly demonstrates what Christina Sharpe expresses in her eloquent elegy of loss and refusal born of antiblack suffering, namely: "The past that is not past reappears, always, to rupture the present."[44] The reappearing past that regenerates racialization-as-black inferiority dates, however, from much earlier and captures not only the reappearing past or a past-present but also a future-past or what lies in the offing.

Make no mistake. As I will show, those on the receiving end are not passive victims of antiblackness. Blackened people must deal with it daily, which also means dealing with those who attempt to invalidate their experiential reality. The post-2005 generation has forced the issues of racism and race in France into the public arena, causing even President Macron, for instance, to reluctantly weigh in on matters of police violence. But critics see Macron's positioning as politically self-serving, and he has proven himself to be a hardliner on upholding French universalism. He has waxed poetically of a France that has not experienced US-style segregation, while ignoring that those "locked in and isolated" in the French outer cities, to revisit Borloo, have not experienced French universalism. A *nouvelle vague* of b/Black academics are also refusing to acquiesce to backlash politics, but it is unclear what the repercussions will be from the former minister of higher education, research and innovation, who has been accused of trampling on academic freedom in the hunt to rid France of ideas supposedly imported from without. As I show in this book, navigating antiblackness or refusing it includes a variety of protective strategies, ranging from resilience to traditional protests and uprisings to the arts to legal recourse through the French and European courts. Promoting an understanding of the history and contributions of b/Black people to France, typically obscured in French national education, is another strategy of refusal, as seen in diverse projects, such as Black History Month, founded by scholar-activist Maboula Soumahoro; *Africultures*, an online publication focused on African and African diasporic arts and cultures, headed by journalist Samba Doucouré; and activities aimed at commemorating enslavement and its abolition(s) in France, along with Black-focused heritage tourism. Building an "undercommons" of Afro/Black French Studies, drawing on Fred Moten and Stefano Harney's notion of fugitive Black Studies, is yet another, which largely occurs in France through activities and events organized by various antiracism, cultural, and political associations. But these studies are not considered legitimate by the powerful French and European academies, though American

Studies in France has become a site where French scholars can perform that labor.[45] At the same time, this backlash, as a sociologist in a French academy put it, has not "seemed to deter those few hundred new scholars every year who are exploring race in new ways (for France)" and in French academies, though he also admitted that sanctions could be imposed, such as not receiving public financing for such projects or research.[46]

France has, nonetheless, sown the seeds for the demise of raceblind republicanism through its very principle of universalism, discussed ahead, which actually seeks not to preserve sameness or efface difference but instead embrace pluralism. Franco Lollia, activist and spokesperson for the Black advocacy collective the *Brigade Anti Négrophobie*, founded in 2005, poignantly and succinctly expresses this dimension in scholar-filmmaker Nathalie Etoké's illuminating documentary, *Afro-Diasporic French Identities*. "To establish the basis of our association," states Lollia, we cite Article 1 of the Declaration of the Rights of Man, as it was decreed in France. In other words, if we cite it, it's not because we believe in it but to show the contradictions that exist between facts and the text (what's written and declared). If we look at the text, France is the most beautiful postcard that has ever existed because it's the country of Human Rights. *We are the living proof* that France has usurped this title, and it's what we try to remind them when taking action [emphasis mine]."[47] What is also obscured by raceblind republicanism is France's role in modern racial capitalism's imperatives of dispossession and extraction, following Cedric Robinson. However negated or invisibilized, the evidence of blackened life occurs precisely at those moments, both unexpected and predictable, that are integrated into the flow of everyday life in French society. This book responds, then, to the real question *Libé* asked its readers: What does it mean to be *racialized-as-black* in French society? It means to suffer antiblackness in the everyday and in other salient ways—an antiblackness hidden in plain sight.

SPECIFICITIES OF ANTIBLACKNESS: BLACK COLOR SIGNIFICATION AND EXPLICIT RACE DENOTATION

In the impressive volume edited by historians Tyler Stovall and Sue Peabody, *The Color of Liberty: Histories of Race in France*, historian Pierre Boulle persuasively argues that the physician and traveler François Bernier (1620–1688) should be recognized among the pantheon of thinkers identified with the modern concept of race. In the seventeenth century, Bernier defines race "as broad human categories characterized by distinct physical traits," particularly "skin pigmentation," and insists "that the transmission of characteristics by inheritance predominates over environmental or cultural determinants," writes Boulle, ideas that were a "startling departure from contemporary beliefs" of the day.[48] In highlighting Bernier's case, Boulle demonstrates that the "origins of modern racial thinking in France," typically associated with the early eighteenth century, are temporally more fluid than canonical theory asserts, which generally inaugurates the destructive career of race during the European Age of Exploration (ca. 15th–17th centuries). However, marshaling evidence from multiple sources from the twelfth through the fifteenth centuries, medievalist Geraldine Heng argues that such periodizing makes "it difficult to see the European Middle Ages as the time of race, as racial time" from which "*homo europaeus*—the European subject—emerges."[49] The same holds for "antiblackness time" in France and Mediterranean Europe prior to the fifteenth century in terms of the invention of racialized black inferiority, defined by negative black color symbolism. This enduring specificity of antiblackness has crisscrossed time and space and has been foundational to "the process of transforming people of African origin into '*Nègres*' [capital his]," that is, "into bodies of extraction and subjects of race, largely obey[ing] the triple logic of ossification, poisoning, and calcification," writes Achille Mbembe.[50] Premodern race and precursors of antiblackness, as Cedric Robinson develops in his classic *Black Marxism*, derive not solely from intergroup contact with peoples on the African continent but from "the internal relations of European peoples," or, more precisely, "the phenomenon of racist attitudes among Europeans toward other Europeans" during that era.[51] As numerous scholars argue, peoples who became racialized-as-white-and-European differentiated and exaggerated differences among regions, dialects, or customs. Value-laden constructs of barbarians, bloodline purity, belief systems, civilizations, and humanity as inferior and superior would also have an enduring impact on the structure of labor under racial capitalism.[52] The legacies of racial enslavement and colonialism are found today in postcolonial labor migration, both solicited and propelled across Europe along with a predictable rejection of such migrants fueled by resurgent anti-immigrant campaigns.

Similarly, Heng documents compelling evidence of "racial thinking, racial law," and other "racial phenomena . . . in medieval Europe before the emergence of a recognizable vocabulary of race" (ca. 5th–15th centuries).[53] Although Robinson locates antiblack antecedents in practices of intra-European racialization, "the fears and terrors of the Occidental were centered on blackness itself," argues Heng, but again not initially from actual encounters with those eventually racialized-as-black.[54] They found their source, rather, in resilient myths, theological exegesis, Enlightenment thought, travelogues, and proto-natural science that often prefigured the blackened body prior to tangible interaction. Consequently, "in the absence of substantial contact with living, black-skinned human beings," these ideas flourished in what is today Western Europe, and this absence of actual contact "freed the hermeneutic development of blackness from being troubled by representatives in the flesh."[55] In the twelfth century, for instance, "the identification of blackness with evil was reflected in . . . the *Chanson de Roland*," writes historian William B. Cohen, adding that "Frenchmen saw the blackness of Africans as symbolic of some inner depravity, since they thought the color aesthetically unappealing."[56] In the thirteenth century, Heng further observes that "[b]lack is damned, white is saved. Black, of course, is the color of devils and demons, a color that sometimes extends to bodies demonically possessed."[57] As various historians show, such beliefs would infect the modern era, shaping how understandings of racialized blackness would evolve. In the twelfth century, carved tympanums and other art artifacts at the dawning of French literature featured entities such as the "black devilish Saracen enemies," illustrated by the epic poem *Chanson de Geste*, "that tap directly into the political imaginary" and extol white as the "the color of superior class and noble bloodlines."[58] "Saracens" and "Moors," racialized categories of difference, are nevertheless deceptive because of their semantic slipperiness. While applied to those perceived as "Arab" or "Muslim" during the Crusades (11th–13th centuries), "Saracen alterity" also inconsistently referred to "dark skin color," writes medievalist Suzanne Conklin Akbari in her analysis of premodern "orientalist types"; but such color "continue[d] to be at least occasionally interpreted as a marker of danger and duplicity."[59]

Classicist Frank Snowden Jr. argues by contrast that ancient times were not "antiblackness times" to the extent that there was "nothing comparable to the virulent color prejudice" or "the germ of anti-black bias" that would ultimately degenerate into a destructive pattern of scientific and structural racism.[60] Cautioning against presentism, and against some competing views of his day, Snowden insists that "black skin color was not a sign of inferiority; Greeks and Romans did not establish color as an obstacle to integration in society, nor did ancient societies make color the basis for determining human worth."[61] Acknowledging that Greeks and Romans associated the color black with death, Snowden maintains, however, that the association with "the Underworld had in origin nothing to do with skin color," and "anti-black sentiment in the ancient association of Ethiopians with death and the Underworld are questionable," though not entirely non-existent.[62] Likewise, historians such as Michel Pastoureau document "a well-diversified [semantic] palette of black" in antiquity that signified a range of meanings, including "fertile black" in Ancient Egypt, a valued sign of fecundity.[63] Eventually, the exegesis of blackness in biblical-based cultures would contribute to notions of polygenesis, a separate origins thesis, and notions of inherent racial inequality from which narratives such as the curse of Ham and black enslavement have been sourced. The undutiful Ham, son of Noah, failed to turn his gaze from his father's naked, drunken state. For this indiscretion, Noah purportedly cursed him and his descendants with everlasting servitude that eventually became synonymous with enslavement as a natural state of blackened peoples. Acknowledging the influence of Snowden on his work, David M. Goldenberg argues further that "by the beginning of the Atlantic slave trade in the fifteenth century Black [capital his] and slave were inextricably joined in the Christian mind," as would Western color binaries migrate across the globe to "China and South Asia . . . black Africa . . . [and] in the near East and Classical world."[64] Indeed, in the "long history on the meaning of color," writes Toni Morrison, it was "not simply that [a] slave population had a distinctive color; it was that this color 'meant' something," something antithetical to that against which it was defined and thereby measured, racialization-as-white superiority.[65] People racialized-as-black become "incarcerated in their own bodies [and] held back by the invisible barrier that separates off those who lack 'civilizational legitimacy,'" writes sociologist Nacira Guénif-Souilamas.[66] In a racialized world, the blackened incarcerated body, like race, is "all so constructed, it's all so made, and it also has some kind of serviceability," states Toni Morrison during her memorable 1993 interview with PBS' Charlie Rose when describing her experiences of racism.[67] Historian Kate Lowe similarly documents, in her analysis of the "stereotyping of black Africans" during Renaissance Europe, that although perceptions of blackened Africans were not set in stone, Europeans "perceived them to be in opposition to the particularly Renaissance vision of white, European culture and civilization"—the yardstick.[68] Although skin color varied, these differences were omitted, as blackened skin color was uniformly damning, writes Lowe, and "manumission could not free black Africans from slavery because society at large equated black skin colour (of whatever hue) with slavery."[69]

European imperial practices of race-making dating from the fifteenth century would by the eighteenth century become reified racial categories and hierarchies produced from racism that ultimately served to rationalize and justify conquest and enslavement in the name of Christendom. Naturalized and practiced in calculated, patterned, and destructive ways, European ideas of race would distinctively brand the racialized-as-black body with antithetical black color symbolism, a hereditary stain and stigma of inferiority, underscored by the seven Ds: darkness, death, depravity, defectiveness, deficiency, disease, and the devil. Determinant of inclusion and exclusion, racialized-as-black color symbolism is all the more deleterious in raceblind contexts because, to return to Morrison, that "long history in the meaning of color" becomes disconnected from inequalities and injustices people suffer not for what they have done but, again, because of their racialization-as-black. This is antiblackness to the core, and its erasure by raceblind republicanism further distinguishes blackened people in the French context.

UNIVERSALIST RACEBLIND REPUBLICANISM: ANTIBLACKNESS WITHOUT b/BLACK PEOPLE

French raceblind republicanism, France's ideological approach to belonging, has rested on a flawed premise that has yet to be proven on the ground, that is, by not identifying ethno-racial differences, social equality follows. As sociologist James Cohen reminds us, "the republican model does not now, nor has it ever in practice, required that all citizens be treated in a strictly equal manner in the service of some abstract republican equality."[70] Indeed, historian Lorelle Semley addresses this point in analyzing citizenship in the French Atlantic world from the late eighteenth century to the demise of the Fourth Republic in 1958 through the narratives of known and lesser-known figures, such as Toussaint Louverture and the *signares*, "elite woman of African descent from the region of Senegal and neighboring coastal regions." Semley demonstrates how race and gender troubled universalist republican citizenship in the French Empire, where "citizenship depended on the distinction between subject and citizen as well as between colony and metropole," adding that "under Napoleon Bonaparte's 1803 Civil Code, citizenship was also defined by the separation between civil status and political rights," with profound effects that lasted well into the twentieth century.[71] Likewise, in the context of France's Caribbean colonies after the abolition of enslavement in 1848, social scientist Silyane Larcher documents how race has historically fashioned French citizenship. The antinomy between practices of civil and political equality left France's "other citizens," the formally enslaved, excluded from common law and from the French citizenship to which they were entitled, argues Larcher.[72] A case in point is the Haitian Revolution (1791–1804), a litmus test of French Revolutionary universalist ideas, whose "other citizens" would be punished by France and forced to pay it reparations to the tune of billions of dollars for refusing racial enslavement in their assertion of actual universalism. Though Tyler Stovall analyzes what he terms "race riots" in the interwar years in France, his insight about the "ultimate goal of strategies of racial exclusion," is not lost in this context, which involves "the consolidation of racial hierarchy through a denial of its existence."[73]

In practice, universalism in the French context, as Pierre Bourdieu argues, functions more as an "imperialism of the universal," that is, "universalizing for a society its own particularity by insisting that it is a universal yardstick . . . a kind of realized ideology: to be French is to feel entitled to universalize one's particular interest, a national interest that has the uniqueness of being universal."[74] Of course, to realize this ideology is to remove from the equation those "other citizens" and constructs of race that make them "other." At issue, however, is not just the falsity of universality, as Robert Stam and Ella Shohat write, but "the very premises by which the West in general has been constructed by the 'universal,'" which, when untethered from a "broader colonial genealogy is myopic, ethnocentric, and covertly nationalist," as well as racist.[75] It is precisely that type of universalism that Fanon abhorred. For him, universalism does not hinge on an abstract grand narrative of human equality and dignity but is more an ecological project to build the very reality that Western universalism corrupted through its project of universalizing, instead, racialized whiteness as superior to all others.

For its adherents, French universalism, the animating force of raceblind republicanism, has sturdy historical and legal legs on which to stand. Grounded in European Enlightenment philosophies and the French Revolution of 1789, this history serves to legitimize France's claims to exceptionalism, equality, and race neutrality. But there has always been a chasm between those principles and their application, which uprisings (past and present), ranging from abolitionism to the revolts of 2005 and 2020, have put to the test only to expose racialism wholly intact. France's core principals of universalism and indivisibility are preserved in the document outlining the supreme laws of the land. The 1958 French Constitution, notably its preamble and article 1, are the legal sources that define human rights, equality, and republican democracy in terms of humanism. The preamble invokes both the *Declaration of the Rights of Man and of the Citizen* (1789), which established the First Republic (1792–1804), and the preamble to the 1946 Constitution, which sets forth those rights as inalienable to all human beings. Yet, in matters of political sovereignty, citizenship is decisive in the republican model largely because the citizen and nation are considered indivisible. But this model posits once more a universal white male subject, the European man, against whom all others are measured, defined, and named.[76] Still, many countries profess ideas of liberation and freedom yet also fail to deliver what they promise. What makes French universalism arguably exceptional, writes Catherine Raissiguier, is "its ability to foreground a strong discourse of universal inclusion and equality along with its unique resistance to acknowledging exclusionary and discriminatory discourses and practices both in its past and in its present."[77] In other words, France professes powerful principles and values of raceless equality while institutionalized and codified race-blind republicanism, enforced by the state, camouflages racialized inequality in daily life.

In the logic of Antonio Gramsci, as sociologists Michael Omi and Howard Winant affirm, "the ruling groups must elaborate and maintain a popular system of ideas and practices—through education, the media, religion, folk wisdom, etc."—in order to sustain their ways of thinking and being in society, despite opposition and often because of it.[78] Such ruling ideologies prevail, then, when the mechanisms and circumstances accounting for their existence are invisible or undisclosed, giving them the appearance of being natural and/or normative, how society unquestionably is and ought to be. This entails suppressing, repackaging, and/or erasing the underpinning power relations and thereby the interests, histories, complicity, and coercion that make dominant ideas possible and seemingly in the collective interests of those whom they are said to serve. In other words, as Sylvia Wynter lucidly expresses it, "by the time your colonizer's flag goes down you have already trained your 'natives.' Trained them, as Sartre noted, in the Word that you own. So you will therefore continue to legitimate your dominance by means of your ruling ideas, even where cast now in new sanitized terms."[79] In his examination of universalism in the evolution of modern French political culture and history, Tyler Stovall writes that "universalism argues that the core revolutionary values of liberty, citizenship, and Enlightenment principles of reason are at the same time central components of French national identity and the province of humanity as a whole."[80] France interprets, then, "its civilization" as specific to its construct of nationhood and as part of the inheritance of peoples worldwide, continues, Stovall. The Enlightenment, as one form of modernity, becomes pivotal in the archaeology of race in

France, a race-making power, not only for the ways in which its doctrines of universalism and humanism structured French republicanism and, thereby, its ideals of raceblindness, but also for its universalizing assertions that encoded whiteness and maleness as normative and racialized blackness by antithesis as anormative, thus ahuman.[81] In this context, Stovall concludes that "in the empire, national and racial universalism blended into each other, crafting a vision of France as a universal white nation," recalling Nadine Morano's assertion in the opening epigraph.[82]

Then as now, French universalist exceptionalism rings hollow for citizens racially othered and thereby deprived of what sociologist Jeanne Beaman terms "cultural citizenship" in her perceptive study of people of "Maghrébin origin" in France whom she also locates in racialized blackness.[83] "Cultural citizenship" desires precisely what raceblind republicanism forecloses as dangerous for the nation-state, that is, admitting into the public sphere differences (i.e., "racial, ethnic, cultural, and religious difference") central to people's ways of being that allow such "outsiders" to feel fully included. The criminalization of Muslim women's covering practices, including expelling them from schools and public beaches for wearing burkini swimsuits, captures this point, as do other issues documented within these pages. In the country of human rights (*le pays des droits de l'homme*), "fabricating slaves and monsters" was also essential to European humanism, in the logic of Jean-Paul Sartre, which for racialized-as-inferior peoples has been nothing more than "pseudo-humanism," asserts Aimé Césaire, something "narrow and fragmentary, incomplete and biased and, all things considered, sordidly racist."[84] But universalism and humanism, like communism, were not ideals that Césaire flatly renounced; rather, he denounced the French execution of them, as he made clear in his letter of resignation from the French Communist Party, to the Party's general secretary, entitled *Letter to Maurice Thorez*.

In condemning the "avalanche of abuse" perpetrated by and under Stalin, which was revealed in Nikita Khrushchev 1956 report, Césaire also denounces the French Communist Party for its Stalinist ways and blindness to the "singularity" of race, not only class, in emancipatory struggles against colonialism and racism, as Robin Kelley and Brent Edwards elucidate in their analysis of the letter.[85] This letter, writes Keith Walker, "protests the slipknot of assimilation that European Communism has put like a noose around the neck of Martinique, Césaire's country."[86] Indeed, Césaire reasons that communism, similar to universalism, should be "placed in the service of black people," not the reverse, and that far from losing himself in an "emaciated universalism," he conceives of it as "enriched by all that is particular" and thereby "rich in all its particularities" with "the coexistence of them all."[87] The deployment of universalism, as today, "obscures the colonial excess of the European and American racism which continues to dehumanise 'non-Europeans' and 'non-whites,'" writes Barnor Hesse, and thereby preserves that "universal white nation."[88]

Though cloaked in the "sanitized terms" of universalism, raceblind republicanism interpellates or addresses people as "French" and "citizen" with seductive notions of fairness, the common good, and a raceless humanity as one. Ultimately, this is a trap.[89] These noble ideas have always hinged on the power to authorize who is human and whose humanity is universalizable while evacuating from humanity and human history of those selected for social death. The force of institutionalized raceblind republicanism has been illustrated to me often in France and still confounds me. I find it difficult to believe that in the face of so much racialized inequality and oppression, people really do extoll the virtues of republicanism and/or react with disdain and/or confusion when I and others insist that race is indeed a lived reality as much in France as in my country, the United States. Then, there are subtle ways that its ingrained character makes itself known. For instance, in 2015, I was struck by a Facebook exchange that a b/Black male student in his early twenties shared with me during an interview when I asked him if his generation subscribed to republican ideas. In the exchange, he both expresses his raw feelings about the killing of Michael Brown and the ensuing revolts in Ferguson, Missouri, that locate antiblackness for him in a global context. However, his interlocutor, of a similar age, draws deeply and directly from the well of French raceblindness in his pushback:

STUDENT: I feel sick about this Ferguson shit. I'm seeing all of this now (mind you, I live in France) and I am so mad. I want to cry because I realize that black people don't matter in the world. Me, a black [lowercase his] person, is not considered worthy of respect. I will never be equal to white people. I can try all I want to be successful in life, but it will never be enough because of my skin color.

RESPONDENT: Though I genuinely understand that you're moved by everything that is happening these days in Ferguson, I think you're ungrateful to France. There have never been such things as segregation here for example, and I don't understand how you can use the expressions "white people" and "black people" to talk about our country. That's not how we have been raised here. We have always been taught we're all equal, and sorry, but as being part of a "minority" too, I think I will succeed in life.

While some may take umbrage with the latter respondent's view or consider it out of step in the wake of the summer of 2020, my point is that it illustrates the naturalization of raceblind republicanism, a hegemonic ideology, that effectively works against the interests of people racialized and minoritized into "racial minorities." On this journey, I have encountered a similar perspective from a variety of everyday people, despite the lived experiences of antiblackness that are part and parcel of their daily life. A near cliché example—cliché because of its ubiquity—is illustrated by use of large b/Black security guards in supermarkets and as night club bouncers who track blackened and brown bodies, particularly youth, with patterned predictability. I can no longer count how many times over the years that I have been followed in varying stores, particularly in Paris, or have witnessed it happening to others. On occasion, I have resorted to a strategy shared by a friend's teenage son— reverse tracking perpetrators of racial profiling—which was born out of frustration but also research interests to see its effects. Often, I encountered anger, shock, and fear from store employees when they realized that I had started following them in a similar fashion, including catching their attention to let them know that my actions were purposeful. But nowhere are the fallacies and absurdity of French raceblind republicanism better exposed than through the experiential reality and perspectives of French people of African descent whose very presence as a *racial* group raises other questions concerning identity politics and specifically capitalization politics born of raceblind republicanism. These sociohistorical constructs along with the lived experiences of the blackened people whom they name are daily reminders that France has been anything but raceblind.

BLACK LIKE WHEN AND WHERE AND THE POLITICS OF THAT CAPITAL "N" OR "B"

An exploration of antiblackness is at once an exploration of b/Blackness on some level, as the two are constitutive of blackened life. However, determining what b/Blackness and a b/Black identity mean, whether in upper or lowercase, for Afro French people is not the aim of this book. In France as elsewhere, these understandings are always already inscribed in unfinished and unsettled identity and belonging politics over recognition and nonrecognition within a *longue durée* of race-thinking and race-making, as I have outlined. However, in her insightful analysis of "Blackness" (capital hers), Michelle Wright argues that to "locate and define" this formation across vast African diasporas, we must understand it relationally, as a mutually generative racial and political formation that is sociohistorically produced. Blackness, she writes, "operates as a construct (implicitly or explicitly defined as a shared set of physical and behavioral characteristics) and in terms of phenomenology (imagined through individual perceptions in various ways depending on the context)."[90] In this way, "Blackness" is less of a "what" (What is it; what are you?) and more temporally and spatially drawn as a "when and where," that is, a dynamic that shapeshifts across time and place thus "cannot be located on the body because of the diversity of bodies that claim Blackness as an identity," or disclaim it for its presumptive solidarity and essentialized connotations.[91] Reinforcing this point at the European level and with respect to discourses of "Black Europe," Essed writes that "different than in the US, Black as a notion is not always exclusively used to refer to people of African descent."[92] Rather, as she argues further, this understanding becomes a homogenizing container concept assigned "to targets of discrimination on the basis of race, culture, ethnicity, religion or a combination of these factors," which makes "Black" not only a "when" and "where" but also a disputed "who." This question often arises in my Afro/Black Paris study away programs in France among my US Black students who have never visited the country or have rarely, if ever, left the United States. Many have expressed a range of emotions from shock to despair when learning that their presumed kinship, based on skin, is not universal. I have witnessed their frustration and dismay on many occasions, such as when, for instance, the head nod of mutual recognition or a hello is not reciprocated. In 2018, one of my students captured this point in an email when describing an encounter between him, his classmates, and a twenty-something waiter at a restaurant in Paris:

Some of us were having dinner, and a black [lowercase his] man (the waiter) asked why we didn't want to learn French. We had been talking to him about our French classes and trying to learn the language. He told us that Americans are mean because when he spoke French in NY, a lady told him to speak English. [Another student] asked, "was she our color, or was she the other color?" He was like "we don't do that here" and "that's your American thing. Race doesn't exist here."

The experience left them stunned but also enlightened. Identity politics involve "challenging, transforming, replacing and/or attempting to preserve identities others wish to impose" or, in this case, negate altogether.[93] Raceblind republicanism operates as a form of identity politics in exercising its power to name and negate entire peoples, as occurs in polemical debates about ethno-racial statistics and attempts to suppress knowledge that challenges France's history of race-making and its connection to present-day unequal treatment. Less interrogated in France is the related issue of capitalization politics, that is, whether to place in upper- or lowercase *noir* or "black," making the use b/Black or *n/Noir.e.s* (or *Noir.e.x.s*), written in a gender inclusive and non-binary style, also a "why" in a raceblind France in light of its b/Black diversity and how b/Black identities have been conditioned by antiblackness operating upon them.

These discourses and subjectivities are not only "ways of speaking about one's perceived and desired location in the social world," writes sociologist Bennetta Jules-Rosette. They are also "complex and deceptive because they appear to be statements of fact and exhortations to act . . . when they are, in fact, expressions of virtual states (e.g., 'wanting-to-be' or 'wanting-not-to-be')," or impelled to be, which is fundamentally indicative of identity politics.[94] Still, the semantics and politics of upper- and lowercase are not easily sidestepped in the writing of subaltern histories and lived realities precisely because the politics of capitalization and identity are entangled with what historian Dipesh Chakrabarty unpacks as the idea of being "major" and "minor."[95] Similar to categories such as "minority," which prescribes what it describes, and "minoritized," which accentuates the process of racialized status diminution, the capacity to authorize these formations is not merely about meaning-making. The politics are also indicative of historical power asymmetries that both underpin and engender political and emancipatory ways of thinking and identifying vis-à-vis shared injustice and oppression.

In 1919, W. E. B. Du Bois confronted the question of capitalization that continues to play out in our time and in this book. Readers of *The Crisis* asked Du Bois why he, as its editor, capitalized the word "Negro" in the articles of the NAACP's official magazine. His prescient response, entitled "That Capital N," seems to anticipate the direction of capitalization politics on the other side of the Atlantic in the wake of 2005. Written in the masculinist, racial discourse of his day, his editorial is, on one level, a cutting rejoinder to entrenched ideas of racialized black inferiority, represented by the lowercase, while, on another, a lucid expression of second sight. Du Bois reminds readers that "rule books" enjoined capitalization to reference *people* and that it was customary during "Negro slavery" to use the lowercase "since Negroes were looked upon as 'real estate' or as moveable property like horses, cows, etc."[96] He also pointed to the role and evolution of printing technologies and "the great distaste" for using capital letters in publishing industries. He then notes that "rule books" of his day stipulated "that capitals shall be used for the names of all nations and races, 'except Negro,'" because "Negro" was not a "race" but "a description of the color of a people." This also implies that "Negroes" are not, in effect, people. For Du Bois, these claims were "manifestly false" because "the persons designated as Negroes are by no means black, even in Africa." Rather, Du Bois reasons that the capital N is indicative of much more, that is, the long dialectal arc of antiblackness and its refusal from which that capital letter has been produced and refashioned over time. For Du Bois, then, that capital letter served to elevate, situate, and celebrate blackened peoples and denoted subjectivity and humanity, the antithesis of racialization-as-black. Fanon made a similar distinction in the French version of chapter 5 in *Black Skin, White Masks* in that the identity discourse *Noir* is in the uppercase while *nègre* is in minuscule. Philosopher Ronald Judy explains that "when capitalized, as it is in Fanon's title, the French *Noir* is an analogue for the English 'Black,' referring to a conscious identity, and not to a phenomenal event. Whether or not that identity is truly a state of being [*a physical condition v. a state of mind*] is the question which this chapter attempts to explore."[97] Sociologist Juliette Sméralda complicates matters, writing that "Fanon hammered home the fact that he wasn't a color, but a man (with a capital H)" for *Homme*.[98] However articulated, these insights are the recognition of a color line, whether visible or invisible, and of the double or "multiple consciousness" due to "multiple jeopardies" also faced by b/Black women, theorizes sociologist Deborah King, whose writings were foundational to intersectional theory in the United States. By this, King refers to the "interactive oppressions that circumscribe our lives and provide a distinctive context for black womanhood" and girlhood alongside the acknowledgement and rejection of those "multiplicative," interlocked, "systematic discriminations of racism, sexism," class, sexuality, cis-patriarchy, and other forms of subjugation illuminated by intersectionality.[99]

In his 2020 article, "The Case for Capitalizing the B in Black," Anthony Appiah weighs in, as does Nell Painter, a month later, in her editorial, "Why 'White' Should Be Capitalized, Too."[100] Recognizing that these "racial identities" are historically constituted, both favor the uppercase to situate, not essentialize, these identities "within the American ideology of race, within which 'Black,' but not 'White,' has been hypervisible as a group identity," argues Painter, as is the case in France. Capitalization, she writes, "simply makes this ideology visible for all" and thereby removes "the comfort of this racial invisibility" for "white people." For Appiah, "the racial designation 'black,' is not a natural category but a social one—a collective identity—with a particular history." He also shares that "black" was in lowercase in his article owing to the capitalization conventions of the magazine in which it was published, the *Atlantic*, which invokes Du Bois's insight while raising the question of that capital "B" as a "why." For the French state, none of these formulations are appealing and would be rejected outright, even as mainstream media employ different casing without explaining why capitalization is used and what it means in the context of universalist principles of raceless equality. Initially, I did not ask interviewees their capitalization practices, but in retrospect, I wish that I had, as it became increasingly clear over time that some were thinking about the distinction, others not at all. I would eventually come to learn that for those who subscribed to political Blackness with that capital "N" (*Noir.e.x.s.*), for whatever reason, capitalization was a way of expressing the idea that "the personal is political," even if inconsistently. For instance, I revisited in 2019 an email written in 2016 with a then graduate student interviewee whose capitalization was a bit all over the place to ask him to help us understand. His response via email, in English, is insightful, as it affirms some interviewees' perspectives and runs counter to others. Here, b/Black should be read as *n/Noir*: "Some people think it is essentialist to put a 'B' for 'Black' and maybe they're right but I tend to write 'Black' when I use it as a common noun and only for distinguishing the 'social color' from the specific color (within the chromatic range). On the other hand, I use 'black' only as an adjective." Others interviewed saw the lowercase as indicative of biological or essentialized race, while others made no distinction or had no particular preference. Inconsistency also obtained among people who have transnational lives and/or traceable names and identities attached to their descendance, heritage, and geographies that race-blind republicanism does not diminish and perhaps even fosters. It is correct that adjectives are not capitalized in France at a grammatical level, but the issue here is about recognition and nonrecognition of a lived experience and how that decision is determined and expressed in terms of capitalization.

More and more in the United States, media outlets, as notes Painter, such as the Associated Press, *New York Times*, *Los Angeles Times*, and *Fox News*, have joined the capitalization band. Brookings Institute President John Allen announced in 2019 that, in recognition of that long arc, the institute had "modernized our writing style guide to capitalize Black when used to reference census-defined black or African American people, with further revisions to a handful of other important racial and ethnic terms," but not "white American," which brings us back to Painter's point.[101] The tendency in the US publishing industry is to assume and, at times, impose a convention of lowercasing "black." In the mid-2000s, I confronted this very issue when editing a volume about b/Black people whose contributors hailed from both sides of the Atlantic and who used different casings for b/Black identity that I purposefully left as indicated when I submitted the volume to the publisher. However, when the manuscript was returned, a copyeditor had systematically put all iterations of b/Black in lowercase throughout the text. The easier fix would have been to put everything in uppercase to also capture a shared political solidarity that I had wrongly presumed. In the end, not everyone agreed. A powerful voice among them gently but assuredly stated that I was in fact imposing my identity politics and US notions of b/Blackness onto people whose self-understandings are not filtered through the same history that made capitalization meaningful for me. For another contributor, that capital eclipsed salient identities that were much more meaningful and themselves hard won, such as expressing a national identity. In revisiting the politics of identity and capitalization that arose from that exchange, the title of Rinaldo Walcotts's insightful collection of essays on Black Canada, *Black Like Who*, kept crossing my mind. Indeed, b/Black like who, for whom, by whom, and against whom, and who ultimately decides about that capital "B" or "N"?

While identity discourses are always in the making, capitalization of racial designation in France, as elsewhere, serves to reframe and resignify imposed racist identity discourses that make what they name. At the same time, capitalization has meant conscious-raising and mobilizing around a shared experience of anti-blackness *against* a robust archive of transtemporal antiblack nomenclature represented by "n-words" in minuscule, be it in English or in French. Unless otherwise explained or indicated in a text, I have opted for the formulation "b/B" or "n/N" to minimize imposing, wittingly or unwittingly, a US frame, even as Black radical traditions from Black Power to Black Lives Matter have influenced capitalization and identity politics among b/Black people in France.

THE CHAPTERS IN THIS JOURNEY

Using a storytelling approach, the prologue serves as the book's entrée, which sets its tone and provides insight into my connection with this subject matter while, this introduction contextualizes my arguments and the cases documented, which derive from recurring themes in this research, themselves indicative of broader debates in society. The key arguments of each chapter are threaded through the opening quotes that provide penetrating insights and glimpses into what lies ahead, and the body of each chapter is prefaced by a summary, titled "Setting a Context," which serves to prepare and guide the reader for the chapter's content. My methods and framing of everyday antiblackness through the lens of Fanon and Essed comprise two separate appendices of this book whose combined chapters explore the difficulties documenting everyday antiblackness statistically and the suppression of race-making knowledge, its expression on the ground, its role in visual culture, and the transversal nature of police violence that targets blackened and arabianized youth, all of which are interlinked by their everydayness. These acts and facts of antiblackness, negated and enabled by raceblind republicanism, are experienced directly and vicariously, that is, by "identification with other groups who are targets of racism" and "racism through the experiences of others because of the very nature of racism," which means that the danger and harm surpass the moment in which antiblack acts are lived.[102] The question of police violence, particularly racial profiling, is an issue that was consistently raised over the years in this work and merits greater visibility precisely because it is the clearest manifestation of the state's monopoly on violence and structural racism. I have therefore devoted the lion's share of these pages to this issue, which, like all the cases and problems discussed, is the surface manifestation of deeper, societal problems. Visual culture has been a powerful lens for exploring antiblackness, including narrative film, which I have at times integrated into chapters as a form of social text. Raceblind republicanism permits and reproduces racist and racialized structures in denying them while attempting to manage their varying manifestations. Each chapter illustrates a dimension of that structure. "The Choice of Ignorance: Equality in Principle vs. Equal Protection" examines the consequences of the official nonrecognition of race by the French state—what sociologist Patrick Simon calls "a choice of ignorance"—and how it obscures both structural and everyday antiblack discrimination, and racism more broadly. Reporting agencies in the European Union have, however, documented antiblack discrimination and antiblack racism, though with great difficulty. I also explore in this chapter a dangerous consequence of the official nonrecognition of b/Black French people in France, the denial of their status as racialized "national minorities," which leaves them without protections against discrimination on the grounds of race in all areas of life. "#YouKnowYoureblackInFranceWhen . . . The Fact of Everyday Antiblackness" returns us to *Libé*'s hashtag, the Twitter storm that it created, and related events in the media that illustrate a pattern of antiblackness in France and in other European societies. I show the harm and effects of these shared, repetitive, familiar, and seemingly small indignities and dehumanizing violations, which are erected on constructs of black inferiority. Among these facts of antiblackness are blackfacing, disparagement humor, and what I refer to as "*nègre* slippage," that is, instances when discourse, typically reserved for private use among likeminded listeners, slips unintentionally into the public domain. In "*Au Nègre Joyeux* and Friends: Everyday Antiblackness Posing as Public Art," I explore the presence of a sign, translated as "The Happy Nigger" which was on public display supposedly from 1748 to 2018. It represents a textbook case for understanding the unwitnessing of antiblackness, preferences for racial sameness, and how history and culture are deployed to legitimize and justify entitlement to these types of everyday assaults. Although it was removed, it has counterparts in other public spaces that I also examine. "On Police Violence" comprises two sections: section I, "'Everyone Hates the Police!' ('*Tout le monde déteste la police!*'): The 'Ceremony of Degradation' and the Logic of Running from Police Violence," examines how raceblind republicanism provides cover for state-driven brutality and cruelty that is rooted in the legacies of racial enslavement and coloniality. Police violence, understood in this book as a "ceremony of degradation," is routinely inflicted on its primary prey, boys and young men racialized-as-arab and black. This "ceremony" includes public humiliation, racists insults, repetitive identity checks, sequestration, beatings, sexual assault, and police custody killings. What has consequently emerged is an underexplored logic among those preyed upon of running not to but from a militarized police force whose abuses rarely come to trial and even more rarely result in conviction. While families are devastated by racial and emotional injustices that result from police violence, they also fight back through the courts where the very principles of raceblind republicanism have also been placed on trial, issues that I examine in section II: "'*Il faut se battre!*' ("You Have to Fight!"): Racial Profiling, Strategic Litigation, and Accountability." Finally, in the "Coda: Universalize to Pantheonize: Scripting Josephine Baker," I return to the bistro where this book began, where I contemplate the ironies, fallacies, contradictions, and seductive power of universalist raceblind republicanism in relation to the pantheonization of Josephine Baker and the mainstreaming of extreme right-wing presidential candidate Éric Zemmour.

THE CHOICE OF IGNORANCE

Equality in Principle vs. Equal Protection

It's a paradox, isn't it. France has such strong ideas about equality but fails to practice them like other countries. Having ideas and practicing them are not same thing, right?
—Social scientist interviewee, 2017

The credo of indifference to differences—the French colorblind approach—leads to promoting what I would call the *choice of ignorance* by removing any reference to ethnic or racial origin from policies or laws (in compliance with the Constitution) as well as from statistics. . . . The omnipresence of references to ethnicity and race reminds us that while France is officially a society without "race," racism and racial discriminations are as widespread as anywhere else.
—Patrick Simon, "The Choice of Ignorance: The Debate on Ethnic and Racial Statistics in France," 2008/2015[1]

France does not recognize the existence within its territory of minorities with a legal status as such and takes the view that the application of human rights to all of a State's citizens on the basis of equality and non-discrimination normally provides them, whatever their situation, with the full and complete protection to which they are entitled.
—UN International Convention on the Elimination of All Forms of Racial Discrimination, 2013[2]

As . . . FRA's EU Minorities and Discrimination Survey . . . confirms, simply "being Black" means often facing entrenched prejudice and exclusion. This situation cannot be

tolerated in the EU, which is founded on the values of respect for human dignity, freedom, democracy, equality, the rule of law and respect for human rights, including the rights of persons belonging to minorities.
—European Union Agency for Fundamental Rights (FRA), *Being Black in the EU*, 2018[3]

SETTING A CONTEXT

Coming from a country in which there is a well-established tradition of studying and tracking the role of race across a wide swath of social institutions, I have long been both infuriated and intrigued by what sociologist and demographer Patrick Simon calls a "choice of ignorance" by the French state, that is, the choice of race-blindness. This chapter examines how this historically rooted model of "equality through invisibility" suppresses knowledge-making and the capacity to generate statistical equality data on the basis of race and/as ethnicity in France where ethnicity is often a race proxy. Such suppression conceals antiblack discrimination and antiblack racism while also disappearing vital evidence in antiracism and antidiscrimination battles, a material effect of this "choice." Among the more deleterious consequences of the nonrecognition of b/Black French people is the concomitant nonrecognition of their status as "national minorities," which leaves them without collective rights and protections authorized by the European Union (EU) of which France is a member state.[4] Put simply, b/Black French people are unprotected "national minorities" in France by dint of this outmoded "choice," and France is not alone in choosing ignorance rather than confronting race.[5] Plenty of evidence from multiple sources, including this book, shows the existence of antiblack discrimination and racism in France and in the EU, and for some time, which gives credence to b/Black people's unprotected status as a racialized and minoritized group. At the same time, national data protection laws and the EU's Data Protection Directive impose strict restrictions on the processing of personal data against abuses. In their interpretation of the directive, some member states classify "racial and ethnic origins" as sensitive personal data, with "racial origin . . . as including ethnic origin," that is, race *and/as* ethnicity.[6] While some states, such as Finland, Ireland, and the United Kingdom, require or promote collecting equality data based on those "origins," not all member states embrace equality statistics disaggregated by race, even with an eye toward antidiscrimination. France is often "seen as a case of absolute prohibition," but important national surveys such as *Trajectories and Origins (TeO1* and the forthcoming *TeO2*) have nonetheless yielded important data—though not without severe restrictions on explicit reference to race and color, causing researchers to develop stratagems to work around these restrictions.[7] Absent these data, race proxies fill the void, but race proxies also obscure race problems.

Member states justify this choice in various ways, but none has been more powerful, enduring, and oft-cited by those rejecting ethno-racialized data than historical memories associated with scientific racism and racial statistics during the Nazi/Vichy era alongside the condemnation of biological racial superiority by international intergovernmental organizations, such as the United Nations. This postwar framing of race has fashioned antiracism laws and cherished principles enshrined in the French Constitution.[8] Consequently, the law of the land is itself a fundamental barrier to the recognition of what exists in the everyday in France, the lived reality of race and specifically antiblackness. Raceblind adherents fail to invoke, however, enslavement and settler colonization by France and its living legacies as race barriers.[9] But here's the rub: disqualifying and rejecting notions of race through discrediting—justifiably—race as biology has become an obstacle to seeing race as socially constructed in other ways and the damage it causes *to* and *in* France and beyond. The daily life of raceblind republicanism in this regard should not be underestimated, as I have seen over the years in France and in my research. Sociologist Michel Wieviorka's observation remains steadfast for many: "If you mention 'ethnic' or 'racial' statistics to a French person, he or she will consider you to be a racist. The French do not consider 'race' as a social construction, they consider it to be a physical definition of human groups and will not accept it."[10] Do not read "white only" for "French," as other racialized groups share this perspective. A thirty-something b/Black French woman whom I interviewed about this issue illustrates the potency of selective historical memory: she describes such statistics as "doing the work of the Nazis" and refuses them altogether.

Challenges to that "choice" result in backlash politics that also attempt to suppress knowing and knowledge-making about the French house that racism built. These politics are inscribed in broader expressions of anti-intellectualism and attacks on critical thought, academic freedom, and so-called "divisive ideas," as we have witnessed in the United States with critical race theory (CRT), intersectionality, and the 1619 Project. Because inconsistencies in categorization are one of many problems invoked by those producing or relying on equality data disaggregated by race in France and the EU, I incorporate the terms and categories used in reports and studies on which I draw to highlight how these empirical and political questions are framed and named in France and in the EU. However, my intent is not to rehash the debate on ethno-racialized statistics or determine whether they should be generated in France; I and others have written about those issues elsewhere.[11] EU and French statisticians have already made the case for generating such statistics through the equality data that they have managed to produce, despite formidable barriers. Meanwhile, those inferiorized by race, and specifically antiblackness, suffer from France's "choice," which officially disappears antiblack violence happening under its very nose.

IN/EQUALITY DATA: DOCUMENTING STATISTICALLY ANTIBLACK DISCRIMINATION AND RACISM

In 2013, the United Nations issued a resolution, declaring 2015–2024 the "International Decade for People of African Descent," emphasizing the importance of "recognizing that people of African descent represent a distinct group whose human rights must be promoted and protected."[12] A daunting statement, to be sure, but one that also highlights two issues at once: the unprotected status of African-descended people worldwide through the very need to make such a declaration and the issue of categorization politics in terms of race proxies that masks diversity as it casts diverse people into a single racialized group. The UN is not alone in sounding an alarm about blackened people's well-being. It reverberates throughout research findings by the European Union Agency for Fundamental Rights (FRA), in particular the first-ever EU-wide survey focused on antiblack discrimination and violence, *Being Black in the EU*, released in 2018. This report documents the lived experiences of "5,803 immigrants and descendants of immigrants of African descent" in twelve member states—Austria, Denmark, Finland, France, Germany, Ireland, Italy, Luxembourg, Malta, Portugal, Sweden, and the United Kingdom—whose overall findings show that

racism based on the colour of a person's skin remains a pervasive scourge throughout the European Union. . . . Racial discrimination and harassment are commonplace. Experiences with racist violence vary but reach as high as 14%. Discriminatory profiling by the police is a common reality. Hurdles to inclusion are multi-faceted, particularly when it comes to looking for jobs and housing. . . . A particularly unsettling pattern is that younger individuals tend to experience more discrimination and exclusion than older individuals. This renders even more urgent the need for intensified efforts to promote the full inclusion of people of African descent in the EU.[13]

Established in 2007, FRA is tasked with providing "independent, evidence-based assistance and expertise on fundamental rights" to the relevant entities in EU and member states. Its purview also involves monitoring the implementation and assessing the outcomes of antidiscrimination laws and measures in those states.[14] Through data collection and survey research, FRA produces equality data, defined as "any piece of information that is useful for the purposes of describing and analyzing the state of equality," whether qualitative and quantitative.[15] These data are not only evidence of racist, exclusionary "unequal treatment," they also inform legislation and policymaking and serve to empower those agitating for racial justice by providing them with actual data. At the same time, the EU must operate "in full respect of national contexts" and therefore cannot really enforce compliance with its data collections' directives when they cut against countries' laws or historical and cultural responses to collecting personal data. The French model of one people, one territory means that "citizens are equal before the law, which implies non-discrimination"—and therein lies one of many difficulties researchers and agencies like FRA face in France and the EU when attempting to generate comparable equality data on the basis of race, let alone data on antiblack discrimination and racism.[16]

Despite those limitations, *Being Black in the EU* shows how equality statistics complement and reinforce observations and studies by an array of social actors and qualitative research about the dangers people racialized-as-black face daily in all areas of life, from education to housing to employment to health to policing to just trying to *be* in the world:

Nearly one in three respondents of African descent (30%) experienced what they perceived as racist harassment in the five years before the survey; one in five (21%) experienced such harassment in the 12 months before the survey (20% of women and 23% of men). . . . Experiences of racist harassment most commonly involve offensive non-verbal cues (22 %) or offensive or threatening comments (21%), followed by threats of violence (8%). . . . Most victims (61%) do not know the perpetrators, but generally identify them as not having a minority background (65%). Some 38% of the victims identified the perpetrators as having a minority ethnic background other than their own. One in 10 of those who experience racist violence say that a law enforcement officer was the perpetrator (11%).[17]

On the "prevalence and frequency of harassment motivated by racism" for "people of African descent" in the study, 32% reported such violence in France five years prior to the survey, though reports were higher in other countries: Finland (63%), Ireland (51%), Denmark and Sweden (41%), and Italy (48%).[18] In emphasizing the "dire picture of reality on the ground" from these results, FRA Director Michael O'Flaherty also noted the "unsettling pattern" of young people experiencing "more discrimination and exclusion than older individuals"; and, as I show in this book, "discriminatory profiling by the police, too, is a common reality."[19] On this point, the majority of victims (63%) under-reported racist police violence because they feared or lacked trust in the police, though researchers observed that victims generally under-reported discriminatory and racist treatment.

In many ways, the *Trajectories and Origins: Survey on the Diversity of the French Population (TeO1)* reinforces and fine-tunes those findings, cited in the introduction, which shows the highest incidences of racism in France against peoples of "sub-Saharan Africa" descent (53%), while the French Defender of Rights (*Le Défenseur des droits*) reported in 2016 the overrepresentation of young "Arab and black" men and boys in cases of racial profiling.[20] The 2020 coronavirus epidemic placed these issues and the difficulty of documenting ethno-racial disparities in sharper relief where pandemics of racism and police violence converged with COVID-19 in impoverished urban areas where people of African immigration and descent appear to predominate, areas pounded by the harsh police enforcement of stay-in-shelter mandates. Seine-Saint-Denis, a department outside Paris where "immigrants and their descendants are over-represented," illustrates this point.[21] Since 2005, this region, where the uprisings occurred and where the poverty rate in 2019 was nearly 30% and unemployment 11%, has become synonymous with racialized inequality, urban blight, and hyper-policing.[22] It also ranks third in terms of population density, that is, "6,802 inhabitants per km^2 (more than 64 times the average density in France)," and, at the height of COVID-19, between March and April 2020, it had "the highest excess mortality rate in Île-de-France . . . approximately 130%, compared to 74% in Paris and 122% in the Hauts-de-Seine."[23] Existing data also show that the lion's share of essential, frontline workers (cashiers, service sector employees, nursing assistants, etc.) reside in this region, which also has the fewest medical facilities. However, what public health data do not and cannot show are *racialized* disparities in COVID-related deaths, as dramatically witnessed in the United States and the UK. High excess mortality coupled with demographics in Seine-Saint-Denis serve as race proxies, but vital race-based data are not really known.

Lacking data to show facts of antiblackness, civil society organizations in France have generated their own "racial statistics" over the years to illustrate what race-blind republicanism prohibits. In 2007, the TNS-Sofres/Representative Council of France's Black Associations (CRAN) issued the "first-ever" survey, as it was called at the time, on antiblack "discrimination" in France, which found that among 581 persons who were 18 years or older and self-reported as "black" [lower case theirs], 67% said yes to the question: "Would you say that, in your everyday life, you personally are a victim of *racial* discrimination" in metropolitan France?[24] Moreover, people who self-identified as b/Black generally reported discrimination more frequently than people who said they were *métis* or mixed, "69% versus 56%," particularly in public spaces and at work.[25] B/black people also reported that they were stopped by the police more often, "an average of 2.8 stops in the last 12 months compared to 1.4 stops for mixed people."[26] In other words, equality statistics from a variety of sources have shown over time a frightening pattern of "unequal treatment" at best, and violent aggressions against blackened peoples in France who, as throughout the EU, appear to be in danger.

FRA's second, extensive EU-wide study places these issues in a broader context. Their 2017 *Second European Union Minorities and Discrimination Survey* (EU-MIDIS II), from which *Being Black* is drawn, "surveyed 25,515 persons with different ethnic minority and immigrant backgrounds in all 28 EU Member States."[27] This study also served to evaluate progress made since FRA's first EU-MIDIS survey in 2008. Overall, findings show "little progress" in the EU where "the prevalence of discrimination on the grounds of racial or ethnic origin remains consistently high, both over time and across different population groups in different Member States." Respondents "with ethnic minority or immigrant backgrounds," reported all manner of everyday antiblackness. "Violence motivated by hatred" cannot be stressed enough in matters of un-protection, and, once more, blackened peoples attributed such treatment to "visible signs of difference, such as skin colour, physical appearance or wearing traditional or religious clothing in public spaces."[28] For instance, in the five years before EU MIDIS II, these findings translated into over eight in ten (84%) of "respondents with a sub-Saharan background" who indicated skin color as central factor in their denial of housing. In the area of employment, 50% reported similarly with other triggers being last name (36%) and linguistic features such as accent (18%). As Maya Smith documents in her perceptive study of France and Italy, *Senegal Abroad: Linguistic Borders, Racial Formations, and Diasporic Imaginaries*, perceived linguistic competence is highly determinant of cultural belonging and legitimacy in those societies, as elsewhere.[29] Overall, results show that "41% of Roma, 45% of persons with a North African background, 39% of sub-Saharan Africans, 60% of Roma and Travellers and 25% of Jews felt discriminated against because of their ethnic or immigrant background."[30] For Romani peoples, these findings give added pause and reinforce beliefs that I have heard voiced many times that the Romani are the most despised people in Europe whom FRA has also surveyed apart. Sociologist Giovanni Picker's insightful study of the centrality of race in Romani lived experience and their disposability in urban European cities also captures how space is always already raced.[31] Still, the broad categories used in these surveys paper over much, including internal distinctions, understudied intergroup tensions, and antiblack, race-based discriminatory treatment. People perceived and treated as b/Black exist within the geo-categories listed (i.e., Jewish, North African, Sub-Saharan African, and Romani,) as do other racialized groups, including whitened peoples, which means that these studies cannot capture internal specificities and dynamics. Based on its data, the FRA concludes that "manifestations of discrimination and racism *that specifically affect* persons of African descent *should be acknowledged to ensure effective responses* to these phenomena [emphases mine]."[32] At the same time, the lack of official ethno-racial data prompted these observers to add that "the survey therefore cannot claim to capture the entire scale and complexity of the experiences of Black people across Europe."[33]

POLITICS AND PITFALLS OF DATA DISAGGREGATION

The EU has adopted legislation since 2000 to battle these problems, but EU authorities also maintain that "without the evidence based on equality *statistics*, it would be *impossible* to track progress in achieving goals towards equality [emphases mine]," as mandated by law for the "promotion of equal treatment."[34] The Racial Equality Directive (RED) broadly "prohibits direct and indirect discrimination on the grounds of racial or ethnic origin," along with the Framework Decision on Combating Racism and Xenophobia, which makes these ills, including hate speech, criminal offenses and subject to criminal law across EU states.[35] The Employment Equality Directive (EED) proscribes such discrimination on the basis of "religion or belief, disability, age or sexual orientation," and gender equality directives, adopted since 2004, mandate equal treatment principles between women and men, though it is unclear if non-binary and transgender people are similarly protected.[36] In their critique of the

Framework Decision, the European Network Against Racism (ENAR), a grassroots "pan-European anti-racism network," also gestures toward a problem raised by FRA researchers about inconsistencies across member states that affect the transposition of laws. ENAR writes that this legislation "sets the bar very low," granting too much latitude at the national level for lawmakers to devise their criminal codes, which makes transposition of the Framework Decision problematic, more so when inconsistencies and lack of clarity prevail across states about definitions of racist, discriminatory behavior and attitudes.[37] Other advocacy groups have also questioned the capacity of the EU to enforce these directives in light of the evidence that its own agencies have produced, evidence that, by their own admission, does not show and cannot show the magnitude of the problem. Much lies with the lack of "reliable, valid, and comparable" equality statistics across states, but the problem is not only there. The European Commission, other EU bodies, and FRA strongly assert that data be "disaggregated on the basis of racial or ethnic origin in order to capture both subjective experiences of discrimination and victimisation and structural aspects of racism and discrimination."[38] On that point, the EU and France fundamentally part ways.

Although race and ethnicity were not officially systematized in France, the two exceptions were the registering of Jewish people under Nazi/Vichy regimes and colonial statistics in countries colonized by France. In the name of the public's interest and its security, the French Constitutional Council, France's highest constitutional authority, "forbids the processing for the purposes of measuring personal data revealing directly or indirectly the racial or ethnic origin of people, as well as the introduction of variables on race or religion in administrative files."[39] But which public's interests are being served and protected by this decision? In short, "ethnic and racial origin" are not considered objective concepts and data, though proxies are allowed, such as "names, geographical origin or previous citizenship," discussed ahead. Even as France's highest judiciary court held the French state accountable for "discriminatory identity controls" by the French police in 2019, France's 1978 Data Protections Law, which prohibits the collection of ethno-racial data, is no dead letter and is enforced by France's Data Protection Authority, the CNIL, the National Commission on Informatics and Liberty (*Commission Nationale de l'Informatique et des Libertés*).[40] In other words, French principles informing its laws and EU mandates for protecting b/Black French and other vulnerable peoples are incompatible, leaving them at risk.

In March 2018, I and eight other researchers of the African diaspora in Europe were invited to a meeting at FRA in Austria to offer feedback on a draft of *Being Black in the EU* before it was launched publicly at the European Parliament in November 2018.[41] Socially constructed race and antiblack racism were central to our respective research, which covered Austria, Belgium, Finland, France, Germany, Ireland, Italy, Sweden, the UK, and comparatively Spain. Overall, we expressed concerns about terminology, categories, concepts, methodology, and the omission of Spain from the report, given the sociohistorical importance of Afro Spaniards and the violence that African migrants to the region have confronted in places such as Ceuta and Melilla. We were particularly vocal about disaggregating data by race for the reasons already outlined, and given my own work in France, I was insistent upon this point only to have the French representative invoke universalism and French constitutional prohibitions as impediments in response. While he may have disagreed, he was clear about it being a formidable barrier. Nearly three years later, I asked a principal investigator at FRA about any updates since then specific to documenting race. She replied in an email that there were "no real changes in the general 'colorblind' approach towards data on ethnic or racial origin in France nor in Germany. . . . There is nevertheless a kind of slow move on the level of the EU to try to push more and convince countries to do more in this regard."[42] In the twenty years since the passing of RED, the dial has not fundamentally moved, which does not bode well for that "push" or for changing the "choice of ignorance."

In their insightful analysis of the RED and the "adaptational pressures" from divergences in national laws and customs and EU legislation, political scientists Terri Givens and Rhonda Evans Case write that such incompatibility "produces contestation, delay, and the possibility of implementation failure," more so when authorities and actors in such states "interpret their interests in opposition to the Directive and actively seek to thwart its transposition" or other EU laws.[43] The longstanding debates, at times vitriolic, in France on ethno-racialized categories and statistics exemplify this point, and passions still run high, as do fears and anxieties of being "racially documented." A b/Black young man in his mid-twenties whom I interviewed expressed it this way: "What if they [the statistics] prove them [the perpetrators of antiblackness] right about us [b/Black people]?"—"right" in the sense of black deficiency rather than demonstrating inequalities and exclusions.

This view is inseparable from the innumerable times that interviewees and everyday people have invoked Nazism and mistrust of government related to that history. The violent opposition in the early 1990s to demographer Michèle Tribalat's study on immigrant "insertion" contextualizes those passions, as it became a lightning rod for attack because it used what were considered race variables (i.e., national origins and native language) to identify "ethnic groups" within African and Arab-speaking immigrant communities in France.[44] For opponents, Tribalat's categories also objectified and ranked lower racialized groups in terms of their supposed capacity to intermarry—presumably with a white French partner—as a key index of assimilation. Tribalat's colleague, Hervé Le Bras, compared her study to the Wannsee Protocols (1942) by the Nazis. Recall that these procedures were used to define a "Jewish race" based on parentage and thus were instrumental in carrying out the mass murder of Jewish people, so the framing of these pitched battles and rejection of these methods derive from entrenched feelings and attitudes that have not dissipated. And keep in mind that a discourse of *racial* discrimination had only entered into public debates in the 1990s in France, as antiracism mobilizations and scholarly work shed greater light on structural inequality and discrimination against the so-called second generation of "postcolonial" African and Asian immigration.[45]

A DIRE STATE OF UNPROTECTION

The UN and the FRA are not the only bodies that paint a "dire picture" of b/Black people as unprotected "national minorities." The *European Parliament Resolution on Fundamental Rights of People of African Descent in Europe*, adopted by the Parliament in 2019, minces no words when pointing out:

Afrophobia, Afri-phobia and anti-black racism as a specific form of racism, including any act of violence or discrimination, fueled by historical abuses and negative stereotyping, and leading to the exclusion and dehumanisation of people of African descent. The Fundamental Rights Agency has documented the fact that minorities in Europe with sub-Saharan African backgrounds are particularly likely to experience racism and discrimination in all areas of life.[46]

Yet the recurrence of the same or similar themes and patterns from varied sources send a clear message that this evidence is not taken seriously, that power forces are either not listening or choose to ignore these grave problems for "an estimated 15 million people of African descent living in Europe."[47]

How French Members of the European Parliament (MEP) voted on this Resolution is both revealing and chilling, more so with Italy's first Black MEP, Cécile

Kyenge, as its architect, who has repeatedly suffered antiblack attacks from right-wing MEP's that mirror broader issues of antiblackness in Italian society.[48] Overall, 535 MEPs voted in favor of the resolution, while 80 voted against it, and 44 abstained. When I asked one of the coordinators of the resolution at the EP why all of the 751 MEPs did not vote, he replied in an email: "It is the normal figure. You only get a full house if it is a really important file."[49] The broader implication of nearly 100 people missing the vote strongly suggests that b/Black people and antiblackness for some states are neither issues nor priorities. Of the 74 French MEPs, 36 (48%) voted against the resolution, and of the 80 MEPs overall who voted no, 45% were French. In other words, 1 in 2 French MEPs voted against a measure "recogniz[ing] discrimination and past injustices" and the "fundamental rights of people of African descent" who "are entitled to protection from these inequities both as individuals and as a group."[50] The vote among French MEPs also reflects how structural antiblack discrimination expresses itself through decision-makers controlling levers of power who need never say race's name. The same could be said of the European Commission, though it acknowledges in its antiracism action plan for 2020–2025 that "upholding values starts at home, in our own institution" where all its Commissioners for 2019–2024 appear white.[51] When viewing the photos of the no-voting French MEPs, they are also white-appearing, which may not reflect how they self-perceive, and they hail from two political parties on the right and far-right respectively, *Les Républicains* and the National Rally (*le Rassemblement national*), formerly the National Front (*le Front National* or *FN*), the Far Right party founded by Jean-Marie Le Pen.

DISMEMBERING WORDS FOR OBJECTS AND THE FAR RIGHT

The popularity of extreme-right 2022 presidential hopeful Éric Zemmour, to whom I return in the coda, overshadowed during the campaigns the party to which he is indebted and whose normalization in France paved his way. As journalist and commentator Rokhaya Diallo writes in her hard hitting *Washington Post* editorial titled "Marine Le Pen Is Now Part of France's Mainstream: That Should Scare Us All," the Far Right is nonetheless an "an unavoidable force in French politics" and "Marine" has "managed to both raise her profile and cultivate an image that white-washed her dangerous agenda . . . [and] has definitely won the 'de-demonization' game," which entails using only her first name which disassociates her from the taint of her family name.[52] It is worth pausing here to recall that the Le Pens were in the running for Élysée Palace (the presidency) on more than one occasion. The first occurred in 2002 when Jean-Marie Le Pen received 17.9% of the vote, followed by his daughter Marine Le Pen who received nearly 34% of the popular vote in 2017 compared to Emmanuel Macron's 66%, and in 2022 when she garnered over 41.5% of the vote in a too-close-for-comfort race that left Macron President of the Republic (58.5%) in an election where a record 28% of the voters abstained in the second round. As reported in *Le Monde*, "If we add the invalid ballots and abstention, Mr. Macron was reelected president with only 38.5% of the votes among the registered voters," which ultimately reinforces the point about the ever-growing force and mainstreaming of the Far Right, a fact reinforced by the National Rally's record gains of 89 MPs in the 2022 parliamentary elections. In its quest for political respectability, "the evolution of the FN owes much in recent years to the efforts of its leaders to rid it of the ideologies of the extreme right on which it was founded and to distinguish it from its trademark anti-Semitism," writes Michel Wieviorka.[53] The price of shedding that inheritance has meant attempting to dilute its white nativist, anti-immigrant, Muslim-phobic supremacist messaging, but its platform and its love fest with Donald Trump's chief strategist Steve Bannon show the new National Front to be little more than old wine in a new bottle, illustrating what Ann Stoler terms "colonial aphasia." This "dismembering of words for objects to which they refer" is a "political condition" in which genealogy and knowledge are occluded, argues Stoler, thereby yielding a "space that has allowed Marine Le Pen and her broad constituency to move from the margin and extreme—where her father was banished—to a normalized presence in contemporary France."[54] Anti-other politics and immigrant dog whistles are a mainstay to rally and secure the base. For instance, capitalizing on the plunging popularity of Emmanuel Macron, Marine Le Pen and her niece Marion Maréchal-Le Pen, a former MEP for the National Front, have particularly set their sights on the younger generation and disaffected workers among the "Yellow Vest" movement (*les gilets jaunes*). In 2018 and 2019, I witnessed firsthand acts 1 through 9 of the protests, vividly captured in David Dufresne's documentary, *The Monopoly of Violence*. However, it was not immigration that ignited the over 200,000 protestors in the uprising's early phases but a hike in fuel prices by the centrist Macron administration that tipped the scale. In a context of 9% unemployment and the long-standing economic precarity inherited from the previous administration, working people were struggling to make ends meet in an economy where their buying power had spiraled downward for some time. The fuel tax was a last straw and a promissory for continued suffering, particularly for people whose vehicles were essential to their livelihood. Enough was enough for Priscillia Ludosky, who launched a Change.org petition in opposition to the new tax.[55] Ludosky, to the surprise of many, is also b/Black. This single act energized a sleeping giant whose chain mail armor was a yellow security vest, worn in case and cause of emergency. The messaging was unmistakable. A simple everyday garment became a powerful visual of economic insecurity and badge of working-class honor. However, the optics of the movement in media depictions, particularly televised townhall-style meetings with Macron, showed the intersection of class, race, and gender through absence or omission. Rarely were b/Black people or nonwhite persons in general visible; nor were connections made with, for instance, the twenty-two-month battle waged by African housekeepers at the Ibis Hotel in Paris who were on strike for better working conditions and pay also in 2019. The power of symbolism was not lost, however, on hundreds of undocumented African people affiliated with a migrant association in Paris that drew inspiration from the Yellow Vests. With the threat of deportation looming, the "Black Vests" occupied the Panthéon in 2019 to draw attention to the long-standing crisis and expulsion of unauthorized African migrants from metropolitan France.[56] This staunchly anti-leader and, for some, anti-Macron social movement with nationalist elements in its midst proved irresistible to Le Pen, who sought unsuccessfully to co-opt and steer the Yellow Vests toward her Party's agenda, including toppling both Macron and the European Union, of which she is no fan. In 2019, the public witnessed a telling twist of fate when Marine Le Pen's party dominated the European Parliamentary elections, winning 23.3% of the vote and ahead of Macron's party (22.1%), though 49.9% abstained, including 60% of those under 35.[57]

The point is that having antidiscrimination laws is one thing; enforcing them is another, especially in a political arena where raceblindness prevails, which leaves the EU between a rock and a hard place.

RACE PROXIES, RACE PROBLEMS

Because most EU member states do not track race in their census or in their administrative statistics, researchers rely on self-reports and race proxies, primarily respondents' country of birth and parents' country of birth (i.e., citizenship, nationality, and immigration status), to categorize populations for equality statistics. This method allows researchers in raceblind states to identify the second generation but not how they may explicitly self-identify or be identified in terms of race, nor do those proxies reveal how hierarchies and inequalities have conditioned their racialization and thereby self-understandings. As we have seen, geographical regions do not map neatly onto socially constructed race, and the container category "sub-Saharan African" is a catchall race substitute for "b/Black," even as this vast region is itself multiracialized. Consider, for instance, the categories used in the 2020 French employment survey on the "descendants of immigrants by country of origin" from the National Institute for the Study of Demographics (INED) and National Institute of Statistics and Economic Studies (INSEE). "Immigrant descendant," the second generation, indicates someone born in France with one immigrant parent, and if both parents are immigrants, then the father's country is the default, an enduring legacy of patriarchy. There is also the distinctive definition of "immigrant" in France: someone who has acquired French nationality and been "naturalized" can still be classified as an immigrant, but "French-born people are never considered immigrants in public statistics."[58] The countries listed in the employment survey are "Portugal, Italy, Spain, Other EU countries, Algeria, Morocco, Tunisia, Other African countries, Turkey, [and] Other Countries," and a variety of studies already show that blackened people are long-standing populations in those geographies or are there as a result of migration.[59] But how are we to understand their treatment in society as people racialized-as-black? In countries with an established track record on producing significant research and scholarship on race intersectionally, its direct role and consequences in social institutions "would not have been possible without data on racial categories," argues for instance the American Sociological Association.[60] This begs the question of the location of race and its effects in the French labor market and economy that go unseen in national surveys. After all, FRA, *TeO*, and diverse organizations show robust and shocking evidence of discrimination and racism in the areas of life covered by RED and other equality directives in France and the EU.[61]

The French census asks questions about nationality and citizenship status, so "immigrant descent" is relatively easy to identify.[62] But descent also has a shelf life because "origins" become less legible by the third+ generation, as French people by acquisition (and otherwise) meld into the majority population. At the FRA meeting in Austria, we particularly emphasized this point in relation to the importance of disaggregating data on race and having it recognized as a specific ground of discriminatory treatment. One colleague put it plainly when stating that the experiences of his children would be totally eclipsed by current data-gathering constraints in this regard. In our follow-up remarks, our group wrote that "the survey could not capture the scale and complexity of Black experiences in Europe, including Black Europeans themselves, who have been erased from the survey. The survey captures 1st and 2nd generation migrants from 'Sub-Saharan Africa (which is itself a problematic term) but does not and therefore cannot be said to represent 'Black Europe.' It entirely erases third generation populations and significantly underrepresents the Caribbean presence."[63] The European Parliament Resolution on the fundamental rights of African-descended people echoes this concern: "Equality data collection in EU Member States . . . *often omits descendants of migrants or 'third generation migrants' and beyond* [emphasis mine]."[64] Despite these limitations, results from the FRA and *TeO1* surveys show that racism and violence in the EU and France respectively are "distinctly" related to skin color. However, it is worth noting that the French data-protection authorities (CNIS and CNIL) also forbade *TeO* researchers from asking skin color questions, effectively making origins the proxy for color and thereby for race. The principal investigators explicitly addressed the impact of suppressing this critical aspect of a study on population diversity and discrimination in France. "The impossibility of tackling this dimension of identities and discrimination head-on in a scientific survey," they write, "raises questions, on the one hand, about the freedom to conduct research on these issues and, on the other hand, about the existing confusion between an 'ethno-racial frame of reference,' used by administrations, and categories, albeit statistical ones, constructed by researchers for the purposes of knowledge production."[65] To be clear, the issue is not only about creating ethno-racialized categories since this is done every day, notably by the state through police databases of victims and offenders, writes sociologist Abdellali Hajjat. These databases, he explains, "contain a racial filter with twelve different 'types' (White or Caucasian, Mediterranean, Gypsy, Middle Eastern, North African, Asian or Eurasian, Amerindian, Indian, Mesoamerican, Black, Polynesian, Melanesian-Kanak). The term 'negroid type' is regularly used in police reports. In other words, police officers and gendarmes use racial categories every day to work," even as data-protection authorities have regularly dissuaded their use.[66] An INSEE statistician explained that making categories is not the same as using them statistically: "It is not because police use ethno-racial categories to characterize offenders etc. that . . . categories in files end up in statistics. Actually, the irony is that these categories are widely used by the police *but their collection into numbers and tables is strictly controlled, so that they are simply nonexistent* [emphasis his]." In other words, as he further wrote, "categorization exists, but not the stats (even though it would be easy to go in that direction)."[67] When I asked the same researcher if he sees any foreseeable change in the future in terms of the possibility of measuring statistically discrimination or inequality in terms of race (not color) and ethnicity within the French population (citizens), he replied in an email: "Nothing will change in a near future. We are collecting data on the 3rd generation in our ongoing . . . survey, but otherwise only a handful of surveys have collected ethno-racial data, and not in the network of public statistics surveys."[68] In other words, the status quo for now, and the lack of a b/Black racial or ethnic category means that the full complexity of b/Black people's experiences cannot be captured, not only in France but also within groups identified as North African/Maghrebin or Asian.

LIMITS OF SELF-REPORTS

The last issue that I wish to raise on these points concerns the identity politics of self-reporting a racialized identity in a raceblind France. While pragmatic, sociologist Wendy Roth argues that self-reports do not help us understand the outcomes and underlying structures of racialized unequal treatment that result from racism. For instance, socially excluded, second-generation Muslim girls in the French outer cities identified themselves as French in my early ethnographic research on French identity politics. But what we also want to understand is how these girls are perceived and treated in society, despite their assertions, and how power, resources, rewards, hierarchies, category formation, and a host of other factors are drawn in society, because they have been racialized in particular ways, as seen in French national education in terms of, for instance, ability tracking. For Roth, "observed race," how others racialize thus classify us, provides more insight into how mechanisms of socioeconomic exclusions operate.[69] But in France, this method would mean introducing into the society what the raceblind state already rejects, a race question.

Moreover, the "tabooing" or outlawing of race and racialized identities can influence both how individuals self-understand and self-report their identities. For instance, in France, mixed (*métis.se*) has long been an everyday category that defines a distinctive experience among people who may be unwittingly absorbed into other racialized groups and who may contest that affiliation or the discourse of *métis.se*. Here, I am reminded of many random conversations and reactions over the years to my self-identifying as a Black American (*Noire américaine*), as memorably occurred in 2019 with a self-identified Tunisian and French taxi driver who, based on my accent, had originally asked me where I was from. When I replied the US, he asked about my lineage—the "Where are you from, *from*" question—to which I casually replied that I am Black American. "You're not black," he insisted and told me instead that I was *métisse*, though I am not, but clearly my ethno-political identity did not correspond to how he racialized me. Similarly, and interestingly, I have confronted sadness, pity, and confusion when I identify as African American but am unable to say from where on the continent I or my people hail. Offering a brief history on US plantation enslavement and identity politics has at times confused more than clarified. Politics of identity and thereby categorization are unstable, messy, stubborn, slippery, and complex. On this point, Stuart Hall writes in "Minimal Selves" that "identity is formed at the unstable point where the 'unspeakable' stories of subjectivity meet the narratives of history," exposing hegemonic forces that we do not fully see nor control.[70]

TeO and FRA have generated crucial equality data, demonstrating that these race matters are neither academic nor statistical questions but lived experiences that profoundly affect the lives of real human beings, navigating treacherous waters in countries where they are factually, not "fake-tually," oppressed. What's lacking is enforcement of equality directives to translate law into practice among all member states. The "dire" condition of b/Black people sounded by these observers also recalls *Libération*'s "call for stories," discussed in the introduction, in which readers were asked what it means to be b/Black in France on a daily basis. In Europe more broadly, the answer, according to FRA, is this: "Being black in the EU often means racism and poor jobs," underpinned by antiblackness that is formally negated and thereby perpetuated by the French state.[71] Whatever the limitations, these surveys are the evidence of blackened people unseen who are racialized, minoritized, and unprotected in France.

UNPROTECTED NATIONAL MINORITIZED PEOPLES IN FRANCE

The evidence from an array of surveys, declarations, resolutions, legislation, and qualitative studies confirm b/Black French citizens are what the Council of Europe calls "national minorities" who have been denied the protections of EU laws and equal protection under the law in France. The French state refuses to acknowledge this fact, for doing so means recognizing "collective rights," an anathema to how

French citizenship and nationhood are conceived and framed by constitutional principles of indivisibility and universalism. Thus, national principles designed to provide equal protection wind up producing the opposite effect, while distorted historical narratives about the causes of inequality and the massive overrepresentation of whitened bodies wielding power and resources in French institutions and society are presented through raceblind ideology as the natural order of things. The zero sum of principles over protection renders moot statements by the Parliamentary Assembly of the Council of Europe on these groups: "Protecting persons belonging to national minorities is crucial for ensuring the equality of all people, preserving social and political stability and democratic security and promoting the diversity of cultures in Europe."[72] However, France has neither signed nor ratified the Council of Europe's Framework Convention for the Protection of National Minorities (Framework Convention), claiming that "constitutional obstacles" prevent it from acknowledging collective rights for minoritized nationals.[73] Adopted in 1994 and put into effect in 1998, the Framework Convention "is Europe's most comprehensive treaty protecting the rights of persons belonging to national minorities," and "the first *legally* binding multilateral instrument [emphasis mine]," dedicated to their protection throughout the world.[74] According to the Council of Europe, which describes itself as the continent's foremost human rights organization, rights enjoyed by national minorities are also the very ones that the French state rejects, namely "freely [read: publicly] expressing ethnic, cultural, linguistic and religious identities."[75] Rejected especially are subjectivities or race-conscious identities that are the fruits of stigma reversal, which have long been a means of self- and group-defense against group-based attacks throughout the b/Black diaspora. Negritude of the past and *n/Noir.e.s* self-understandings of the present exemplify this point.

Challenges to French indivisibility, particularly in terms of race, religion, co-national identities or hybridity (e.g., Malian-French) are "defined only in negative terms: as what the French society is *not* and should not become [emphasis his]," asserts Simon, because it cuts deeply against "Republican values and national cohesion," which are elusive in practice.[76] In other words, one can express all sorts of particularism, but there are material consequences for doing so in the public sphere. For instance, state actors have regularly sanctioned those who cross that raceblind republican line by typically branding any presumed ethno-racial mobilization or gathering as "communitarian" (*communautaire*), a pejorative label and discourse that serves to delegitimize ethno-racial identities and activity in public space by painting its embracers as promotors of divisibility and thus threats to

French principles and values. Ultimately, the failures of raceblind republicanism both block and create ethno-racialized communities, but when branded communitarian by statist forces, the consequences are real, which has included state actors canceling the events of b/Black citizens in state-controlled venues and rescinding public funding. This style of shock combat rained down in 2017 on Mwasi, an Afro-feminist collective, from strange bedfellows, which vividly captures at once the material consequences of raceblind republicanism and how weaponizing it and its discourse can result in antiblack discrimination. The Twitter exchanges that ensued got very ugly, to use the vernacular, while also demonstrating the anxieties and aggressions that surface when someone asserts a race-conscious subjectivity at odds with raceblind republicanism.[77]

It all began when the public became aware of three breakout sessions during an Afro-feminist festival organized by Mwasi devoted to (1) b/Black women only, (2) b/Black people and women of color (i.e., *femmes racisé.es*), and (3) another open to everyone, respectively. Far right groups and the media quickly described the event as "forbidden to whites" (i.e., "*interdit aux blancs*") and accused the group of anti-white racism, while others joined the trend in condemning the groups as *communautaire*. Their high-profile detractors also included the International League against Racism and Anti-Semitism (Licra) on the right; SOS-Racisme on the left; the white left-leaning mayor of Paris and 2022 French Socialist party presidential hopeful, Anne Hidalgo; the first b/Black woman hired in 2005 to anchor prime time news in metropolitan France and 2022 presidential contender on the left, Audrey Pulvar; and the w/White left-wing former Secretary of State for the Family, Laurence Rossignol, who in 2016 engaged in what I call "*nègre* slippage" during a televised broadcast when referring to enslaved black people in the United States as such. I return to Rossignol and slippage in the chapter, "#YouKnowYoureblackInFranceWhen . . .".

Nevertheless, the strategy of non-mixing to create safe spaces has been used by marginalized peoples, including white feminists since the 1960s, to mitigate the interference of entitled voices that tended to highjack their conversations and agendas.[78] Sociologists Christine Delphy and Sylvie Tissot cut to the chase when describing what became an overblown media event: "In 2017, in Paris, supposedly a world city, the reunion of a few young black women among themselves became a matter of state, as if they were endangering the Republic and its proclaimed universalism."[79] If one has international name recognition like Rokhaya Diallo, all the worse. Ms. Diallo has also been routinely subjected to all manner of violence, including lawsuits and threats of rape and death for her speaking racial truth to raceblind power, causing a range of attacks from local governments withdrawing promised financial support to associations inviting her to speak in government-controlled public locales. These attacks have only strengthened her resolve, making her one of France's keenest social critics of intersectional antiblack racism in her diverse films, writings, and public forums. Trying to silence her, to douse her flame, has only allowed a phoenix to rise.

In France, antiracism laws have been in effect since the French law of 1972, which was shaped by the post–World War II years. Political scientists Erik Bleich writes that in 1990, the next key antiracism legislation, the Gayssot Law, emerged with the rise of the Far Right and anti-immigrant campaigns.[80] In other words, France has antiracism and antidiscrimination laws and an equality body, the French Defender of Rights, as well as EU-level protections, but something is not working for racialized, minoritized groups within the existing framework where a variety of evidence shows that they are unprotected. The ravages of COVID-19 and police violence in under-resourced neighborhoods in France have also prompted academics and activists to double down on demands for the recognition of race and ethno-racial statistics in France. This included the first b/Black and short-lived government spokeswoman under President Macron, Sibeth Ndiaye (April 1, 2019 to July 6, 2020), who in an op-ed called for revisiting "in a calm and constructive manner the debate on ethnic statistics" in the battle against "racial discrimination," adding that "today we are paying the price for the erasure of republican universalism."[81] Some observers viewed Ndiaye's position as secretly expressing the wishes of the president, but Macron ultimately undercut her when asserting that the "ethnicisation of the social question" amounted to "breaking the Republic in two," following the reshuffle of his government and resignation of his prime minister after pivotal regional elections.[82] The consequences of this choice of ignorance are multiple and include the suppression of equality data and attempts to suppress supposedly "divisive ideas" imported from the United States, ideas that state authorities and raceblind adherents see as "tear[ing] France apart."[83] Equality data are not recognized as such but they are, by definition, a threat to raceblind republicanism in efforts to identify and disaggregate race.

ANTIRACISM AS RACISM AND KNOWLEDGE SUPPRESSION

To explain the logic of race neutrality in the French context, philosopher Magali Bessone and political scientist Daniel Sabbagh invoke, along with others, the power of historical memory and how "the de-legitimation of racism has led to the disqualification of 'race' as a term with descriptive or analytical validity."[84] The United Nations and UNESCO Conventions and Declarations from 1948 to 1967 are indicative of this point and played a pivotal role in denouncing and discrediting scientific racism, racial discrimination, and genocide with the aim of making them punishable by law. Those atrocities convinced member states, elaborate Galonnier and Simon, that "any doctrine of superiority based on racial differentiation is scientifically and empirically false, morally reprehensible, socially unjust and dangerous and that nothing could ever justify racial discrimination wherever it occurs, neither in theory nor in practice."[85] Bessone and Sabbagh argue that the term and concept of race in France did not undergo the type of semantic transformations that occurred in the United States, and that thus in France, race remains fraught with essentialist notions that make the concept and term more the reserve of the extreme Right and "a minority of social science practitioners, inspired by its prevalent use in the U.S."[86] In French social science, Bessone and Sabbagh maintain, "the view that race is only a 'collective fiction' largely prevails," but the next generation of scholars have thrown down the gauntlet by challenging this perspective through their research, though not without reprisal from powerful academics and state actors.[87] In an email exchange in 2019, I asked an established sociologist in France his thoughts about those observations and the persistence of race taboos in the French academy. In his response, he acknowledged their weakening but saw no end in the foreseeable future. His email is worth quoting at length, as it echoes concerns raised by other interviewees and references polemics that would intensify on both sides of the Atlantic around questions of academic freedom and what some observers in France called "intellectual terrorism" by state actors and the French intelligensia:

The taboos, it is true, are *slightly* less omnipresent in university research than in the mainstream media and in mainstream politics, where we all know how strong they remain. Lately I've seen some truly horrendous McCarthyistic rhetoric developing against any attempt whatsoever to legitimize the use of race as an instrument of analysis, or to combine that with gender, or to speak in the name of minorities whose origins within the Republic may be traced to colonialism and slavery etc. There have been petitions to condemn the language of "decolonial" struggles and even the language of "intersectionality" as some sort of mortal ideological poison that the Republic must never accept. . . . It's no doubt true that there are a few more spaces now than 20 years ago in the French university in which it's possible to discuss race, and slavery and colonialism and their legacies etc., not to mention antiracist struggles etc. Such pockets may be found in the social sciences a tiny bit (Fassin brothers and others); in anthropology and history a little (depends on where), and in also, as you note, in my current niche of American studies more than in most places. But to say that there is frank and open debate on public policy on the basis of this kind of knowledge. . . . *oh là là, on en est loin* [far from it]. Nasty atmosphere in general.

Over the years, I have witnessed powerful adherents of raceblind republicanism reprimand, critique, and sanction French scholars and students who have attempted to use concepts and frames of race and racialization in their work and/or organize events explicitly on those ideas. "My dissertation advisor warned me not to refer to race in my work," one junior French scholar shared during a conference on critical race theory (CRT) in 2019, so he resorted to euphemisms in his research by referring to "white informants" with "French-sounding" names and people of African descent with names ethnically inflected. This event was met with hostility by some at the university where it was held because of its theme. One work-around has been to invite speakers from "race-conscious" countries to validate or legitimize interventions on race. Or non-French scholars have brought the battle directly to France by organizing events that foreground the sociohistorical realities of racism's production of race in the French landscape, as I and others have done over the years.[88]

However, as with efforts in the United States to cancel "divisive ideas," particularly CRT, intersectionality, structural racism, and any thought informed by such thinking, decolonial, postcolonial, and race studies more broadly in France have been met with similar backlash politics in tandem with these theories gaining ground in French academies and among civil society actors. Notably, in November 2018, eighty predominantly white French "intellectuals," some longtime arch defenders of raceblind republicanism, voiced this so-called threat when penning and/or endorsing a declaration publicly denouncing the "alarming situation" posed by

colloquia, exhibitions, shows, films, "decolonial" books, reactivating the idea of "race" [which] continue to exploit the guilt of some and exacerbate the resentment of others, fueling inter-ethnic hatred and divisions. It is in this way that decolonial activists have strategically entered into higher education (universities; elite Colleges and teacher education; national schools of journalism) and into the culture.[89]

These attacks on academic freedom would intensify in 2021 when Minister of Higher Education Frédérique Vidal (2017–2022) called for an investigation of the so-called identitarian "Islamo-leftists" (*Islamo-gauchistes*), "infecting" French society and higher education with "dangerous, poisonous" ideas and fields of study supposedly imported from the United States.[90] *Islamo-gauchiste*, a term used by Far Right politicians to discredit the Left, is particularly vile for invoking Islamophobia to invalidate and stigmatize counterviews by calling them apologies for "terrorism" in a country still reeling from terror attacks on its territory. International scholars expressed solidarity with French colleagues, including Angela Davis, Gaytri Spivak, Achille Mbembe, and over 18,000 people who signed a petition calling for the resignation of Vidal.[91] Unrelenting, Vidal doubled down on her threats of having researchers investigated for "looking at everything through the prism of wanting to fracture and divide," namely those scholars working on race, coloniality, or whatever these detractors deem "poisonous" and "a threat to French identity and the French Republic."[92] Lacking better ideas or stronger arguments, fearmongers retreat to suppression and oppression rather than confronting the problems that these theories and studies illuminate. Historian Gérard Noiriel and sociologist Stéphane Beaud have long held presumed US imports of race and "identity politics" responsible for a "racialization of public discourse" in France and for eclipsing class as the rightful ground of inequality and discrimination in French society.[93] Social scientists Abdellali Hajjat, Silyane Larcher, Audrey Célestine, Lionel Zevounou, and others' spirited response to these false dilemmas in a special edition of the journal *Mouvements* represents more than a defense of intersectionality.[94] They and other scholars of their generation are clapping back at the state's academic nobility and these tiresome attempts to censure ways of thinking and silence opposing voices about race through wielding academic, political power and titles. "Of course, we do not associate Gérard Noiriel with these challenges to academic freedom," write Hajjat and Larcher, "but given the scientific authority he has acquired, the questionable arguments that he uses to denounce feminist or postcolonial studies contribute to the overall disqualification of these fields of study. This raises the question of power relations within the academy, the role of public intellectuals, and their relations with so-called 'minority spokespersons.'"[95] Pap Ndiaye, the historian and specialist on questions of race in the United States and France and President Macron's choice for Minster of Education in 2022, was slammed by the Right (Far and otherwise) before he made it out of the gate for his stances on race and asserting that structural racism exists in France. His appointment seems, however, like a setup for failure, as he has been tasked with addressing those very issues in the institution where enduring racialized inequality has festered over generations: the raceblind French national educational system, as I show in my first book, *Muslim Girls and the Other France*.

What we are rewitnessing is a rebranding of the battle for racial justice in which "antiracism is the new racism," argues Kimberlé Crenshaw in her public responses to assaults on herself and theories with which she is synonymous, CRT and intersectionality. Such classic misdirection is nothing new, as we have witnessed throughout history, from abolitionism to decolonization to civil and human rights struggles worldwide, in which calling out racism makes *you* the racist. Displacing histories and critiques of racism elsewhere also conveniently sidesteps and ignores race-based enslavement, white settler colonialism, and other legacies and continuities of French and European imperialism, analyzed in these studies. Also obscured are archives of critical studies on race, racism, and antiblackness linked to French coloniality by those whom we might call CRT theorists today whose thought disrupts laying the "blame" anywhere but at France's feet. While not an exhaustive list, they would include the eighteenth-century orations and writings by Toussaint Louverture and Jean-Baptiste Belley, Anténor Firmin's 1885 *Of the Equality of the Human Races* that rebuts Arthur de Gobineau's *On the Inequality of Human Races*, Négritude thought, and work by the organizers and participants in the 1956 Congress of Black Writers and Artists, along with libraries of material published by Présence Africaine, L'Harmattan, and Karthala. Similarly, many civil society organizations and advocacy groups over time have shown that the history of the republic is littered with the so-called "race question," but exposing how and why race has been made to matter sociohistorically fragilizes nations. These "debates" recall the polemics against scholars such as Éric and Didier Fassin in the wake of 2005 for supposedly racializing social questions of exclusion and inequality.[96] Let us not forget that Pap Ndiaye encountered a similar backlash when he showed against the grain in his 2008 book *The Black Condition/La Condition Noire* how social race rendered visible b/ Black French people effaced by the state and the structural racism that they suffered, a fact that activists and scholars across the diaspora had previously demonstrated for years.[97] Ultimately, the issue is not the invented threat of critical thought and theory but the very questioning of French raceblindness as a banner of equality, flying over rampant racial inequality and oppression. A French sociologist whom I interviewed in 2017 seemed to anticipate Crenshaw's point in an email about refashioning antiracism as racism: "This is a nonsense debate about anti-white racism . . . to attack all those scholars who are talking about race because they are supposedly paving the way for racism. . . . So, the real enemy is those who are talking about racialization—but racialization created these conditions," and raceblindness provides cover for the ways that social systems, including legal ones, maintain the interest of the dominant whitened group to the detriment of inferiorized nonwhite people. This may sound like nonsense, but it has had real consequences beyond questions of academic freedom, as backlash politics of this nature are ultimately about power and authority used to preserve racial sameness.

Nothing better illustrates the explicit suppression of race in France than the lawmakers from the Left and Right who voted in 2018 to replace the word *race* with *gender* in article 1 of the French Constitution. Many cite this article to justify or explain raceblindness, as it contains those fundamental, cherished principles of the republic: "France shall be an indivisible, secular, democratic and social Republic. It shall ensure the equality of all citizens before the law, without distinction of origin, *race* or religion. It shall respect all beliefs." Recall that the inclusion of the word *race* in the post–World War II French Constitution served to send a forceful message about France's intolerance of scientific racism, but in the world that it colonized, the racial contract remained operational.[98] That gulf of hypocrisy would draw Aimé Césaire's most scorching condemnation in *Discourse on Colonialism*, described by historian Robin Kelley as "a declaration of war." Césaire connects the "barbaric, brutal violence and intimidation" of European colonialism specifically to race in his indictment of colonial racism, encapsulated in a single sentence: "Europe is indefensible."[99] For Césaire, colonial violence—racialization to justify dehumanization—"decivilizes" the colonizer and produces what he called the "boomerang effect" of fascism and Nazism:

Before they were its victims, they were its accomplices; that they tolerated that Nazism before it was inflicted on them, that they absolved it, shut their eyes to it, legitimized it, because, until then, it had been applied only to non-European peoples; that they have cultivated that Nazism, that they are responsible for it, and that before engulfing the whole edifice of Western, Christian civilization in its reddened waters, it oozes, seeps, and trickles from every crack. . . . At the end of formal humanism and philosophic renunciation, there is Hitler.[100]

Ten years later, Fanon would echo that analysis in his tour de force, *Wretched of the Earth*, writing that "Nazism turned the whole of Europe into a veritable colony."[101] These "racial temporalities," writes Crystal Fleming in her study of the racial legacies of French enslavement, entails not only "making claims about the content of the racial past, present, and future, as well as the *relationship* among racial categories"; it also means invisibilizing race to sidestep racism.[102]

Many viewed swapping *gender* for *race* in article 1 as a purely symbolic and/or political maneuver to give the appearance of being gender-forward but without addressing gender issues, such as the wage gap or domestic violence that caused thousands to take to the streets in protest in 2019. As reported in the media, "every year in France, an estimated 219,000 women aged 18 to 75 are the targets of physical or sexual violence by current or former partners."[103] Gender parity laws, in effect since the 1990s in France, created a permissible quota system to redress an imbalance in political representation that even some feminist decried as anti-universalist, thus *anti-républicain*. While gender parity laws fly in the face of universalist equality, replacing *race* with *gender* disappears the intersectional oppressions operating in the everyday life of women of color, including their near absence in French political life. Consider that in 2019, of the 577 deputies elected to the French National Assembly (the lower house of French Parliament), 228 are women. Of those 228, 15 appear b/Black, while of the 359 male deputies, 14 appear b/Black, based on my visual perception.[104] For the Senate (the upper house of French Parliament), racial representation dramatically shifts: of the 348 senators, 117 are women of which only 2 appear b/Black who hail from France's overseas departments of Martinique and Guadeloupe.[105] Of the 231 male senators, 9 appear b/Black who similarly represent French overseas territories, but neither category of race nor gender may fully capture how these individuals perceive themselves and how they are treated in French society.[106] While it is true that constructing race in this way is scientifically meaningless, it is precisely how race gets made in the everyday. Moreover, as philosopher Elsa Dorlin shows, with the expansion of revolutionary principles, race and gender were not merely biological markers but categories of alterity that cut fundamentally against the founding ideals of equality at the core of French republicanism.[107] Although lawmakers justified their action on the grounds that race rightly has no biological existence, the same holds for gender, which is similarly an invented social category whose supposed fixity is easily disintegrated by non-conforming bodies.

The banning of the word *race* from French law began under the socialist president François Hollande (2012–2017) as part of his campaign promises when appealing to nonwhite voters, some of whom were also denouncing ethno-racialized statistics.[108] At a meeting dedicated to the French overseas departments, of all places, he confidently declared, "There is no place in the Republic for race. And that is why I will ask Parliament the day after the presidential elections to strike the word 'race' from our Constitution."[109] A certain irony accompanies Hollande's declaration in those territories where the descendants of slaveholders—the minority population—have long controlled the local industries and economies to the detriment of the majority, the descendants of the enslaved who were defined by race, territories where racial inequality and precarity are omnipresent and long-standing. The uprisings in November 2021 in Guadeloupe and Martinique were not only about mandatory COVID-19 vaccinations but also about coloniality, and where, in what some saw as anti-Macronism, Marine Le Pen won over 60% of the vote. Ghosting race and its proxies has not, however, resulted in raceless equality before the law, nor has it prevented discrimination and racism, indeed antiblackness, in French society. On the contrary, suppression has only made it more difficult to identify, measure, and redress the very problems that are actually tearing France apart, including those expressed in response to the hashtag #YouknowurblackinFrancewhen . . . .

#YOUKNOWYOUREBLACKIN FRANCEWHEN . . .

The Fact of Everyday Antiblackness

I was haunted by a series of corrosive stereotypes: the *nègre*'s sui generis smell . . . the *nègre*'s sui generis good nature . . . the *nègre*'s sui generis naïveté.
—Frantz Fanon[1]

It's always the little things, like "ah blacks are always late" or "blacks are . . . fill in the blank," or "it was just a joke; don't be so sensitive." [*Partner interrupts:*] But watch out! Your jokes don't make me laugh!
—Couple interviewed in 2017[2]

"We are witnessing a real awakening to inequality and discrimination," says Prisca, a 38-year-old Parisian, a victim of "ordinary racism." "They touched my hair without asking me; they took me for the cleaning lady when I moved into my new building; they told me I was beautiful for a black woman," she says. Orlane and Maureen, 22, are also fed up with a form of "ordinary racism," with people who "hold their bags tight when they see us getting on the subway."
—*Le Monde*, 2020[3]

Everyday racism is, thus, racism from the point of view of people of color, defined by those who experience it.
—Philomena Essed[4]

After the attacks at Charlie Hebdo and the Bataclan concert hall in 2015, I returned to Paris filled with apprehension about continuing fieldwork for this book. I had already experienced in France, my country, and other regions how terrorist violence condemns entire groups of racialized people in the courts of public opinion for crimes committed by others. I steeled myself for what I would both witness and hear from the people whom I planned to interview, following that coordinated assault that left hundreds murdered and injured, and families and communities traumatized and destroyed in the wake. At the same time, life-affirming displays of international unity seemed to signal a change. Heads of state of every political persuasion walked arm in arm down the boulevards; the masses quickly reclaimed their streets and proclaimed on signs, at times in English, "Not Afraid!" And who could ever forget that poignant, defiant moment when pianist Davide Martello rolled his grand piano outside the Bataclan the day after 130 people had been massacred and so many wounded inside? He played John Lennon's "Imagine" and asked us to do the same. I wondered if working on antiblackness at that moment was ill timed. One of the attackers was b/Black and b/Black people were among the many victims. I concluded that it is precisely during such times, when public attention is drawn elsewhere, that we must lean into this work. Antiblackness does not disappear at such moments or give way to other suffering. There is no bad time for shining a light on racist violence or studying the mechanisms of institutional forces that allow it to thrive.

In this chapter, I explore the material, everyday life of antiblackness and how blackened people in French society identify and experience racialization-as-black inferiority, directly and vicariously, in ways that upend raceblind republican ideology. To this end, I return to the Twittersphere generated by Boni-Claverie's film and *Libération*'s hashtag, #YouKnowYoureblackInFranceWhen, which sets the tone for the many expressions of antiblackness taken up in this chapter. These include disparagement humor, attributions of animality, slippages and other uses of the French n-word *nègre*, and blackfacing in the France with reference to other European countries. By slippage, I mean instances when discourse, typically reserved for private use among likeminded listeners, slips into the public domain, thereby blurring the lines between what sociologists Leslie Picca and Joe Feagin further analyze and refer to as the "frontstage and backstage" in their study of white racial framing.[5]

Lived experience coupled with events and representations in the media reveal a pattern in shared, repetitive, and familiar accounts of vertical and horizontal oppressions that are erected on constructs of racialized inferiority whose perpetrators try to invalidate, justify, and/or dismiss by resorting to claims of entitlement, innocence, and ignorance. Inculcated through varying systems of education (e.g., family, schooling, religion, and society itself), entitlement racism reflects the naturalized ways and preferences of the dominant group. Essed writes further that "people feel they are allowed to say whatever they want, whenever they want, about whomever they want, in the name of freedom of expression."[6] To justify entitlement racism, perpetrators often resort to unconscious or casual antiblackness that capture both Wekker's notion of "white innocence" and what Naomi Murakawa refers to as "racial innocence," that is, a "blamelessness" and "a way of knowing fueled by the desire for unknowing."[7] Such articulations of a Millsian epistemology of ignorance reflects not an "absence of knowledge," argues Murakawa, but more "the cultivation of institutions, ideologies, and rhetorical mazes that *unwitness* racism [emphasis mine]," and specifically antiblackness.[8]

In the wake of 2005, the ground was already prepared by various and sundry activities focused on what in France is called "ordinary racism" that turned a spotlight on this issue and lived experiences of antiblackness in French society. In 2007, for instance, the antiracism association founded by Rokhaya Diallo, *Les Indivisibles*, deployed satire to battle the ordinariness of racist discourse in the media by public figures, notably through its sharp-witted Y'a Bon Awards, which recognized "the best of the worst" of these speech events from 2009 to 2015. Personal blogs emerged, such as *Vie de Renoi* in 2011 (*Living while Black*) and *#VismaviedeFemmeRacisée* in 2013 (*#LifeasaRacializedWoman*) that addressed specifically everyday antiblack discrimination and racism.[9] One "been there, done that" posting stood out for many: a photo of a Navigo metro pass where the picture of the passholder is literally so black that it is impossible to make out the person's features. Such representations become the butt of all jokes imaginable, including those from smirking metro employees who insist that nothing can be done or that nothing is wrong with the lighting or camera. What's wrong is the racial bias that results from lighting that is calibrated for white skin, as seen also in films with b/Black actors. Another post recounts an incident when a b/Black woman was asked by a coworker if she was okay because apparently no one had seen her at work for a few days, to which she responded: "What, I've been here; you probably confused me with Karen (the other black woman)." In 2013, *Libération* (*Libé*) launched its Facebook page,

Assez (Enough), on racism and hate speech, the same year that far-right politician Anne-Sophie Leclère compared Christiane Taubira, the first the Black French minister of justice (2012–2016), to an ape on her Facebook page. When asked about the photomontage during a documentary that aired on France 2, she resorted to innocence/ignorance/entitlement, asserting that there was no racist intent, after all: "I have friends who are black." According to her, her aim was simply to illustrate that Taubira was a "savage," adding: "I'd prefer to see her swinging from a tree than in government," an attribution of animality to which I will return.[10] By 2014, France TV (France 2) would join fray through a collaboration with its overseas department channel (France O), which resulted in the hashtag *#RacismeOrdinaire: Les mots qui font mal (#OrdinaryRacism: Words That Hurt)*. This public awareness campaign was designed not merely to sensitize the public but also to provide educational, cultural, and legal resources "to fight everyday prejudice . . . in order to learn, understand and move forward together."[11] Ultimately, the institutional, recurrent, and routine facts of everyday and other-way antiblackness discussed in this book and chapter revive Fanon's query about the actual source of cultural pathologies typically attributed to blackened people: "How does an oppressing people behave?" While traditional and social media both play an important role in combatting antiblackness, they also paradoxically perpetuate it by dint of their intended design. Their content is meant to be shared. Consequently, these media amplify and transform, albeit at times unwittingly, everyday antiblackness into a vicarious experience, one also lived and relived in virtual time. Even as we relive those experiences through these pages, I am reminded of an interviewee's reflections in 2018 who said with insistence: "I want people who are not directly concerned by racism to feel what it is like from people on the inside; how hurtful and destructive it is, that it's not only a political and sociological matter, but something that affects you intimately" and extends beyond the individual to engulf an entire racialized group.

TWEETING EVERYDAY ANTIBLACKNESS: *"THE FEELINGS WHEN YOU SEE AFRICAN OR B/BLACK NANNIES"*

Despite the relatively low use of Twitter in France in 2015, *Libé*'s hashtag still trended among the highest on the day of its release, with throngs of tweets and retweets.[12] In other words, this hashtag deeply resonated with its audience who seized this rare mainstream opportunity to purge itself of the very lived experiences that are ghosted by French raceblindness. One vignette featured by *Libé* from Isabelle Boni-Claverie's film, *Too Black to Be French*, is classic antiblackness from a man who states: "You know you're black in France when you're waiting for a friend outside a pub, and everyone thinks you're the bouncer, or say things to you like: 'Good evening, we're here to eat; *bonsoir*, we're here for drinks; [or] party of two,' and you respond: Sorry, that's not my job tonight." Perhaps due to word count limitations, *Libé* truncated the segment after "bouncer" in its online article, which taps into commonsense stereotypes that equate certain occupations with blackened bodies with which they become identified, typically low-wage jobs indicative of systemic racism. This representation illuminates similar racial logics in the French film industry, for instance, in terms of the roles typically reserved for b/Black actors. Sociologist Marie-France Malonga notes in her analysis that among them are the helpers, such as the house cleaner, "nanny/*nounou*," or "African mama," in contrast to those problematized and pathologized in society as threats and/or pariahs, particularly outer-city youth (*banlieusard*) and undesired migrants.[13]

Over the years, I have discussed this issue with friends in Paris and interviewees precisely because the b/Black-nanny-white-child phenomenon is indeed "a thing" and not limited to France. Upper Westside Manhattan could be any day Paris in this regard, where b/Black women pushing strollers of white children was part of the daily routine so much so that photographer Ellen Jacob devised a photo series, *Substitutes*, to denaturalize this practice. The series takes the perspective of a w/White woman who had a b/Black nanny, and in explaining her project, Jacob writes: "My images are about the things we don't notice that we should; the things that seem natural but aren't. The women in these photographs perform parenting duties. They are substitute parents."[14] This project, as its title conveys, demonstrates that these women are not mere caregivers but also emotional proxies for parents and mothers. Their employment results and relies on historically produced intersections of economic, gender, migrant, and racial domination and inequality, as sociologist Tamara Mose shows in her instructive study of Caribbean domestic childcare providers in Brooklyn, New York.[15] In this way, their bodies become simultaneously hyper-visible and invisible in predominantly white or gentrifying public space.

In France, similarities abound. In my interviews, b/Black mothers of mixed, white-appearing children especially expressed their anger and/or resentment over continually having their motherhood questioned by strangers when going about their ordinary activities. The mistaken identity issue was something that seemed to plague Emilie most, an attorney in her late thirties whom I have known for many years. The fact that she is an upper middle-class professional living in a predominantly white neighborhood amplified her anger because she felt that her cultural and socioeconomic class standing meant acceptability and inclusion. She recounted her experiences this way:

So, I have two little boys, and one has lovely, wavy light brown hair with little hazel eyes, and a second son is a tiny, tiny bit darker with a little more curl to his hair, brown eyes. Beautiful, beautiful little boys, and whenever I am walking with them, people always think that I am the nanny, for sure //How do you know?// Because here in France it is a tradition for black women to take care of white children . . . It reminds me of [former companion's name], the white professor that I dated years ago. His sister, when she got pregnant, told me that she couldn't wait to hire a b/Black nanny, and I asked why . . . [she said:] Because everybody understands that they care for children so much more, love children so much more [in a mocking tone]. I said, you've got to be kidding me! It's like this misconceived notion or perception; I don't know what you call it because if you go to the park at 3:00 or 4:00 you will see a congregation of darker-skinned women, not just the black nannies, but also the Indian nannies, Filipino nannies. They're all together and they're hanging out chit-chatting. Those kids are running wild! It's not like black people are taking care of them any better. Anyway, even walking down my own street, I had the woman at my shoe shop ask me something like how I liked working for my family and about "my charges"! *My kids*! I almost went crazy. Because I was like, I wanted to invite her to my 150 square meter apartment so that she realizes that I'm not the babysitter or the *nounou*! You know, it's like they see the color of your skin and that's it!

Her case and others like it reveal, however, how race invisibilizes class, even as the latter is historically entrenched and omnipresent in French society. Here, we also recognize Fanon's present-day echo in terms of the anger, humiliation, and frustration that arise from everyday epidermalization. But we also see the emotional toll of everyday racism and how the ideology compels complicity with it through strategies of racial distinction. The irony is that Emilie works on migrant issues and is a strong advocate for migrant rights, but she is continually placed in the position of saying, "I am not them," which further reinforces the racism against which she battles on the job but cannot escape in her everyday life. Ultimately, those placed in this situation find themselves in Kipling's racial logic: "All nice people, like Us, are We; And everyone else is They."

In her study of Ivorian nannies in Paris, sociologist Caroline Ibos also analyzes the belief that b/Black nannies supposedly "love children so much," finding that employers whom she interviewed considered the capacity to "love" one's ward an important attribute of a good nanny. But this same aspect also evokes slavery tropes and imagery of blackened "mammies," wet nurses, and cissexist stereotypes about African women's natural and instinctual vocation to mother and display love above all others.[16] "African women are great with children," exclaims an informant in Ibos's study: "they bond to kids like Scarlett O'Hara's nanny in *Gone with the Wind*. The dream nanny!" Further, as Ibos uncovered, "Scarlett O'Hara's nanny [was] a recurring reference on online forums devoted to hiring nannies," suggesting that prospective nannies were expected to be mammies, that is, the asexual caregiver and female version of an "Uncle Tom," the docile, submissive, self-sacrificing racist trope immortalized in Harriet Beecher Stowe's *Uncle Tom's Cabin*.[17] Although the labor market offers limited, often low-status and low-wage opportunities for undocumented migrant women in France, Ibos also found that even these positions provide some refuge from everyday racism because these occupations require minimum contact with employers. Nannies, however, often cannot escape that fate in rigidly controlled households, where "the bosses' grip on the personal life of their domestique distinguish[es] the condition of the African nanny of the twenty-first century from that of the 'little maid' of the nineteenth century."[18] At the same time, sympathetic and empathetic b/Black onlookers witness the hypervisibility and daily optics of this everyday coloniality, that is, of b/Black women pushing strollers of white children or caring for them in public in order to provide for their own.

For many years, I have witnessed this ritual at a school adjacent to the residence where I stay in Paris when doing research. It was remarkable to see, in a predominantly white neighborhood, often older b/Black women waiting outside at the end of the day for white children in their charge or strolling with them through the neighborhood when their own homes and neighborhoods in the outer-cities were economically light-years different and must have felt light-years away. Though less ubiquitous now, I also recall the advertisements for nannies featuring b/Black women smiling while holding a blonde, blue-eyed child, which only reinforced how naturalized this practice had become in France.

An everyday, common variation on the bouncer-nannie-service theme occurred in 2016 while I was interviewing an actor at a restaurant in Paris. Overhearing my generic, introductory questions to this person about the film industry, our young w/White waitress curiously asked if my interviewee was an actor, to which I responded,

French Babysitter/Nanny Advertisement/
Flickr.

French Babysitter/Nanny Advertisement in
Parisian Metro. Photo: Trica Keaton.

"a wonderful one, and a singer." From the expression on her face she was delighted by the news, and then said, "Great! What kind of music, Zouk?" Without missing a beat, my interviewee's response was classic. "No," she answered, smiling wryly, "French songs, of course." Catching the drift, the waitress replied with her own "*Bien sûr*," and abruptly left our table, leaving my interviewee clearly vexed over an assumption that "happens all the time" and "pisses me off." In other words, "you know you're black in France when" you are a classically trained singer but are stereotyped as a jazz or hip-hop artist because a b/Black performer is unimaginable outside those genres.

Although the perpetrators in the vignettes featured in Boni-Claverie's film are racially unmarked, the experience of a woman attending an event at an "Indian restaurant" gestures to the equal-opportunity aspect of antiblackness transcending neat black/white dichotomies, since the agents of antiblackness can look like the very face staring back at in the mirror. "You know you're black," states this person, "when [. . .] the girl who greets you [at the restaurant] accompanies you quietly [to the kitchen] and tells you what dishes are left for you to do." Another example in the film worth mentioning here is: "You know you're black when you're a group of three people but referred to as 'two guys and a black' (i.e., *un noir* or *un black*)." This particular form of casual and unthinking antiblackness dehumanizes through a type of negation that is historically rooted in deep-seated notions of black inferiority that removed blackened people from humanity itself.

"YOUR JOKES DON'T MAKE ME LAUGH!"

Shortly after *Libé* launched its call for testimonials, the responses were almost immediate and continued through 2018, though with less vigor. As illustrated by the "#uknowurblackwhen" hashtag in the United States by Ashley Weatherspoon in 2009, early engagement with its French counterpart showed how b/Black people are rendered problems, marginalized, or ridiculed in the everyday.[19] But their recognition of this antiblackness also problematizes France in turn, that is, race-blind republicanism is rendered the problem from the b/Black perspective. Many tweets and retweets on the day of the hashtag's release focused on disparagement humor, that is, attempts to amuse or entertain through denigrating or humiliating a social group. As studies show, this type of humor "creates a normative climate of tolerance for discrimination" and racism that its conflicting message reinforces.[20]

However, perpetrators dismiss or dispute their seriousness and harm by retreating into race neutral explanations. For instance, perpetrators claim "non-serious intent," using catchphrases guised as innocent teasing (i.e., "It's only a joke" or "Just kidding"), which "impact[s] the degree to which participants may be legitimately held accountable for the potentially serious implications of the tease in question."[21] Consequently, such claims not only preempt calling out an offense, "but represent[] a deeply moral claim," argue researchers, in that partakers of such humor acknowledge the possibility of offending their targets but seek at the same time a type of moral high ground when "sanction[ing] the recipient for taking themselves (or things) too seriously."[22] Once more, the inadvertent effect of sharing these racists comments and representations is that they wind up reproducing the selfsame antiblack violence that now live on in perpetuity online. Reflecting on that point, an interviewee responded this way when I brought up the issue: "Listen, people say these things to us and about us, and they find every excuse imaginable to dismiss what we say, but we need to keep saying it over and over until they get it; we're not making this up." Another emphasized "the disrespect that you feel, of being black in your body. You know, you feel like crying; you feel like slapping somebody; you're shaking," when describing the feeling of being misrecognized and/or a site of ridicule: "and then people feel like they can do whatever they want because it's *you*! You know something is happening because it's you, because of how you look," because of racialization-as-black.[23] This frustration of having their lived experiences dismissed or denied by well-intentioned family members, friends, colleagues, and others was quite prevalent in this research. Infuriating reactions include reversing the blame and projecting racialist attitudes onto the messenger. Accusations of "oversensitivity" or "paranoia," or being called a "killjoy" (*casseur* or *casseuse d'ambiance*)" or anti-white, were among the most common.

Tweeters shared varying examples of disparagement humor, mined from the media and everyday life, often linked to skin tone, accent, hair texture, haircare, or, at the extreme, animality. No example better epitomizes the association of blackened people with animality in disparagement humor than the French humorist Michel Leeb's ever-popular, forty-year skit, "The African" (*L'Africain*), which is something straight out of the archive of antiblack representations. Through gestures, accents, and facial expressions, Leeb imitates for laughs an ape that he calls "African," a metonym for blackened "Africans." In so doing, he foregrounds the underanalyzed intersections of antiblack racialization and animalization that inhere in racist constructs of blackened identity that Bénédicte Boisseron analyzes in her insightful book, *Afro-Dog: Blackness and the Animal Question*. The analogy is not with animal suffering, however, as Boisseron writes, but b/Black dehumanization, here for the price of a laugh.[24] Humor in this way serves not to ridicule antiblackness but rather reinforce it, and Leeb, like others, resorted to white innocence/ignorance claims in its defense, arguing that "there is obviously not an ounce of racism!"[25] Leeb's brand of humor lies at the core of tweets and retweets, particularly on the first day of the hashtag. To minimize the vicarious effect, I offer a small but illustrative sample of antiblackness in the everyday: "#YouKnowYou'reBlackInFranceWhen they ask if you can speak African" (270 retweets and over 75 likes); or "tell you 'but you're black, you should be able to stand the heat' (240 retweets and 69 likes)"; or variations on this theme: "on hot days, people tell you: 'Well . . . you can't be hot; you're used to it'" (337 retweets; 114 likes); or "they ask . . . if you get sunburned" (274 retweets; 78 likes). The excess focus on the blackened body is also evident when someone wisecracks: "When you smile at night, we can only see your teeth. . . ."

When thinking about this type of humor and how b/Black people are perceived in French society based on it, another interviewee attributed these representations to a "colonial imaginary that refuses to die," one that still constructs b/Black people as a menace but not a danger on par with "Arabs." Perpetrators consider these insults harmless and certainly not racist because of the customary racialization of b/Black people as brutes, on the one hand, and thus prime fodder for employment as security guards and bouncers, but on the other hand as "good natured," helpers who are thus less easily offended. As the interviewee put it: "In France the Arab is imagined as someone with a knife in his teeth, plotting revolts, etc., while *le noir* is the one who makes you laugh, makes you dance and sing; he's the one who is easygoing, like the *Banania* [i.e., a sambo figure] that you mentioned. Yes, blacks are seen as big and strong, but the threat they pose is more linked to immigration; if there's too many of them, that threatens the national identity, national purity, etc. But it's a collective menace; it's not *un noir* who's the threat. It's when there are too many b/Blacks that it's a problem."

For others interviewed, it was less about being b/Black and more about being perceived and treated as an "African" in France that initiates antiblackness. One explained it this way while reinforcing earlier insights: "I think that African is worse than black //Why?// I think it's, you know, because of the perception that the entire world has of Africa, including Africans, I think. It's like the worse you can be in the world, in history, you name it because you can be black, but if you come from the States, if you're African American, that's cool, right. If you're an African, it's like you're a beast, an animal, you're uncivilized, you're stupid. You're not even scary like the Arabs; you're not a terrorist, and you don't get on people's nerves like the Chinese. You're just backward; you're just backward! That's Africa; that's how Africa is perceived." Here, we see an antiblack civilizational hierarchy that ranks African-descended people with Leeb's "Africain" occupying the lowest rung. Later in our conversation, I asked this interviewee about the specificity of antiblackness, and she returned to this point. Keep in mind that she is also French: "It's like I said in the beginning. I think the French really do hate the Arabs. I don't know if it's about Algeria, but they hate them, and they're scared of them. But at least they respect them. I think the specificity of antiblack racism is that they think, and this what I said at the beginning, that black people are just stupid, and Africans, they're just crazy people, animal-like. That's all. No respect, no respect. Not even fear, unless it's the primitive fear, like the Africans will beat you." She explained that the last point was not calculated but indicative of "Africans'" supposed uncontrollable violent nature and unpredictability which are likened to a wild animal. Indeed, racism generalizes from the individual to the entire racialized group, so that it's not a b/Black person at issue but rather an entire "b/Black race." Again, refusing these and similar abominations elicits a common response of displacing the problem onto b/Black people and their presumed inability to take a joke because we are supposedly so hypersensitive.

NÈGRE ENTITLEMENT, INNOCENCE, AND SLIPPAGE

On the heels of the Black Lives Matter (BLM) Summer of Reckoning in 2020, the French publishers of Agatha Christie's 1939 best-seller, *And Then There Were None*, announced that the French title, *Les Dix Petits Nègres* (i.e., *Ten Little Niggers*) would become *Ils Etaient Dix* or *They Were Ten*. In the United States, the rebaptism of Christie's book title occurred in 1940, three months before the release of Richard Wright's *Native Son*, but not before trying out its offensive penultimate title, *Ten Little Indians*. Forty years later, in the 1980s, Britain followed suit, but it would take France eighty years to do likewise. The public defense of the original title with the French n-word (*nègre*) intact and the backlash that the title change provoked in France and beyond illustrate how the lines between the mainstream and the extreme discourses blur in ways that allow everyday antiblackness to roam freely, even during periods of overtly battling antiblack injustice.

Christie's great-grandson, James Prichard, approved the title change, explaining that the book was written for a different time, when "language was different, and words were used that are now forgotten. . . . My point is that Agatha Christie was all about entertainment, and she wouldn't have liked the idea of anyone being hurt by one of her turns of phrase. . . . Today, fortunately, we can remedy that without betraying it and still be acceptable to everyone. . . . It makes sense to me: I wouldn't want a title that distracts from her work. . . . If only one person felt that way, it would be too much! We should no longer use terms that might hurt. . . ."[26] Reminiscent of the furor in the United States over calls in 2011 to expunge *nigger* and *injun* from Mark Twain's *Huckleberry Finn*, defenders of the original Christie title in France decried the dangers of imported US "political correctness" gone wild. "You can't say

George Floyd solidarity protest in Paris, June 6, 2020. Photo: Jerome Gilles/NurPhoto via Getty Images.

anything anymore" becomes the enlightened, entitled response for those pitting freedom of expression against antiracism. Tweets by French philosopher and TV and radio show host Raphaël Enthoven sum up that reaction: "A few months ago, there were thousands of us laughing out loud at those uncultivated people [*incultes*] who were offended by this title. Nowadays, the uncultured triumphs and reigns. #dixpetitsnègres"—retweeted 1.2K times and liked 4.1K times in 2020.[27] When attempting to invalidate dissent and justify maintaining the title, defenders also resorted to the ruse of false equivalencies. In other words, if Christie's original title is racist, would not the same hold for classics by b/Black creators, such as Négritude literature, or, for instance, filmmaker Euzhan Palcy's film *Rue Cases-Nègres* (*Sugar Cane Alley*, 1983); Dany Laferrière's novel *Comment faire l'amour avec un nègre sans se fatiguer* (*How to Make Love to a Nègre without Getting Tired*, 1985, reissued in 2020); or hip-hop artist Kery James's *Musique Nègre* (2016)? Missed, however, is the distinction between promoting or reproducing racist ridicule and critiquing the system that produced it.

It is tempting to see this case as an outlier. However, it is not the first time that this racist term has reared its ugly head in blackened people's daily life in France through "slippage" or become an international media event that we have had to suffer and navigate on the ground or vicariously due to its public life. The eighteenth-century sign, *Au Nègre Joyeux*, that I analyze in the next chapter is arguably among the most egregious of the latter in shared public space. There are also legendary cases of prominent figures publicly uttering "*nègre*," defined by Achille Mbembe as "this massive coating of nonsense, lies, and fantasies [that] has become a kind of exterior envelope whose function has since then been to stand as substitute for the being, the life, the work, and the language of Blacks [*capital his*]."[28] Such slippage by renowned parfumier Jean-Paul Guerlain in 2010, discussed ahead, was not forgotten among tweeters who posted and retweeted images of b/Black-led protests and boycotts that this assault provoked.[29]

In 2016, the former French minister of families, children, and women's rights, Laurence Rossignol, joined this inglorious club. During an interview on BFM TV, Rossignol was asked about "Islamic fashions," adapted for the covering choices of Muslim women that were entering the public mainstream. In denouncing them as oppressive, Rossignol ultimately and matter-of-factly compared Muslim women who cover to "des nègres afric . . . des nègres américains qui étaient pour l'esclavage" ("Afri-niggers, American niggers who were for slavery"), to the shock of many.[30] Note the word on which she stumbled was not *nègre*, whose offense neither she nor the

Protest against Jean-Paul Guerlain, October
23, 2010. Photo: Bertrand Langlois/AFP via
Getty Images.

talk show seem to register at the time. When later explaining her remarks, Rossignol burrowed deeper into the antiblack hole by claiming that she only used the term in the context of slavery: "I used the word *nègre* in the only way that one can, to talk about slavery in America and the slave trade. But I did not consider the more common understanding, that we don't say *nègre* even when it's allowed in connection to slavery. Aside from that language mistake, I don't take a word back of what I said" about the clothing.[31] Although she conceded that "the reference was not obvious," Rossignol, an outspoken feminist, retreated into innocence and entitlement to unwitness her antiblack, sexist, and patronizing views about Muslim women's agency, a view that discounts covering as a choice.[32] What's more, any redemption that Rossignol was attempting to find was obscured not only by the misdeed but also by the very act of retelling the story in the media while continuing to repeat the injurious term after acknowledging its racial offensiveness. The immediate injury became eclipsed by its indirect effect through its recycling and replaying in multiple media and social commentaries at the time that felt inescapable and recalled the epic *nègre* slippage known as the "Guerlain Affair."

During a televised interview on a major French network, the then-septuagenarian patriarch and "the nose" of House Guerlain was explaining how he developed the scent for one of his highest-selling perfumes, *Samsara*. In identifying the ingredients, he casually states: "This time, I started working like a *nègre*. I don't know if *nègre* have ever worked so hard," at which the host of the program on France 2, Élise Lucet, seemed bemused; she later claimed not to have heard the remark. But b/Black people who experienced the insult in real time and in replays did hear.[33] Describing this moment in her autobiography, also titled *Too Black to Be French*, Boni-Claverie writes, "The interview ends as if nothing had happened, in the same playful tone and without any clarification from the journalist. Immediately, the excerpt goes viral on Twitter and Facebook," along with its vicarious antiblack effects.[34] Expanding on the everyday nature of these "racist slips," Boni-Claverie writes that they "ha[ve] become a category unto themselves which regularly make the headlines. . . . Alleged racist slips express with great authenticity what its perpetrators think deep down inside" about b/Black people.[35] Politicians, French television, and audiovisual authorities (i.e., CSA) largely attempted to "unwitness" that assault through silence and/or inaction, which essentially invited the public to follow suit. Such indifference conjures in the process the immortal words of Dr. Martin Luther King Jr.: "In the end, we will remember not the words of our enemies, but the silence of our friends." That silence would compel Audrey Pulvar, the first b/Black woman news anchor, to respond by channeling Aimé Césaire's legendary riposte from a selfsame assault derived from his classic essay, "Nègre je suis, nègre je resterai" ("*Nègre* I am, *nègre* I'll stay"). In a similarly titled essay, Pulvar writes: "Well, you know what this *nègre* says, F . . . you!" (i.e., *Eh bien le nègre, il t'emmerde*!).[36] Guerlain was convicted of "racist injury" and the courts fined him 6,000 euros, albeit two years after established antiracism groups filed a lawsuit. But neither House Guerlain nor France anticipated the swift and coordinated b/Black mobilizations that Guerlain's everyday antiblackness ignited. The Guerlain case would be a tipping point for Boni-Claverie and an important impetus for her film, but it was her call to action on Facebook in solidarity with Rokhaya Diallo, the *Brigade Anti Négrophobie*, and other antiracism organizations that resulted in an unprecedented, powerful moment of b/Black refusal in France in front of the Guerlain perfumery on the Champs-Élysées in Paris. Apologists resorted to race neutrality to explain away Rossignol's and Guerlain's remarks. They were excusable gaffs, slips of the tongue, a consequence of age in the case of Guerlain. But these "slips" and silences in response also speak to the naturalization of antiblackness in a society where blameless innocence operates in the service of masking racial sameness and the white supremacy underpinning it. Guerlain, himself, described his remarks as "an imbecility" (i.e., *une imbécillité*) that he regretted saying, and I am sure he did once that initial protest evolved into an international mobilization and boycott, catching even the attention of Al Sharpton, who offered his assistance and platform.

Nègre slippage also has cousins, namely *bamboula*. Although this offensive term may have originally meant "drum" in languages spoken in colonial Guinea, by the eighteenth century it reportedly migrated to the Ivory Coast and became *danse de nègres* ("nigger dance"), with its obvious antiblack connotation. Linguists Marie Treps further explains that today, "bamboula designate[s] in a particularly pejorative and racist way Black people," information lost on Luc Poignant, a representative of the French police union, in his televised defense of the term in 2017.[37] Shortly after the rape-by-police-baton that year of Théo Luhaka, taken up in the chapter on police violence, Poignant was interviewed about deteriorated relations between outer-city youth and police in general and specifically about accusations that the police spat on young people in Luhaka's neighborhood and called them *bamboula* and *négro*, another French n-word.[38] In response, Poignant retreated into innocence, entitlement, and slippage: "*Bamboula*, okay, it shouldn't be said, etc.," offered Poignant, only to undercut that insight by saying, "but it's about right [*convenable*]." This time, the host replied swiftly. "No," she said and pushed back on his attempt to explain away his "gaffe" for which he was roundly condemned, including by the minister of the interior among others. Recall that racist insult is a punishable offense in France and includes *nègre*, as Guerlain learned. The next day, Poignant attempted to apologize on France Info, a public radio network, but only dug himself deeper in the same antiblack hole when stating that *convenable* but not *bamboula* was ill chosen. That such glaring antiblackness can be so casually stated in the media without fear of sanction tells us much about how deeply entrenched these ideas are in society. Maboula Soumahoro further illuminates the everyday lived experience of this antiblack formation in her instructive book, *Black Is the Journey, Africana the Name*: "It is no longer just a 'simple' case of police violence, but a case of racist police violence. The case of Theo and the debate over 'bamboula' particularly caught my attention because my own first name is Maboula . . . the ensuing debate sent me back to my French childhood, when the sonorous resemblance between Maboula and bamboula made me—in the eyes of French or foreigners, blacks or whites—the unexpected embodiment of African savagery," *nègre* by another name.[39] In referencing Fanon's interrogation of the lived experience of *nègre*, Mbembe, like Fanon and Soumahoro, addresses not only the everydayness of these cuts. These inventions that the West has universalized and naturalized thrive through raceblind ideologies that seek to conceal institutionalized racial structures linking these offenses "profoundly [to] unequal redistribution of the resources of life and the privileges of citizenship," writes Mbembe.[40] Even as Fanon asserts that "the *nègre*" exists no more than "the white," co-constitutive though they may be, obviously neither is this fact without material consequences. Offenses cloaked in storytelling, disparagement humor, or simply unvarnished antiblack insults indeed tell us something about what French society "thinks deep down inside" about people racialized-as-black.

Consider the fictional slave narrative and slave portrayal of Danièle Obono, a self-identified Black French member of Parliament from the left-wing Party France Unbound (i.e., *La France Insoumise*), in *Valeurs Actuelles*, a right-wing weekly news magazine. Released in August 2020, around the time of the public outcry over Agatha Christie's title, the editors similarly retreated into innocence and entitlement and eventually accusations of political correctness. In other words, antiracists were the racists for denouncing the depiction of Obono—one of precious few b/Black deputies in the 577-strong National Assembly—as a bare-chested enslaved "African woman," weighted down by a heavy iron collar locked around her neck that enslavers used to identify, punish, and animalize the enslaved. The editors of this magazine, whose circulation surpasses 100,000, insisted that the story and image were part of a summer series in which political figures were depicted in differing historical periods with no malice intended. Public condemnation was swift, even from a top official in Marine Le Pen's Far Right National Rally Party who wrote on Twitter: "The political fight does not justify this type of humiliating and hurtful representation of an elected representative of the republic," advice this party would do well to heed when blowing anti-immigrant dog whistles that fan white nationalism in France.[41] Similarly, President Macron expressed repugnance for the material and sent a personal note of support to Obono. However, in 2019, he accorded *Valeurs Actuelles* an exclusive interview, focused on immigration, Islam, and the unavoidable confrontation with the Far Right in the next presidential elections. This move— similar to paying homage to Nazi collaborator Philippe Pétain during a World War I centenary commemoration and honoring Napoleon Bonaparte, who reestablished enslavement in France, on the 200th anniversary of his death—was read by many as one of many flirtations with extremism for political gain that abets its creeping acceptance at the expense of racialized, minoritized people.[42]

But let's imagine that the authors of the piece about Obono really "meant no offense" or that their actions were neither racist nor retaliatory, as they claim. That would beg several questions: Why select that particular period? Why not depict her as Joan d'Arc or Olympe de Gouges, for instance, if there were no racist intent? Why write a fictional story aimed at aggrandizing African participation in transatlantic enslavement by sidestepping Europeans' enslavement of Africans, at a time when the world is reexamining systemic antiblackness? To accuse Obono of participating in historical revisionism that minimizes Africa's role in the trade as justification for the representation is precisely, as she called it, an insult to everyone's intelligence and an attempt to retreat into white innocence to mask badly an attack on her activism aimed at exposing the present-day socioeconomic and political effects of the transatlantic enslavement in French society. But ultimately, why return to the antiblack toolkit and represent her as an enslaved person among the universe of possible characters and stories that could have been published during a summer of Black Lives Matter protests? In effect, the magazine called Obono a *nègre* without ever having to explicitly use the term because it is already calcified and implied in the very representation of her as a "slave," a word historically synonymous with *nègre*. Obono answered *Valeurs*' "apology" with a lawsuit that resulted in the courts finding the responsible persons guilty of racist injury in September 2021. Still, she had to suffer that injury and all that goes with battling it in a context of raceblindness, and we, vicariously, suffered by extension, both virtually and in real time. "I'm wounded by my Republic, I'm wounded by my France," she stated at the time. "This image is an insult to my ancestors, my family, my parliamentary group—*La France Insoumise*—but it is also an insult, I believe, to the Republic," which also chooses to unsee the coloniality of antiblackness.[43] In the end, perpetrators and their allies of *nègre* entitlement, innocence, slippage, and the disparagement humor often interwoven through them demonize refusers of antiblackness as PC police because we deprive them and institutions of their presumed right to be antiblack.

ANIMALITY ATTRIBUTION

While catering an event for the extreme right National Front party for reasons unstated, a young woman in Boni-Claverie's film says, "You know you're black that day, when you're met with a hail of insults, when they call you cheetah or *négresse*, when they throw sugar cubes and cookies at you, and then tell you to pick them up." First, why was a b/Black woman catering such an event, one wonders. When I asked Boni-Claverie, she replied, "Her boss told her she did not have to go, but she felt she should be able to do her job whatever the circumstances, and not be obligated to take into account the color of her skin."[44] But alas, the color of her skin mattered, and this lived experience of being treated as a beast returns us to the case of Christian Taubira and other b/Black politicians subjected to antiblack attacks and, indirectly, ourselves. In the European context, historian Dienke Hondius documents a pattern of racialization as animalization, which underscores the importance of including animality in the analysis of antiblackness. Hondius uses instead the term *bestialization* to refer to a historically entrenched system that inclines "Europeans to regard and treat African and Asians as animals," which Hondius alternates with two other practices, "infantilization and exoticism," all inscribed in long-standing practices of "paternalism" in many European countries.[45] While these entities are interconnected, my focus is more on how antiblackness is constitutive of animality, which, when combined with patriarchy, has allowed for the worse treatment and representations of blackened people worldwide.

The bestial-animality dimension of antiblackness in France takes many forms whose perpetrators always resort to stock-in-trade antiblack toolkits when targeting notably b/Black political figures and football players. As with Danièle Obono, Sibeth Ndiaye, the first b/Black spokeswoman for Élysée Palace and for President Macron by extension, became a lightning rod for criticism because of her hairstyle and clothing, which highlight multiple intersections of antiblackness in France. Preferring bright colors and fun prints while sporting full-blown natural hair, Ndiaye, a dark-toned and thick woman, embodied and embraced her contrast to the typical styles and body types of French women in politics. But this also made her a racialized target. For instance, in a 2019, Jordan Bardella, the twenty-something vice president of the Far Right *Rassemblement National*, tweeted excerpts from his interview on France 2 television, describing her "Teletubbies" clothing as an affront to French national identity (read: white) and France. "What shocks me is the way @SibethNdiaye expresses her contempt for our identity, and arrives in official ceremonies dressed as a Teletubbies," he tweeted. "When you represent France, you have to be well-dressed and exemplary"—retweeted 1.6K times and liked 3.5K times.[46] Days before, Nadine Morano, who referred to France as "a country of the white race," returned to the antiblack archive to attack Ndiaye's political views by racializing her citizenship and linking her clothing to circus garb, which also conjured images of nineteenth- and twentieth-century public expositions of Africans in "human zoos." Morano tweeted: "Outraged but used to hearing her ineptitudes often in circus clothes," adding ". . . Indeed, born Senegalese and only received French nationality 3 years ago . . . visibly with major gaps in French culture. unworthy of this official position in France," retweeted 2.3K and liked 3.8K.[47]

Well in advance of these high-visibility cases into which we, as b/Black people, were once more absorbed, b/Black French women politicians during the mid-twentieth century were not only victims of antiblackness, they were largely consigned to the dustbins of French history, as Annette Joseph-Gabriel illuminates in her book *Reimagining Liberation: How Black Women Transformed Citizenship in the French Empire*, which documents the fascinating contributions of two of the first Black female senators in France, Eugénie Éboué-Tell (1891–1972) and Jane Vialle (1906–1953).[48] However, nowhere is animality attribution better captured in contemporary France than in the multiple public attacks in 2013 and 2014 against Christiane Taubira, Minister of Justice (2012–2016). Madame Taubira is also known for having drafted the landmark legislation bearing her name, which recognizes Atlantic enslavement and its trade as crimes against humanity, the Taubira Law. Similarly, her case exposes at once several aspects of everyday antiblackness, erased and thereby abetted by raceblind republicanism, notably its naturalization, its gender and class intersections, its vicarious nature, but also its inculcation and transmission to the young. In Taubira's case, condemnation from her colleagues was not swift. Rather, many initially chose to "unwittness" glaring antiblack attacks, which only prolonged the effects. In 2013, the "Protest for All" (*Manif pour tous*) against Taubira's same-sex marriage bill (*le mariage pour tous*) in the French city of Angers illustrates inculcated antiblackness in particular.

When children at the demonstration were allowed, in full view of their parents and the police, to brandish a banana peel and scream repeatedly "a banana for the monkey" (*une banane pour la guenon!*) and "monkey eat the banana" (*la guenon mange la banane!*) as Taubira's car passed, we bear witness to learned behavior that derives from the impossibility of disappearing through raceblind republicanism the antiblackness that is "deep down inside" of French society.[49] Two weeks later came the grotesque cover of the right-wing magazine *Minute*, featuring Taubira with her mouth ajar vis-à-vis the taglines "cunning as a monkey" (*maligne comme un singe*), and another in larger font that literally translates as "Taubira finds the banana" (*Taubira retrouve la banane*) but is supposedly a play on words for being "in good form" or a smile.[50] Once more, any number of words could have been used to convey that thought without drawing on antiblack animality references. The double entendre and Kingian "multiple jeopardies," which resulted from the positioning of those words adjacent her open mouth seemingly in readiness for a banana or phallus, is indicative of a historical pattern of dehumanizing and beastializing b/Black women while objectifying them as a sexualized objects. Then Socialist minister of the interior, Manuel Valls, with whom Taubira had a tense relationship, claimed, according to media reports, that he had intended to stop the magazine's distribution. That didn't happen. This magazine circulated widely and was on display in kiosks, another site of the everyday. The image of the cover itself was recycled in the media, so it was impossible to escape its public life on the street, in the metros, on television, and on social media, where it was debated but also reproduced. In step with everyday racism, *Minute*'s cover had the added effect of not only ensnaring its intended "game" but also assaulting indirectly all b/Black women who were reduced to an inferiorized black race. These images were retweeted in *Libé*'s Twittersphere, whose message was not only "you know you're black in France when . . . ," but also "you know you're less human when . . . ." Moreover, what lessons did young people and society writ large garner when seeing that image among others on public display?

Elsewhere, Michelle Obama, America's first Black First Lady, was similarly targeted, as was Cécile Kyenge, Italy's first Black minister who at the time was only one of three b/Black members of the 751-strong European Parliament (MEP). Minister

Kyenge's case took on an entirely surreal dimension in 2014 when the Far Right minister of the interior, Matteo Salvini, filed a defamation lawsuit against her for allegedly calling his political party racist. Similarly, Kyenge has been subjected to the banana treatment and has had racist epithets hurled at her. But on the occasion for this allegation, she was reacting to antiblackness, specifically a comment at a public rally in 2013 by Roberto Calderoli, who is a member of Salvini's party and who likened her features to those of an orangutan. Later, according to media reports, he called it "playful banter."[51] In short and ironically, Kyenge was being sued for racism and forced to navigate death threats for calling out racism in the Italian government. Calderoli, like Guerlain and *Valeurs* magazine, did not get off scot-free. The Italian courts issued an eighteen-month prison sentence for making racist remarks, which he appealed, but no one seriously expected him to serve time for antiblack racism. The recurrence of these lawsuits for public racist injury also are glaring signs that official raceblindness is out of step with daily reality.

SPORTING ANTIBLACKNESS

Tweeters' responses to the hashtag also invoked animality in relation to b/Black football players in French and European soccer leagues and long-standing antiblackness in the grandstands. This aspect is coupled with the persistence of scientific racism and its wielding by those who make genetic links between athleticism, intelligence, and race. Projectile bananas, monkey chants, blackface, and nigger-calling are among the common and preferred weapons used by perpetrators of antiblackness in the stands and opponents on the field. Some players and fans deny racism and explain away these assaults as psychological warfare, that is, a means to demoralize and provoke b/Black players which disconnects these practices from antiblackness while also instrumentalizing it to achieve an antiblack end. In November 2019, 140 largely left-leaning MEPs were prompted to sign a letter to the European Football Association (UEFA), denouncing ongoing racism in European soccer and calling upon the association to "combat racism in European stadiums more vigorously, following a string of incidents all over Europe."[52] Despite such petitions, fines, and antiracism campaigns, this violence persists.

Other flagrant uses of race in total violation of French raceblind law include the scandal involving the advocacy, recording, and use of "ethnic" quotas by recruiters for the French Football Federation (FFF) and its prestigious club, Paris Saint-Germain (PSG). As early as 2011, the independent journal *Mediapart*'s investigation revealed a secret quota process to reduce initially the number of b/Black but later also "North African" (read: "Arab") youth from entering its training camps in order ostensibly to privilege the recruitment of more white players, whom the former outnumbered. Then later, from 2013 to 2018, reporters uncovered that PSG racially profiled its prospective recruits and kept illegal "ethnic files" in which they categorized and documented their so-called "origins," a race proxy, to restrict similarly the number of b/Black and Arab players.[53] Some officials rationalized this practice not in terms of diversity or equal opportunity but rather, once more, in terms of the old-stock antiblack trope of brain versus brawn, which, as reported in the media, concerns "established beliefs" or the "hard facts of life," that is, "blacks are strong but dumb as a doornail and white people are weak but have a Platini's insight of the game," ideas also conveyed in newspaper headlines.[54] The latter point is in reference to the football star Michel Platini who, in 2015, was banned from soccer for eight years amid a corruption scandal. Perpetrators denied such allegations of racism only to confirm their antiblackness when stating that they "were looking for players who had a high level of intelligence for the game," in step with scientific racism.[55] Then, there is the naturalized absence of b/Black people in positions of authority and power in the sport. This aspect only accentuates the everydayness of systemic antiblackness in European football when the "'thinking' chain, from club presidency to scouting, is predominantly white. An ethnic homogeneity which, in this case, does not seem to worry decision-makers."[56]

The victims of antiblackness and antiracism associations fighting on their behalf have not only protested but also harnessed the power of the courts, at times with limited success, to demand the enforcement of French laws that have been on the books since the 1970s. However, perpetrators are rarely prosecuted and, if they are convicted, the penalties, once more, are often symbolic. A telling illustration occurred in 2015 when four British Chelsea football fans forced a b/Black commuter off a metro train in Paris, chanting: "We're racist, we're racist, and that's the way we like it." Although convicted of the crime of racism, they received suspended sentences, but not before invoking the innocence/ignorance factor. In media reports, one perpetrator apologized to the victim, "but denied there was any racist aspect to what had happened" and concluded that "I was not racist in any way."[57] Two years later, the victim confessed to ongoing feelings of humiliation, stress, and indeed emotional injustice from hollowed-out antiracism laws that are not fully enforced.[58]

La soirée des policiers déguisés en Noirs fait scandale

UNWITTNESSING BLACKFACING

Blackfacing, the "white racist caricature" of blackened people for its entertainment value, is a "performance tradition in which whites perform their idea of blacks," writes Louis Chude-Sokei in his instructive analysis of blackfacing.[59] This theme also figured prominently among *Libé*'s tweeters, who fiercely defend such entitlement antiblackness in the name of merriment, cultural traditions, or homage-paying. This "ritualized degradation," writes Wekker in her searing critique of Zwarte Piet/ Black Pete, has become so naturalized in the Dutch context "that it requires no explanation or justification," and these formations exist and persist "when there are gross inequalities of power; we are dealing with a violent hierarchy here."[60] This fact of antiblackness was stunningly illustrated in a grotesque screengrab tweeted and retweeted of a so-called "*négro* party" (*une soirée négro*) in 2014 hosted by a French police officer with fellow officers in attendance.

No antiblack stereotype was spared in their literal denigrating representation of the so-called *négro*. This included donning blackface makeup with exaggerated red lips, a wide white-toothed grin, afro wigs or something akin to braids or locks, and clothing and props consistent with their imaginings of "Africans," which one

Tweeted *"Soirée Négro,"* 2014.

described on Facebook as innocent "harmless fun," begging the question of links between this "fun" and what has been naturalized through Michel Leeb's skit of the "African." These acts also render explicit ingrained ideas of antiblackness and feelings of entitlement to these representations and the ideas underpinning them. That the perpetrators are police officers only heightens the abuse and the injury.[61] Or consider the case of then twenty-six-year-old French soccer player Antoine Griezmann in 2017. For a party to honor the Harlem Globetrotters, Griezmann tweeted out an image that went viral of himself supposedly dressed as a member of the team, which, like the "*négro* party," is yet another manifestation of entitlement racism, white innocence/ignorance, and ritualized degradation all rolled into one.

Later, Griezmann apologized, citing "clumsiness," but also added: "Calm down guys, I'm a fan of the Harlem Globetrotters and the good times . . . it's a tribute"—a tribute to antiblackness.[62] Shortly thereafter came images in varied media of employees at Altran, a prominent engineering consulting firm, who had blackened up during a teambuilding session that was posted on Twitter.[63]

Displayed in these cases are the social acceptability and comfort with blackfacing that are characteristic of a certain preference for racial sameness. In 2017, the Representative Council of France's Black Associations (*le CRAN*) would document more cases and mobilize against their recurrence, but it is difficult to battle a problem that goes misrecognized and misdiagnosed as isolated slurs by individuals rather than indicative of an antiblackness that lives deep within society. Despite these examples and public awareness campaigns by antiracism groups about blackfacing, it is telling that in 2019 director Philippe Brunet would interpret *The Suppliant Maidens* by Aeschylus, an ancient Greek play, with the actors wearing darkened makeup.[64] Scheduled to take place at the celebrated Sorbonne University in Paris, the CRAN and other Black activists not only condemned this interpretation as blackfacing, they also stopped the performance by physically preventing the actors and public from entering the building. The response of the director, government officials, university heads, and everyday people was a predictable condemnation of the protest and protesters that, at times, turned violent. Frédérique Vidal, then minister of higher education who has waged war against critical theorists in France, discussed in the chapter, "The Choice of Ignorance," and Franck Riester, minister of culture, issued a joint statement that ironically decried "an unprecedented attack on freedom of expression and creation in a university, which is contrary to all academic values and republican principles."[65] But is not blackfacing also contrary to academic values and republican principles? In defense, Brunet seemed to suggest

Antoine Griezmann ✓
@AntoGriezmann

Follow

80's Party 🏀 🤣

6:16 AM - 18 Dec 2017

3,183 Retweets **5,217** Likes

Antoine Griezmann's tweet, December 2017.

tique France : E. Macron s'apprête à débattre avec une fausse représentante du CRAN   Le CRAN se réjouit de la panthéonisation de

SCANDALE : BLACKFACE CHEZ ALTRAN

📅 13 DÉC 2017   👤 PUBLIÉ PAR   0 COMMENTAIRE

1 j

Viens rejoindre notre dynamique équipe niortaise
dans le cadre d'un stage commerce et RH de 6 mois!
Envoie-moi ton CV : axelle.leroux@altran.com
#stage #Niort #commerce #RH #IAEdePoitiers
#GroupeSupdeCoLa Rochelle

17 J'aime • 6 commentaires

👍 J'aime   💬 Commenter   ◁ Partager

★★★★★

RECHERCHER

to search type and hit enter

LE CRAN TV

12 Novembre 2019 : Ghyslain VEDEUX,
président du CRAN sur 1ère outre-mer

SUIVEZ NOUS SUR FACEBOOK

*Nouvelle affaire de Blackface. Des internautes ont alerté le Cran à
propos d'une des plus grandes entreprises françaises, en l'occurrence,*

Altran blackface scandal, December 2017.

that because the coloring was not actually black, it was not blackfacing, to which Louis-Georges Tin, the honorary president of the CRAN, replied: "There is no good or bad blackface in the same way there is no good or bad racism. However, there is a conscious blackface and an unconscious one. Racism isn't just an ideology reserved for the far-right, that would be too simple. And that's why we fight."[66] In response, the Sorbonne's production went ahead, but instead of using blackened faces, they staged the piece with actors wearing masks, in keeping with practices of ancient Greek theater. Nevertheless, why blackening up in this way was offensive seemed to escape the protest's detractors, illustrating a Millsian epistemology of ignorance, a logic of "successfully unknowing."

Analogues in other European countries are plentiful, and practitioners similarly justify blackface in the name of cultural traditions, charities, and tribute or entertainment. These paternalistic practices infantilize b/Black people in stunning displays of ignorance/innocence/entitlement while inculcating antiblackness as normative and "fun" from a very young age. Decades of implicit bias research shows that the effects are lasting and sustain racism outside of people's conscious awareness, making the practices even more deleterious, a point I return to in the chapter, "*Au Nègre Joyeux* and Friends." The cherished, "harmless" tradition of Black Pete (Zwarte Piet) in the Netherlands is but one infamous example that government officials sought to progressively "de-negrify," to borrow from Fanon, by using blue instead of blackface. Again, this action fails to acknowledge and address the issue of naturalized antiblackness in these societies that connects to broader structural inequalities and discrimination confronted by blackened people in terms of employment, housing, education, health and wealth, politics, and cultural representations linked to racialized black inferiority. The fact that children are socialized to see such oppression as harmless and joyful entertainment only heightens its perniciousness while illustrating, similar to the banana-brandishing children in Taubira's case, how antiblackness is socially transmitted and internalized from a very young age.

Not to be undone by the Dutch, Belgium has its version, Saint Nicholas (*Sinterklaas*), a blackfaced servant/slave, dating from the nineteenth century. Similarly, it transforms the holiday season into a Christmas nightmare for b/Black families and their allies, particularly in locales where their numbers are few and where the cost of speaking out against this tradition is public scorn. The same is true in places of employment. For instance, in 2018, an interviewee shared a heated email exchange at the European Commission, following the circulation of a Christmas celebration announcement and photo posted on its intranet site by a workplace social group,

Cercle des Loisirs de l'Enfant et de la Famille (Child and Family Leisure Circle) or CLEF, comprised of coworkers at the Commission. In the photo, some members of the group and their children had blackened up for the occasion.

"As an employee of African descent in the European Commission," wrote a person offended by the image, "I am appalled and saddened that adults and children alike were dressed in blackface to portray the caricature of Zwarte Piet. In an environment that is supposed to stand for mutual respect within a multicultural environment and representing all European citizens, of which I am one, this antiquated notion continues to perpetuate ideas of discrimination which the European Commission is duty bound to work against as well as the protection of the dignity

Image from the Christmas celebration announcement, December 17, 2018.

#YOUKNOWYOUREBLACKINFRANCEWHEN . . .

of all of its citizens. Shame on you, CLEF!!!" In this case, some coworkers expressed empathy, one stating: "In my kids' Francophone Belgian school, Père Fouettard is never ever blackfaced. He is a normal person, dressed up in an outfit, just like St Nicolas. There's no need for him to be blackfaced, just like there's no need for St Nicolas to be whitefaced. You can still have the tradition and the characters without the racist slur." However, this comment was met with the typical innocence/ignorance/entitlement claims: "Thank you for your attempt to explain how this tradition is racist, but I still don't understand. What negative (colonial) stereotypes exactly does a black child helping Dutch Santa perpetuate? And how does Black Pete negate Black people's humanity? In the text, these things are asserted, but not explained." The response by a spokesperson of CLEF captures fundamentally how raceblindness cosigns racial innocence, ignorance, and entitlement: "Dear colleague, It is precisely because CLEF is a multicultural circle in a really open family friendly environment that we, families from all over the world, are sharing the cultural Belgian event of the beloved St Nicolas. My family is Spanish and obviously we do not have black slaves helping Saint Nicolas. In clef we do not distinguish colours, race or religion and the best thing our children have to share is exactly that. We play together in whatever event we organize. We would be delighted to share with your family your traditions and ideas, as everybody is always welcome. Please come and enjoy an event and you will also have fun without judging anyone. Have a lovely Holiday time!"[67]

In Belgium, there is also the *Noirauds* ("The Blacks"), arguably one of the oldest charities for disadvantaged children, whose members don blackface every second weekend in March in the name of a tradition, dating from the late nineteenth century. Blackening up was supposedly a way for the wealthy to hide their identities when doing charitable work, but b/Black families are left navigating sambo, coonish imagery during those weekends. They are also expected not to be offended by this "tradition" in which even the minister of foreign affairs and defense participated in 2015, and proudly tweeted out to the world.[68]

With the growing outcry against these traditions from antiracism groups in Europe, this organization settled on a workaround that maintains blackfacing in another form, similar to the solution found in the Netherlands. In the Netherlands, it was blue-facing; in Belgium, the *Noirauds* adopted the colors of the Belgian flag.[69] Left unaddressed is the emotional trauma and injustice of antiblackness in a country that, as a colonial power, perpetuated unthinkable, well-documented atrocities on African peoples who were racialized-as-black.

Charity Fundraising Parade and Festivities—
The *Noirauds*, Brussels. Photo: Kotomi
Yamamura, 2016.

Charity Fundraising Parade and Festivities—
The *Noirauds*, Brussels. Photo: Kotomi
Yamamura, 2016.

Charity Fundraising Parade and Festivities—
The *Noirauds*, Brussels. Photo: Kotomi
Yamamura, 2016.

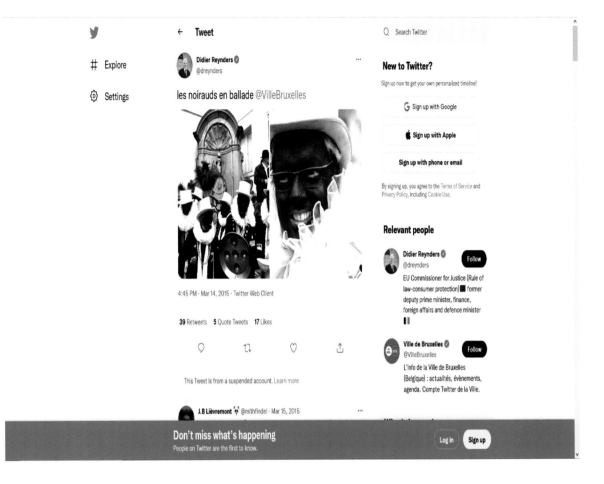

Tweeted selfie by Didier Reynders,
minister of foreign affairs and defense,
March 15 2015.

Then, there is the *Nuit des Noirs* ("The Night of the Blacks"), a celebration that takes place in the former slave trading port of Dunkirk in France that is organized by a self-identified philanthropic association called the Blacks (*Les Noirs*).[70]

Like other groups, its members contend that their use of blackface has no racist connotations but aligns instead with the Dunkirk Carnival, dating from the 1800s in France. Dunkirk is also less than 20 kilometers from the Belgian border. In 2018, when confronted by protests from antiracism associations during its fifty-year anniversary, Dunkirk's mayor and other proponents insisted that blackening up during *les Nuits* was "[their] right to caricature," a cherished tradition, and ultimately about having fun. This disparagement "fun" once more conveniently ignores an entire history and legacy of antiblackness-making and does so again at the total expense of b/Black people.[71]

In the twenty-first century, blackfacing has morphed into the phenomenon of "blackfishing" among white female social media influencers who market themselves as racially ambiguous or appear to masquerade as b/Black through hairstyle, makeup, and filters to darken their skin and/or claim natural tanning. The poster child in 2018 was Emma Hallberg in Sweden. Unlike Rachel Dolezal, Hallberg and the German model Martina Big, who "Africanized" her name as "Malaika Kubwa," are not claiming to be b/Black or "African."[72] Similar to Kim Kardashian in the United States, who has also been accused of blackfishing, Hallberg and others have rejected this charge. As Hallberg put it in the media, "I do not see myself as anything else than white. . . . I get a deep tan naturally from the sun."[73] Nonetheless, their racialized representations conjure the age-old tradition of appropriating blackness for financial gain but without the burden of actually being b/Black. In 2019, the European Parliament's resolution "on the human rights of people of African descent in Europe" put the perpetrators of blackfacing on notice by identifying it as a human rights violation: "The persistence of discriminatory stereotypes in some European traditions, such as the practice of blackening one's face, perpetuates entrenched preconceptions about people of African descent and may thus exacerbate discrimination."[74] Yet these practices show no signs of disappearing.

The revolts of 2005 supposedly generated greater awareness and sensitivity to both race and racism in French society, but what I have witnessed and documented over the years are persistent patterns and consistent themes of antiblackness in people's everyday life. Take, for instance, a memorable, unexpected, and tone-setting interview in 2010 that I had while conducting pilot research for this book. A friend insisted that I "must" meet a twenty-seven-year-old b/Black French woman

Nuit des Noirs, 2018. Photo: Edouard Bride/
La Voix du Nord/Maxppp.

of Caribbean descent who lived in Bordeaux and Paris. "Her life is your book!" she emphatically said. My curiosity was naturally piqued. When Céline arrived at my home with four handwritten pages of examples of everyday antiblackness, some categorized, I realized that I needed to attend more closely to the many ways, as Céline put it, of being "always reminded that I'm black in France," that is, racialized as such in the everyday. She covered a gambit of experiences that other interviewees and friends would also echo over the years, concerning "fixed ideas" about b/Black people in French society. At the top of Céline's list was the impoverished French curriculum that diminished France's role in African enslavement. As a descendant of enslaved people in Martinique, she was particularly sensitive to this issue. She noted categories for racial profiling and "insults," namely, *sale noire/nègre*, a "dirty or filthy nigger," and another for "origins," as in "being asked where I'm from because of the color of my skin." Under "body and beauty," she noted short sentences such as: "You're pretty for a black girl"; "You have pretty hair for a black person"; and "You're 'café au lait' colored so not really black," along with references to her body as a b/Black women, in particular her butt, "like I'm an animal or something." Revisiting these data, as someone who teaches courses on antiblackness in French cinema and society, I am reminded of the nineteenth-century French surgeon general Georges Cuvier's dissection of the so-called "Venus Hottentot" (Saartjie Baartman) in Abdellatif Kechiche's controversial 2009 film, *Vénus noire*. "It impacts how I think, talk, walk," she said, adding, "it hurts." Céline included recurring racial distancing remarks made by white coworkers, such as: "You're not like the others" and "Antilleans are different"—different from "Africans," she explained, because "they see us as more culturally French, you know, meaning more civilized sometimes." She also noted comments not said to her directly but intended for her to overhear, as when coworkers would talk about an "African odor" in the room or say dramatically, "What stinks or smells!" when she or a coworker referred to as "the African" brought lunch from home. *Tu/vous* was another category, that is, being routinely addressed by the informal you (*tu*) in overly familiar or infantilizing ways, noting how *vous*, the formal form, was used frequently to make racial generalizations akin to "you people" or "those people," referring to b/Black people. But what she ultimately found "most violent" was that Fanonian "gaze" or "look" (*le regard*), "that look from people in my neighborhood in the 14th arrondissement of Paris. I've never experienced such violence. //From whom?// From old white people and shopkeepers especially who clearly make you feel that you don't belong. //How exactly?// Simply by *le regard*, a cutting look, a look that says you're an outsider, a contemptuous look, that you don't want this person in front of you, a look that makes you stand out . . . these micro-encounters accumulate and hurt very, very much."

The expressions of antiblackness in everyday life, examined in this chapter, did not emerge in a vacuum; nor are they isolated one-offs, reflecting individual prejudices or preconceived views. Rather, they are symptoms of racist ideologies and structures in sites that self-narrate as raceblind in the name of equality. And who is ultimately hurt? Many, indirectly and in real time. In denying or unseeing these facts of everyday antiblackness, they become naturalized and thereby persist in society. In French visual culture, the subject to which I now turn, everyday anti-blackness indeed finds fertile ground.

AU NÈGRE JOYEUX AND FRIENDS

Everyday Antiblackness Posing as Public Art

Au Nègre Joyeux. Photo: Michelle Young/
Untapped New York.

In Europe, *le nègre* has a function: that of representing the lowest feelings, base instincts, [and] the dark side of the soul. In the collective unconscious of the *homo occidentalis, le nègre*, or, if one prefers, the color black, symbolizes evil, sin, wretchedness, death, war, [and] famine.
—Frantz Fanon[1]

If the white man contests my humanity, I will show him . . . that I am not this *Y a bon banania* that he persists in imagining I am.
—Frantz Fanon[2]

Artistic production and discourse in the eighteenth century produced tools of observation and analysis that allowed human beings to be differentiated as well as implicitly classified on a moral scale, an enterprise that would later veer into explicit racism.
—Anne Lafont[3]

It's between an "ethics of looking" and an "ethics of sharing" that we see how black subjects are visualized. I feel like people aren't pausing to ask how this might add to the violence already taking place.
—Kimberly Juanita Brown[4]

SETTING A CONTEXT

During my early stays in Paris, I loved areas like *La Mouffe* (rue Mouffetard), one of the oldest and liveliest neighborhoods in the Latin Quarter. Its old-world charm, meandering cobblestone streets, and endless people-watching for the price of a *café* or *verre* are the stuff of dreams, indeed "a moveable feast," wrote habitué and former resident Ernest Hemingway. But that postcard quickly faded when I spied for the first time on 14 rue Mouffetard the business sign *Au Nègre Joyeux (ANJ)* at Place de la Contrescarpe in the 5th arrondissement. It was one of those moments of disbelief, when you look around and silently ask: "Are you seeing what I'm seeing?" From ostensibly 1748 to 2018, this sign, for "one of the first establishments where Parisians could taste the exotic flavors of chocolate," held center stage in a public square frequented by locals, students, and tourists in a neighborhood that is walkable distance from some of the most prestigious universities and schools in metropolitan France.[5] According to another source, "this famous sign, depicting a black waiter broadly smiling in shorts and white stockings with a carafe in hand, serving a seated lady, is inspired by someone called Zamor, a servant whom Madame du Barry particularly cherished."[6] Note for future reference the grinning representation of the blackened figure who is also the only one racially marked in this description. On that day, however, what stopped me dead in my tracks was not this erstwhile eerie scene but the sign's large, imposing title board, which read "Chez/ At the Happy Nigger [or simply: The Happy Nigger]." Perhaps more startling was the fact that it had become so interwoven in the fabric of daily life that passersby seemed to pay it scant attention, even as it trumpeted out a rage-inducing antiblack epithet that also constitutes legally a racist injury. Although *ANJ* no longer occupies public space, I focus on it in this chapter because its long presence is a textbook case for understanding a consequence of raceblind republicanism's negation of antiblackness, that is, the unwitnessing of antiblack visual culture in everyday French life. Preserved in the process is a preference for racial sameness, a "taken-for-granted desirability of certain types, the often-unconscious tendency to comply with normative standards, the easiness with the familiar," along with the refusal of such alienating formations.[7] *ANJ* is not alone; it has friends. In this context, proponents have deployed history, culture, and cultural patrimony to legitimize the presence of these objects, as illustrates the "Zamor" (or "Zamore") thesis, the identity attributed to the blackened figure on a sign that is arguably the oldest in a genre of *nègre* signage in France. *ANJ* is gone from the street but not from public view, as it now resides at the writing of this book in the Musée Carnavalet, one of the oldest museums in Paris, devoted to the city's history. But it has contemporaries, notably artist Hervé Di Rosa's painting, *1794: 1ère Abolition de l'Esclavage* (*1974: The First Abolition of Slavery*), at the French National Assembly, a house of Parliament. Through this piece, the defacement in broad daylight of artist Combo's 2015 mural *Jeanne de Panam* a.k.a. *Les Françaises aux Africains* (*French women for Africans*), and artist Alexis Peskine's 2006 protest oeuvre *La France "Des" Français* (*France of the French*), I examine how innocence/ignorance/entitlement claims, discussed in previous chapters, also provide cover for antiblack visual culture in shared public space.

ANJ did not merely exemplify and radiate everyday antiblackness for 270 years, it also *taught* it implicitly at Place de la Contrescarpe, which effectively became a centuries-old classroom in the instruction of antiblackness. Research on implicit bias shows that "the human mind's tendency to generalize from instances to sets is an essential feature of learning and categorization, but this feature may produce unanticipated problems when the characteristics of individual people are generalized to their social groups," so a *nègre* ultimately becomes all who are so-racialized, as discussed in the introduction.[8] Or, in the words of Lewis Gordon, "anti-black racism marks the black, who is, in the end, 'anonymous' in a perverse way, which enables 'the black' to collapse into 'blacks' as parcel of the process of dehumanization."[9] Further, researchers have also found that dark skin color is implicitly associated with beliefs about deeper psychological attributes, such as violence, anger, and aggression, that connect to notions of animality—all of which have been projected onto blackened people with deleterious effects, ranging from subtle discrimination to lethal force. These unconscious beliefs and stereotypes, developed and honed at an early age, become transmitted over generations.[10] I am not suggesting that exposure to *ANJ* and other antiblack visual culture automatically translates into discriminatory treatment, but a wealth of implicit bias research shows such biases can influence actions. This aspect alone leaves us to wonder what possible racialized associations may have developed and were reinforced over the years owing to *ANJ*'s protracted public life and the lack of historical markers explaining its existence, another issue discussed in this chapter.

For a b/Black interviewee who lived in the neighborhood, the sign "is an eyesore, and this painting has no place in any Parisian museum; it's not like it's a work of great artistic value." He added in his email in 2020 that "people who live in the neighborhood see it as a symbol of what we like to naively call 'le vivre-ensemble,' but I see a '*nègre*' without a name, nationality, history, or will of his own. And he's 'happy'!!??, which allows residents to feel comfortable in their belief that it's a positive symbol." Although this person and I are overjoyed to see the sign gone, opinions vary dramatically about the removal of *ANJ* from public space, including among b/Black people, which represents one of several unresolved questions about the strange career of this relic. In this chapter, as throughout this book, I am straddling the fine line that Kimberly Brown highlights in the epigraph, while trying not to err on the side of the raceblind French state and thereby perpetuate what could be called the politics of silence and mis-seeing that contributes to the unwittnessing of antiblackness in French society. "Social practices of looking" and un/seeing, to draw on Marita Sturken and Lisa Cartwright, involve relations of power and access to it, as illustrates *ANJ* and other objects explored in these pages.[11]

There are many unknowns about this remarkably preserved sign, and archival and other research did little to solve lingering mysteries about *ANJ*. For instance, the decor, clothes, and table setting in the painting, including the style of the chocolate (as opposed to coffee) pot, gesture to the eighteenth century. But does the sign actually date from 1748? What of the business it advertises? Precious few sources that I uncovered recycle the same narrative in which *ANJ* was an establishment, at times a café or *chocolaterie* (chocolate shop) where Parisians could sample chocolate, a product of enslaved labor (child labor today) like coffee, cotton, indigo, sugar, and tobacco, whose naturalization in everyday life masked the material conditions of their production. By the nineteenth century, writes anthropologist Susan Terrio, "the word *chocolat* signified a black man" in French argot, and "French chocolate manufacturers sold their products using images of blacks often depicted as naïve and childlike inferiors."[12] These representations of the smiling Fanonian *nègre* reinforced myths of the "happy slave" and the joys of servitude, for, as Fanon writes: "We like to depict the black man grinning at us with all his teeth. And his grin—such as we see it—such as we create it—always signifies a gift. . . . An endless gift stretching along posters, movies screens and product labels . . . playing the fool . . . service always with a smile," and ultimately not a threat.[13]

Product trademarks and advertisement for mass public consumption have long been vectors worldwide for the dissemination of colonial racism and specifically antiblackness. Such iconography and visual cultural accentuated racialized alterity that significantly advanced the normalization of antiblack representations and perceptions of blackened peoples, particularly age-old associations of blackness with filth and whiteness with cleanliness and purity.

Topsy Tobacco, Négrita Rhum, chocolate sweets and beverages, and various food brands in the United States (e.g., Uncle Ben's, Aunt Jemima, or Mrs. Butterworth's), Europe, and in European markets were well integrated into daily family life. However, left by the wayside was the pesky history of French colonial conquest on the backs of racially inferiorized groups. Take, for instance, the "bamboula cake," which has variations in other European countries, or the chocolate covered tea cake once called *le tête de nègre* ("nigger head"), which has become simply "chocolate cake." But even here, perpetrators act out passive-aggressively by diving into the antiblack archive when renaming the cake, for instance, "Mamadou" and decorating it so that it resembles a "golliwog" doll straight from the annals of European

Dirtoff Soap, ca. 1920. Collection IM/
Kharbine-Tapabor.

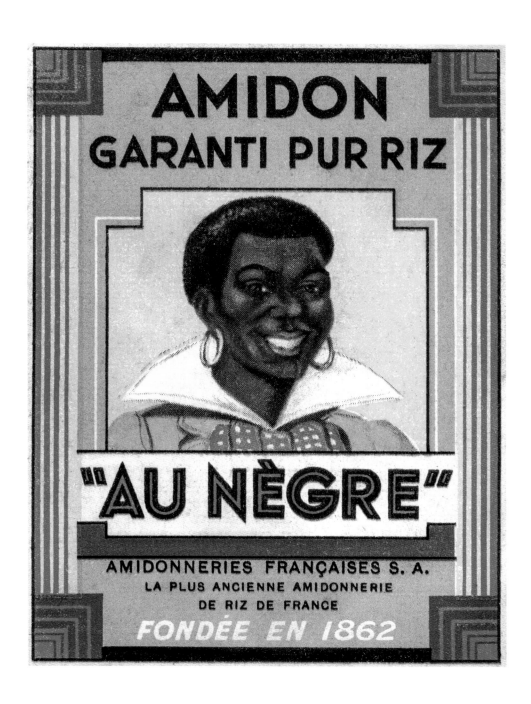

Label of a box of rice, brand "Au Nègre,"
ca. twentieth century. Bridgeman Images.

Gossages Magical Soap—USA, ca. 1910.
Collection IM/Kharbine-Tapabor.

Italian publicity for soap, ca. 1910–1920.
Collection IM/Kharbine-Tapabor.

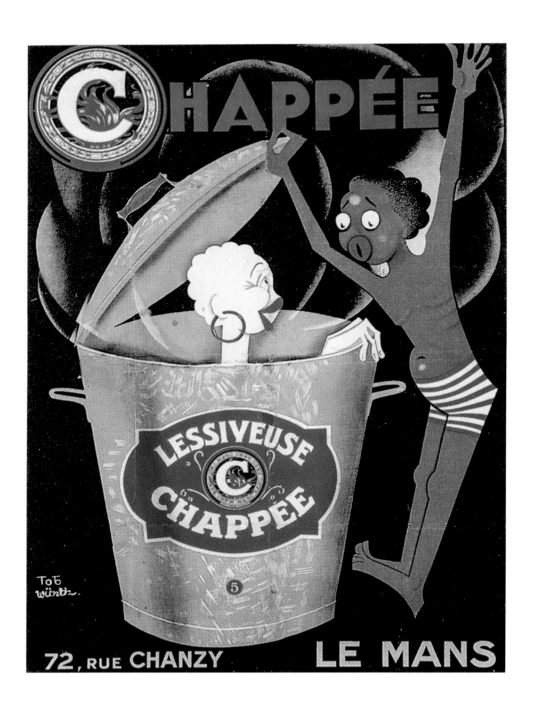

Chappee washing machine, ca. 1925.
Collection IM/Kharbine-Tapabor.

imperial antiblackness. Similar to the so-called "pickaninny" that was popularized in North America, it, too, is another racist caricature that dehumanizes b/Black children. No longer omnipresent, this cake still resurfaces now and then, as it did in 2019 at a bakery in Lyon, whose owner apologized but still unwitnessed the effects of that representation on staff, clients, passersby, and especially children with that name.[14] In 2015, a friend sent me an image of a "Mamadou" cake that he stumbled across in the south of France. I dare not write his reaction but suffice it to say that much swearing was involved, punctuated with: "Here's when you know you're black in France; you'd never find this in the United States!" Au contraire, in the United States, a baker at a French pastry shop invented a cookie supposedly in honor of President Barack Obama's election in 2009, one he dubbed "Drunken Negro Face."[15] It, too, was another golliwog representation whose racist offense the baker claimed not to see when defending his abominable creation.

The use of an infantilized, animalized, and thus inferiorized grinning black body to sell chocolate, however prepared, may have arguably originated in France with *ANJ*, but it is part of a long line of such representations of which the Banania logo (1914–present) is iconic. As historian Dana Hale writes, "The Banania soldier's grin remains one of the most recognized and popular trademarks in France," one that reduces African colonial conscripts to a "stereotype of the *bon noir* or *bon nègre*—a harmless, infantile black figure who was devoid of power despite his military role."[16] Political scientist Franck Freitas-Ekué's powerful 2021 doctoral dissertation examines the materiality of race in relation to the commodified blackened body across the Black Atlantic, including in France, which shines needed light on this issue in the French context. He and others represent the next wave of b/Black French scholars who are researching and analyzing the very questions France should run toward, not from.[17]

However, Banania's lesser-known cousin, the Félix Potin chocolate ad attributed to French painter and humorist Joë Bridge, spares no stereotype in featuring a grinning simian-*nègre* type that supposedly depicts the famous Auguste clown known as Rafael Padilla (ca. 1865–1917) whose stage name was Chocolat.

Who better to represent Potin's confection than the once-enslaved Cuban-born Padilla who rose to stardom by portraying a happy-go-lucky subservient butt of slapstick routines not unlike performances by African Americans in minstrelsies? Those deeply antiblack acts were precisely what made Chocolat "digestible" for the public that consumed them and this clown an ideal subject for these types of

Banania book plate, France, 1950s. © The
Advertising Archives/Bridgeman Images.

Chocolate advertising poster for Félix Potin.
Wikipedia Commons/Joë Bridge, ca. 1922.

La Hêve, featuring clowns Footit and
Chocolat, ca. 1895. Collection IM/
Kharbine-Tapabor.

advertisements. Though rooted in scientific racism, such visual culture intimately knits antiblackness to everyday consumption and connotations of childlike innocence and maternal comfort associated with sugary treats and warm milk, which only further normalized the unwitnessing of everyday racism and its vicarious effects vehiculated by these monstrosities. These effects were not lost on director Roschdy Zem in his 2016 biopic *Chocolat* (*All Out*), which showcases the Bridge poster in a memorable scene that not only captures the past-present of naturalized antiblackness. It also recognizes its rejection by b/Black people in ways that recall protests of *ANJ* and other antiblack visual culture and discourse in France. Taking some historical liberties, Zem depicts a meeting in which Potin's ad managers proudly show a logo mock-up featuring the Bridge poster to Chocolat, played by Omar Sy, who is caricaturized as ape-like, while Foottit, his white counterpart, appears more human. "Ah formidable! Magnifique!" ("Wonderful! Magnificent!") exclaims the owner of the circus where they perform. His appreciation extends to the wordplay in the ad, namely "whipped and happy" (*battu et content*), that signified at once Padilla's portrayal of Chocolat and the idea or sensation of drinking an actual beverage composed of melted chocolate poured into warm milk or cream. Foottit cosigns his boss's assessment, but, as they are being told that the poster would be plastered "everywhere, kiosks, the news columns, billboards," all the spaces of everyday life, a repulsed Padilla pushes back: so "hard to miss." "A good submissive *nègre*, happy to get kicked in the ass," he bitterly says, to which Potin's son casually replies, "Yes, people are very fond of that." Padilla retorts, "You've made me *un animal de foire*" (a beast at a county fair), the very role to which he is consigned and confined in their act. As Kimberly Brown expressed to me when communicating about this aspect: "It is so psychologically destructive to see yourself in the visual dysmorphia of others' perception of you. The degradation is meant to grind you down, and how could it not?"[18] The same applies to the so-called "Venus Hottentot," Sarah (Saartjie) Baartman (ca. 1789–1815), as historian Robin Mitchell documents in her insightful analysis of distorted representations of racialized-as-black women in post-Revolutionary France.[19] Padilla's fame also provides no protection against police violence in Zem's film whose storytelling on matters of racism are comments on current French society that would see the police-custody killing of Adama Traoré months after the film's release. In another scene, an established and beloved Padilla is stopped by the police and imprisoned for lacking identity papers. Wearing fine clothes but handcuffed, a blackened body stands before the white-appearing warden and guards who would become his tormentors. Padilla offers meekly, "I'm the clown, Chocolat," as if that should settle the affair. Instead, he is told to undress. Next, we see a half-naked blackened body doused with water and held underfoot in the prone position by the warden and a guard, while another sadistically and mercilessly scrubs Padilla's back with a rough-bristled contractor's broom to the point of drawing blood. All the while, the police guards sadistically laugh. "*Blanchissez-moi ça*" ("Whiten/clean it [vs. him]"), screams the warden, evoking racist soap ads that equate blackened skin and people with disease and, again, filth. "Plus fort" ("Harder!"), he says, as Padilla cries out in pain in a scene reminiscent of the vicious, perverted beating of Solomon Northup, depicted in the 2013 film *12 Years a Slave*. Thoroughly dehumanized, Padilla is thrown into his cell, where the warden's last words to him returns us to *ANJ* and Fanon when he states in a calm and deliberate tone, "*Tu vois; on a tout essayé. Un nègre reste toujours un nègre*" ("You see; we tried. Once a nigger, always a nigger").

"ALL BLACKS ARE ZAMOR": ABUSIVE ATTRIBUTIONISM AND THE MYSTERIES OF *ANJ*

Two mysteries about *ANJ* that particularly caught my attention concerned the lack of historical markers near or at Place de la Contrescarpe to explain the sign and its significance to the public and the identity of the blackened figure in the painting. In researching *ANJ*'s origins, I have come across rare gems, such as a photo confirming its presence ca. 1908–1910, but historical depictions proved elusive, and given its longevity, businesses with the same address have changed over the years I learned when reviewing old French directories.[20]

In his 1955 rendering for *Time* magazine, artist Robert Sivard shows the sign perched above a café similarly named, adding that "*Cafe Au Nègre Joyeux* on the left bank was once a famous artists' hangout and favorite haunt of Hemingway."[21] Hemingway lived around the corner from Place de la Contrescarpe on rue du Cardinal-Lemoine, where a plaque is affixed on the building that commemorates his residency from 1922 to 1923. Indeed, historical markers describing the area mention the existence of "some signs," but absolutely nothing explained this imposing entity called "The Happy Nigger" in a city where commemorative plaques abound.

In 1988, the owners of the building on which the sign was mounted donated *ANJ* to the City of Paris perhaps for reasons of historical preservation.[22] In so doing, they also relinquished all responsibility for an entity that seemed to violate French

Au Nègre Joyeux grocery store, corner of rue
Blainville and Mouffetard, ca. 1908. Photo:
Eugène Atget, Musée Carnavalet.

antiracism laws against public insult of a racist nature (*injure raciste*), a punishable crime in France, as illustrates the Guerlain Affair and other cases previously discussed. Over the years, Black activist groups and mobilizations that rose to prominence in the wake of the 2005 revolts (e.g., *le CRAN*, *Brigade Anti Négrophopbie*, Circle of Action for the Promotion of Diversity/CAPDIV) have turned an international spotlight on antiblack discrimination and racism in French society that would eventually find *ANJ*.[23] For instance, the Guerlain scandal in 2010 and the ironic expulsion of the Brigade from the commemoration ceremony for the abolition of slavery by the French police in 2011 and 2013, which went viral, would converge with other dynamics specific to *ANJ* that risked creating a public relations nightmare for the City of Paris, thereafter accountable for the sign.[24] Among those dynamics were the Brigade's three-week protest of *ANJ* in 2011, to which I return ahead; critical public scholarship of the sign; and heritage tourism to Contrescarpe, which brought people from across the African diaspora to see and reflect upon "public art" called "The Happy Nigger" in a raceblind France.[25] Eventually, the Historical Committee for the City of Paris (*Comité d'histoire de la Ville de Paris*) proposed text for a plaque in 2013, which takes us to the central mystery of *ANJ*. Who is the blackened man portrayed in the sign? Far from clarifying that mystery, the text by the City of Paris's Historical Committee only heightened it:

Au Nègre Joyeux is one of the first chocolateries that opened in Paris (1748). This sign, dating from the end of the 18th century, represents Zamor (around 1762–1820). A slave from Bengal who was a page of the Countess du Barry. A committed revolutionary, he contributed to the death sentence of his mistress (1793). He was freed on February 4, 1794, thanks to a first law abolishing slavery.[26]

The legitimizing inscription of "Zamor" in the text and his ennoblement as a figure in the French Revolution—the source of French principles of universalism and freedom—minimizes and misdirects us from the facts of antiblackness, namely the sign's name and Zamor's enslavement. At the same time, this description falls prey to what art historian Anne Lafont calls "abusive attributionism," that is, assigning identities to "exoticized" characters in eighteenth-century European portraiture such that "all Black people look alike" and "all Blacks are Zamor."[27] Many whom I interviewed about the sign also attribute the blackened figure to Zamor, who is the subject of various eighteenth-century portraits. The subjects look nothing alike and are light-years from the representation in *ANJ*, which only contributes to the mystery and reinforces classic antiblackness.[28]

Paintings depicting blackened people as "pages" or in similar servile roles during the Enlightenment were not uncommon, according to historian Pap Ndiaye and Lafont; roughly "1,000 to 5,000 blacks are estimated to have lived in France in the 18th century, most of them in the area of the Île-de-France," writes historian Kaija Tiainen-Anttila.[29] Expanding on this point, Tiainen-Anttila returns us to *ANJ* and its environs, writing that "the Paris upper crust used to strut with their black servants in Faubourg Saint-Germain at the beginning of the century. On Rue Mouffetard from 1748 one could drop into a restaurant called Au Negre Joyeux. The Africans in France clearly had the role of servants."[30]

Attempting to authenticate the Zamor thesis felt like a fool's errand. The archives were unyielding and working with archivists turned up nothing; nor could the City of Paris substantiate its own narrative. One city official described it as "a rather widespread urban legend," adding "personally, it seemed credible enough to be defended," he emailed, but offered nothing in its defense.[31] Each question that I raised led me to other officials, archivists, and private collectors, but never to any actual evidence that verified the Zamor thesis. Still, a Louis-Benoit Zamor appears to have existed, according to an oft-cited source, the 1896 biography of the Countess du Barry by Baron Étienne-Léon de Lamothe-Langon, which describes Barry referring to "Zamor," as her "little *nègre*" for whom she professed motherly love. In this same text, she is said to have listed him among three "objects" for which she had the greatest "affection," the first being her dog Dorine.[32] Indeed, the celebrated de Creuse painting of Barry shows her in the company of another Zamor figure who is reduced to a "decorative accessory." In eighteenth-century portraiture, continues Lafont, "young black slaves" were commonly "pushed to the edges of the paintings and smaller than their mistresses [as they] gaze at them in adoration, as if the painter felt compelled to show their agreement regarding the authority of the white race."[33] These obeisant, adoring looks, Lafont writes, "respond to a frequent strategy put in place to remove . . . the moral embarrassment regarding this violent hierarchy of populations."[34]

These portraits depicting enslaved blackened individuals in Westernized clothing dissolve their identities as human beings and efface their pre-enslavement lives and the backstory of violence that accounts for their presence in Europe. In their analyses of the "performance of identity" among blackened figures in European

Zamor, the *nègre* of Madame du Barry, or
Narcisse, the *nègre* of the Duke of Orleans
(no date). André Pujos/Musée Carnavalet,
Paris, France.

Presumed portrait of Zamor (18th c.). Musée
Carnavalet, Paris.

Madame Du Barry and Zamor, ca. 1771–
1800. Credit: Lebrecht History/Bridgeman
Images.

portraiture of that era, art historians Adrienne Childs and Susan Libby write of the racial fluidity and contradictory representations of these subjects. Racialized blackness was, however, "a constant factor in determining the social order."[35] Childs and Libby write further that "Barry was well known for dressing up Zamor in plumed turbans and luxurious costumes, not unlike Soliman, while he carried her parasol and accompanied her on her travels to the king's country château."[36] How Zamor might have felt about such treatment is not part of the narrative, but his role in having the countess guillotined during the French Revolution's Reign of Terror may harbor some clues. That Zamor was a native of Bengal, thus Asian not African, also raises questions about his actual blackness vis-à-vis his portrayal, though he was referred to as both *asiatique* and *nègre*. Put another way, Zamor may have been from South Asia where a variety of pigmentation is found, but he is represented with blackened skin in eighteenth-century French portraiture, which moves the pendulum closer to *nègre*: "a person without a soul or a mind; a dirty person; the opposite of a white person, of a human being," writes Manthia Diawara, when defining the term.[37] The rationale floated to justify the sign's presence was that *ANJ* is officially designated a historical monument. Turns out, it was not: "The sign is neither classified nor registered as a historical monument," according to the City of Paris.[38] *ANJ* was, however, registered in the inventory of signs at the *Musée Carnavalet*. But here's the rub. Without the legitimizing theses, all that is left is an indefensible public artifact of everyday antiblackness laid at the feet of the City of Paris to explain and defend. But let's assume that the figure is actually Zamor. There remains the issue of the actual signboard screaming out *nègre* in our time, keeping in mind that it hung above a supermarket before its removal, a site of daily life, in a predominantly white neighborhood and near some of the most revered sites of higher and secondary education in France.

NÈGRE SIGNAGE

It is important to note that *ANJ* is not the only controversial expression of French visual culture of a bygone era. But it is arguably the most egregious with the addition of its signboard. *Au Planteur*, a sign for an emporium that sold colonial goods in the 2nd arrondissement of Paris, is also of the *nègre* signage genre in its depiction of colonial racism. Represented is a shirtless black-appearing man with pronounced red lips who wears a red-beaded necklace around his neck and gold bracelets on

Street scene, *Au Nègre Joyeux*. Photo:
Michelle Young/Untapped New York.

his forearms and wrists. He stands while serving a cup of some unknown beverage to a white-appearing man seated at a table who is fully clothed. In contrast to the "native" attire of the blackened figure, who wears red-and-white-striped shorts cut above the knee, the white-appearing man is dressed in a white suite, tie, and hat, evocative of colonialists, whose clothing communicates racial superiority and "civilizational legitimacy" to the observer.[39] The sign's caption, "*Aucune Succursale*," indicates that no other Parisian shop sold its wares. But unlike *ANJ*, *Au Planteur* is registered as an historical monument—which does not make it any less offensive and perhaps even more so because it is legitimized by the state.

Back in a time when there were no street names or house numbers, signs were eponymous and thus functional, the most prominent landmarks to distinguish a particular merchant, trade, or personal address. Moreover, street names derived at times from a business sign, such as the famous rue du Chat qui Pêche. Once a fish tackle shop, this is the narrowest street in Paris, measuring 1.8 meters wide and dating from the sixteenth century.[40] But legend also has it that the shop's name is from a paranormal tale about a cat with an uncanny ability to catch fish out of the Seine. Even knowing the name of a street, one would still need to know the exact place of residence and floor where someone lived, a convention that remains true to this day in many apartment buildings. Although *ANJ* is abominable, it may have also been absorbed into rivalries among merchants of the era who used their signs to distinguish themselves based on originality, size, shape, materials, and colors, as signs "were made of sheet metal, wood, and stone representing objects, figures, animals, and landscapes, each more varied than the last."[41] One strong wind could also send a sign crashing down onto an unsuspecting passerby, which led to laws requiring that signs be attached with strong supports or long gallows.

Signage of the *nègre* genre was used to sell anything from clocks to shirts to furniture to libations, "concrete objects of everyday life with which and from which ordinary people invest and draw extraordinary meanings," write historians Leora Auslander and Thomas C. Holt.[42] Or, they become normalized and thereby largely unquestioned by the mainstream public.

Racialized iconography, as Auslander and Holt describe in their sharply titled essay, "Sambo in Paris," included an array of statues, statuettes, and antiques that they encountered in their research during the 1990s from a variety of countries. Although the "unambiguously racist representations of blacks as dumb, servile, and comic" were not the sole examples, they were the most numerous. Then there are

Au Planteur, Paris. Photo: Michelle Young/
Untapped New York.

Au Planteur (close-up), Paris. Photo: Michelle
Young/Untapped New York.

"A la couronne d'or (II)," Golden Crown, an
innkeeper's sign, ca. 1815–1830. Musée
Carnavalet.

Au Petit Nègre, shirtmaker, 30 rue Brochant,
Paris. Photo: Robert Doisneau, 1967.

Au Petit Nègre, shirtmaker, 30 rue Brochant,
Paris. Photo: Robert Doisneau, 1967.

Au Nègre de Charonne, factory supplies,
137 rue de Charonne, Paris, 1967. Photo:
Robert Doisneau.

Au Nègre de Charonne, factory supplies,
137 rue de Charonne, Paris, 1967. Photo:
Robert Doisneau.

a paucity of existing data show that young women and girls of African descent are also killed at the hands of law enforcement in France, and that their experiences are not often reported nor taken seriously, as is generally the case when reporting abusive policing.[5] This invisibility, as sociologist Patricia Hill Collins writes, locks girls and women of color into spheres of isolation and vulnerability.[6] Yet they are visible in their roles as mothers, sisters, aunts, and daughters, that is, as the surviving family members who demand "truth and justice" for loved ones killed, maimed, and traumatized by this long-standing systemic problem in France.

The police force is centralized at the national level and overseen by the French Ministries of the Interior, Defense, and at local municipalities, which for advocacy groups means that the state and these state actors are responsible for the conduct and misconduct of their police. The police force is comprised mainly of the *Police nationale*—notably its Brigade Anti-Criminalité, infamously known as the BAC in at risk outer cities—the *Gendarmerie nationale*, and the *Police municipale*; throughout this chapter, I generically use the referent "police" or "law enforcers," since everyday police violence—particularly identity controls that result from racial profiling—renders those differences irrelevant from the perspective of those on the receiving end. At the same time, I want to be clear that my critique of police violence should not be read as "anti-police." I am not seeking to point fingers at individual police officers, attribute these ills to "a few bad apples" (which is often the explanation given by policing authorities), or equate police violence with issues of morality, though this brutality points to a mislaid or nonexistent moral compass. Focusing on the misconduct of individual officers has done little to change the institution of policing and the lack of accountability that enables these behaviors. Instead, the police are often venerated and upheld by those invested in sustaining the status quo, including politicians during election cycles who reinforce as they echo typical vote-fetching narratives: urban violence justifies harsher policing. Police violence is also urban violence.

Corentin, a self-identified "Noir" Frenchman, has a long track record of community organizing and youth advocacy, which has earned him the respect and confidence of young people under his supervision. As examined in section II of this chapter, for well over a decade, together with young people, their families, activists, various attorneys, and civil society organizations, he has been on the front lines of battling to expose the "ceremony" of police violence in France and to hold the French state accountable for the misconduct and brutality of its police force. While running is but one response, the French and European courts are another. Advocacy groups are strategically helping victims and their surviving families to fight back, and at times win, through the courts, where they are armed with the very universalist principles and values that daily fail them. In the process, as with previously discussed facts of antiblackness, it is French values and principles that are effectively put on trial.

TELL LAMINE

On June 17, 2017, I witnessed firsthand the effect of those words—"Everyone hates the police"—when I participated in a march in memory of Lamine Dieng, organized by *Vie Volées* (Lives Stolen), a "collective of families affected by police crimes," founded by the Dieng family in 2010.[7] On that day, I and sociologist Jean Beaman, journalist Samba Doucouré, and others found ourselves in the company of hundreds of people of all origins who had gathered to support the Dieng family and demand, as was written on the T-shirts we wore and banners we held, "truth and justice for Lamine" and "for all victims of police crimes." Without justice, as was also written on the banner, there could be "no peace": No peace for the families, no peace for the police, and ultimately no peace for the French state.

The banner we held was a familiar roll call of death. Though the names differ across geographies, the feelings of loss and pain do not. This time, it was Lamine on the banner, alongside Mahamadou Marega (stolen in 2010), Tina Sebaa (stolen in 2007), Baba Traoré (stolen in 2008), Youcef Mahdi (stolen 2012), and Abou Bakari Tandia (stolen in 2005)—the names and likenesses of loved ones whose families joined Lives Stolen in its early years and who had unwittingly become members of an unfortunate global network of broken families and shattered lives. As we continued our march that day, the chant "Everyone hates the police" went from a whisper to a thunder once we drew closer to the police station where police implicated in Lamine's killing worked. The procession stopped on the street leading to the entrance of the precinct. We, the banner holders, stood on the front line and found ourselves facing a phalanx of officers who formed a barricade across the street that led to the station. Their shields were up, batons raised, and weapons were at the ready. As we faced off, chants of "Everyone hates the police" continued to roar thickly through the crowd. The tension was palpable but intensified when, every so often, a Maghrebin-appearing adolescent boy would dart his head between me and the person to my side and shout at the police with all the venom that he could muster: "I haaaaaate you! We all hate you!" He never went around us

Ten-year-anniversary march for Lamine
Dieng and other victims of police violence,
June 17, 2017, Paris. Photo: Journalist
Samba Doucouré.

to confront the police directly. We seemed to be his shield, or perhaps like "aunties," there to protect him from what his words and actions might ignite. Clenching their weapons each time he darted in, the police glared back with ever-narrowing eyes and tightened jaws. They looked furious. However, one directly in front of me appeared pained each time those words penetrated the air. His expression matched the look I have noticed on the faces of friends who are police officers and who carry the added weight of wearing a badge that fellow officers' attitudes and actions have tarnished. Before moving on, the kid returned one last time to voice his rage, which seemed to come from somewhere deep in his gut. Reflecting on it later, I wondered if he had experienced the worst aspects of the "ceremony of degradation," the treatment reserved for boys and young men that Corentin, just the week before, had described during an interview. I will never know, but I will also never forget the look of contempt on his young face or the sound of malice that drenched his words. It, too, was familiar.

The chant "Everyone hates the police" should not be taken only literally in this context, nor does it exist in a vacuum. It is the recognition of naked domination and brutality by law enforcers that has turned policing into "a relationship of abasement and mortification" in which individuals are "captives of a situation that forced them to submit to torment," writes anthropologist Didier Fassin.[8] Lamine's case, like many discussed ahead, tragically captures this point. What began on June 17, 2007, as a nighttime noise complaint or disturbance of the peace (*tapage nocturne*) ended with the violent arrest and police custody killing of Lamine, vividly recounted in the biographical documentary *Dire à Lamine* (*Tell Lamine*), written and directed by a self-identified *Noir* collective, *Cases Rebelles*. *Tell Lamine* "is not a film about police violence. It's a film about Lamine, about ten years of absence, ten years of life stolen," and more than ten years of the family's battling for truth and accountability.[9] The film opens with Ramata Dieng painstakingly describing the last moments of her brother's life, a description that takes on an allegorical quality in conjuring imagery reminiscent of the dehumaninizing shackling of enslaved people by slave patrols. While attempting to contain extraordinary, inescapable grief and heartache that we absorb vicariously, Ramata's rehumanizes her brother who, at the hands of his captors, had been reduced to the condition of a thing, in the words of Aimé Césaire. Periodically, the camera fades to black at these difficult moments, allowing, it seems, her (and us) time to recover from the dolor and tears that flow faster than words:

On June 17, 2007, at 4:29 a.m., my little brother Lamine Dieng, then twenty-five years old, was killed by police officers in the 20th arrondissement. These policemen were eight in number. They intervened that night for a nighttime disturbance. According to the hearings, when they arrived at the scene, they found Lamine lying on the ground between two vehicles. They claim to have arrested him for his own safety. They placed handcuffs on Lamine's hands and ankles. The ankles were tied with a leather restraining belt, then they dragged Lamine to the police van. They threw him into the van and there five policemen knelt on him. One knelt on his left shoulder blade, one on his right shoulder blade, one on his pelvis, one on his legs bent up toward his rear, and one on his head. The forensic medical examinations found about thirty bruises on Lamine's body. Lamine died of mechanical asphyxia by suffocation due to facial pressure against the ground and pressure on the top of his head.[10]

"What tortures me," shares Ramata elsewhere, "is to think about the last thirty minutes of my brother's life, the suffering, the helplessness he must have felt, everything that must have gone through his head at that moment."[11] As with Amadou Koumé (killed in 2015), Adama Traoré (killed in 2016 on his birthday), and Cédric Chouviat (killed in 2020 with a broken larynx) in metropolitan France, and Frankie Ann Perkins (killed in 1997), Kayla Moore (killed in 2013), Eric Garner (killed in 2014), Elijah McCain (killed in 2019), and George Floyd (murdered in 2020) in the United States, along with far too many others worldwide, Lamine was deprived of life-saving air. In a police van, far away from probing eyes and cell phone recording, Lamine suffocated at the hands of the police. He, too, could not breathe.

I met a determined Ramata at a press conference held by Stolen Lives where *Tell Lamine* was scheduled to be shown. She warmly greeted everyone who attended, at times walking among us to say hello or offer and receive an embrace from the many supporters gathered that day. Exhaustion was etched in her face, as was her anxiousness palpable, perhaps in anticipation of what happened next, which is why I decided not to formally interview her. The press conference was also devoted to reconstituting the events that led up to Lamine's death to dispute the officers' version of events and their use of deadly force. Based on the case file to which surviving families have access, Stolen Lives created a slideshow of drawings that were projected while Ramata narrated in detail the "over thirty long minutes," to use her words, of the arrest, capture, shackling, and eventual killing of Lamine. Tears welled in my eyes as I took it all in. How gut-wrenching it must be to relive a loved one's death in this way with each recounting of it, as Ramata has done over the years.

Not knowing what was going through Lamine's mind, as he lay dying, tortured her, she said. Did he, like George Floyd, plead for his life and call out for his mother? Or, in Lamine's case, for his big sister? As fieldwork dictates, I should have leaped on the opportunity to interview her, but it felt like I would be asking her to relive that trauma.[12] During the slideshow, Ramata's narration often paralleled the film, and, as in the film, she struggled to hold back tears but ultimately failed, as do we who bear witness. In one of the most heart-wrenching and powerful scenes in the documentary, she sums up the unbearable weight of being a family survivor in cases such as these: "The duty of the living in society is to seek justice for the victims," she said, "and I would like to tell my little brother that I am sorry that I couldn't get justice for him. I'm sorry for all the other victims and other families who are going through the same things we are."[13] Eventually, she would get perhaps not justice for Lamine but some closure for the family, not in the French court but in the European one. In June 2020, the French government reached a settlement with the Dieng family over Lamine's wrongful death, albeit thirteen years after the fact. Thirteen years of suffering amounted to 145,000 euros ($162,000) in damages for a life stolen.

HISTORICAL CONTINUITIES OF PREDATORY POLICING

Although this book is about everyday antiblackness, those racialized-as-arab inhere in the calculus of police violence and cannot be parsed out.[14] But make no mistake, other racialized-as-inferior peoples are also targeted, namely the Romani, the unhoused, real and perceived immigrants, and Asians, illustrated by the case of Monsieur Shaoyao Liu who was fatally shot by the police in his own home in Paris in 2017. The police claimed he assaulted another officer with scissors, and as often happens, the police version was disputed by the family. According to them, their father was using the scissors to clean fish for a family meal, and, as often happens, the charges against the police were dismissed. The prey also includes undesired migrants. In Paris at Place de la Republique in 2020, nearly 500 mainly Afghan migrants were inhumanely evacuated in the dead of winter and in the middle of the night. Mostly asylum seekers, they were already suffering from physical and emotional exhaustion and had little at that point beyond the shelter of a single-layered tent, donated by aid associations and collectives. Even that precious item was savagely confiscated by police, operating on orders from their superiors.

Video shows police beating people, and in one vivid and telling incident, one officer purposefully trips a man desperately trying to flee. Witnessing this, journalists and/or migrant aid workers screamed, "What the hell!! That was gratuitous!! Fuck, fuck!" until the law enforcer turned toward them.[15] Outcry from others who saw the video and photographs of these evacuations would cause the mayor of Paris, Anne Hidalgo, to write the minster of the interior to demand an explanation when denouncing "a disproportionate and brutal use of force." Similarly, Ian Brossat, deputy mayor of Paris in charge of housing, emergency accommodation, and refugee protection, castigated the state for making a deplorable spectacle of itself.[16]

Like the chant of hating the police, violence by enforcers of the law directed at African-descended people in France also does not exist in a vacuum. Political scientist Emmanuel Blanchard and sociologist Mathieu Rigouste document, for instance, how colonized Algerians and people perceived as such were the primary targets of specialized colonial-inspired units in metropolitan France and colonial Algeria that used fear, intimidation, and violence, not unlike today, to dominate and control arabianized and blackened bodies. Here, I refer to *La Brigade Nord-Africaine* (BNA, 1923–1944) and its successor, which was modeled on it, *La Brigade des Agressions et Violences* (BAV), whose name needs no translation. Citing Blanchard, Rigouste writes that "from 1958 to 1962, the BAV, like other police services, systematically fired on all Algerians who seemed threatening, who refused to submit to an arrest or who ran away."[17] Indeed, these patrols cannot be delinked from mobilizations against French colonialism in Algeria that would culminate in the Algerian Revolution of Independence (1954–1962). Those continuities resurfaced during the horrifying Paris massacre in 1961, when an estimated 200 to 300 hundred pro-Algerian independence demonstrators were beaten to death, shot, or thrown into the Seine to drown by the Paris police on October 17 under the orders of not only the notorious Maurice Papon but also the French state that authorized those crimes. The graffiti on the walls alongside the river spoke truth to power about an event that the French government had tried to suppress and/or misrepresent for over half a century: "Here, we drown Algerians" (*Ici on noie les Algériens*). This same Papon would also be found guilty in 1998 of complicity in crimes against humanity for his role in the deportation of Jewish people to the death camps during World War II, a fact that came out during the investigation of the Paris massacre.[18] Laila Amine's illuminating analysis of the "postcolonial other" in French society and specifically Leïla Sebbar's *The Seine Was Red* similarly recall the conscious attempt by the state to erase this defining moment of French history and specifically its history of racist policing with race.[19]

The enslavement of racialized-as-black Africans would provide fertile soil for policing legislation for regulating the presence and mobility of these aggregated peoples. For instance, in the eighteenth century, Louis XVI implemented the *Police des noirs* to control the growing presence of enslaved and free blackened people in metropolitan France who also resisted these laws through many successful lawsuits for their freedom, as historian Sue Peabody demonstrates.[20] Unlike previous edicts in 1716 and 1738, which had restricted the life and actions of the enslaved brought to the metropole, the *Police des noirs* barred the entry of all "blacks, mulattoes and other people of color" (*noirs, mulâtres ou autres gens de couleur*) from mainland France and thereby erected a bar based on *color* rather than slavery.[21] As noted in the 1777 law:

We are informed today that the number of *noirs* here has greatly increased due to the ease of passage between America and France; that the colonies are deprived daily of this group of men most needed to cultivate the land, all the while their stay in the cities of our kingdom, especially in the capital, causes the greatest disturbances. And when they do return to the colonies, they return with a spirit of independence and indocility that makes them far more harmful than useful. It therefore seems to us that the best course of action is to defer to the entreaties of the inhabitants of our colonies by forbidding all *noirs* from entering our kingdom.[22]

It is the first immigration ban based on *blackness*, or more precisely antiblackness, to be erected anywhere in the world, observes Peabody. Historian Laurent Dubois also captures the continuities of identity checks in relation to the *Police des noirs*, which, in the 1780s, "required blacks who lived in France to carry identity papers (*cartouches*) proving their status and right to be in the country; they could be stopped and questioned on the streets, then deported to the colonies if they lacked papers."[23] French policy controlling the mobility of Afro-descended people—on the basis of color or slave status—continued to fluctuate widely until slavery was abolished.

While some of the weapons and methods of abusive police repression and oppression have evolved over time, some have not. Those that have not include what has become a refrain in testimonies collected from multiple watch groups and researchers who study French society, a refrain of being insulted, humiliated, slapped, punched, beaten with a police baton or fist (i.e., *arrêté, insulté, humilié, tabassé—coup de matraque ou de poing*). Throughout Euro-American and French coloniality, ceremonies of degradation, from the whip to the nightstick, have long been exercised by enforcers of law alongside other repressive tactics that give the self-same cause to run. Ultimately, the "ceremony of degradation" is an intentional police strategy of domination that relies on dehumanization to establish authority, instill fear, and force unearned and therefore ungiven respect. Fassin describes this logic of running as "embodied memory" at whose foundation lies "irrepressible fear" to which the body reacts before the conscious mind: "What is manifested in these frantic flights is past experience of interactions with the police. . . . In short, a sort of immune reaction which, unlike that produced by vaccination, allows the danger to which one is exposed to be recognized, but does not protect one from it."[24]

THE LOGIC OF RUNNING FROM THE "CEREMONY OF DEGRADATION" IN DAILY LIFE

The "ceremony of degradation" invoked by Corentin and scholars in France derives from sociologist Harold Garfinkel's notion of a "status degradation ceremony" in which "the public identity of an actor is transformed into something looked upon as lower in the local scheme of social types."[25] Citing Garfinkel, Blanchard writes that these ritualized practices "are old tactics used to control certain populations . . . in the long history of relations between the French police and certain 'degraded citizens,'" in this case African-descended people.[26] That degradation also entails "devaluing the social and political identity of people whom discrimination and stigmatization prevent them from fully asserting their rights," rights that include the right not to be discriminated against or brutalized.[27] Highlighting these practices during the Algerian War, as did Fanon, Blanchard argues that the "ceremony" establishes that these convenient enemies do not belong to the "French community" (read: white and Judeo-Christian) or to the humanist-universalist principles that govern that "community," beliefs used to justify oppressive treatment.[28]

The "ceremony of degradation" is pure police violence and "regular routine," in the words of sociologist Nikki Jones, that is, "a set of patterned interactions that structure the daily lives of young men in the neighborhood" that forces them to "accept a 'submissive or supplicant' role."[29] In French society, the "ceremony" encompasses a range of routinized, naturalized, counterproductive (as a deterrent), and illegal practices that are initiated by racial profiling whose targets apprehend as an inevitable and odious part of daily life. At its extreme lies not only death but also lasting damage to victims' mental health. These practices include racist and hetero-sexist slurs (e.g., *nègre-négro-noir*/the n-word; *bougnoule*/*bicot*/a slur for "Arab"; *pédé*/ the f-word, in reference to Queer people, among others); hours-long detentions at police stations; sexual assault on adolescent males during pretextual pat-downs; beatings; death-dealing strangulation holds; and threats of retaliation for refusing, denouncing, and/or seeking legal recourse against these forms of domination and control. *Street Press* journalists in 2020 uncovered what they described as "hun-dreds of racist, sexist or homophobic messages and calls for murder" on a private Facebook group whose over 8,000 members were primarily French police.[30] During confinement under COVID-19, many testimonials revealed that people of color in France were most susceptible to the converged pandemics of a killer virus and the global phenomenon of violent policing that often accompanied it.[31] Arguably, nowhere was this better illustrated in France than on November 21, 2020, when sev-eral white-appearing plainclothes and uniformed police officers savagely beat for several minutes music producer Michel Zecler in his studio, located in upscale 17th arrondissement of Paris. The officers claimed that Zecler drew their attention be-cause he was not wearing a mandatory facemask and because he allegedly smelled of cannabis. As the forty-one-year-old b/Black man was entering his studio, the officers bum-rushed him at the door and illegally attempted to force their way in with such force that Zecler believed he was being attacked by unknown assailants. His natural reaction was to protect himself, so he tried to fend them off. The officers, in turn, claimed self-defense. They accused Zecler of trying take an officer's weapon and "resisting arrest" to justify their use of force and thereby explain away the inju-ries sustained by Zecler and several young artists who had been rehearsing in the basement of the studio and who came to Zecler's defense. In an interview with the investigative journal, *Mediapart*, these young men recounted being "kicked in the head with a shoe," "punched," "hit for several minutes," and "dragged handcuffed on the ground" during their traumatizing arrest. One added: "Outside I cried; I didn't understand. I thought that someone was going to die, that Michel was going to die. It really hurt me because Michel had done nothing."[32] CCTV security cam-eras in the studio and smartphone footage from a neighbor roused by the sounds of the arrest refuted the officers' version of events and showed one officer endangering everyone's lives when he recklessly threw a canister of tear gas into the studio to force out the occupants. The beatings stopped only when the police realized they were being filmed. Once it went viral, millions witnessed and vicariously experi-enced that violence, onto which insult was added when hearing an officer further dehumanize Zecler by calling him "a dirty *nègre*" during the altercation, according to the producer and one of the artists. Through the lens of Fanon, all the victims had been overdetermined by race long before the first blows. Thanks to that footage, believes Zecler, the officers' version did not win the day, and they face multiple charges, including filing a false police report. But will justice ultimately be served?

The beating of Rodney King in the United States over thirty years ago and the many more recorded acts of violence since then demonstrate that video evidence is only as good as the legal system judging it. The timing of the Zecler footage could not have been worse for proponents of a controversial "comprehensive security" bill, specifically its article 24, which would have made it punishable by prison and a fine to diffuse images of the police in action. However, without that film, Zecler, those young men, and their families would have likely suffered a common fate of debilitating fines and prison time. While their bodies may eventually heal from the physical injuries, which for Zecler included a head wound, a torn tendon, and a long period of rehabilitation, a full recovery from the thousand and one cuts of emotional injustice is much less certain. Police violence—whether physical or psychological—is *violence*.

Although film footage is no guarantee of exoneration for the victims, many cases in France have shown that without video, the police's version of events, outright lies, and attempts to frame the victim as the violent aggressor would likely be upheld. Beyond Théo Luhaka and Michel Zecler, there are many more, including the mutilation of Adnane Nassih, a nineteen-year-old whom a policeman shot in the face in 2020 with a flash-ball launcher (LBD). Typically, the officer claimed self-defense and was backed by his superiors, while video surveillance footage, which went viral, showed that Adnane presented no danger.[33] Chancing upon a group of militarized police in his neighborhood triggered the logic of running, as it did for twenty-year-old Sélom and eighteen-year-old Matisse in 2017, who were hit by a train when fleeing the threat of police violence.[34] In Adnane's case, the police shooter was faster. Or consider the man in 2020 who jumped into the Seine rather than face a beating from the police, which he apparently received once caught. Chilling video filmed by a resident in the area shows several police nonchalantly sauntering about, laughing, and saying racist, colonialist slurs that invoke the 1961 Paris massacre. As the man cries for help, one says: "A *bicot* like that doesn't swim," and another, perhaps in reply, says, "You should have hung a ball and chain on his foot."[35] In Adnane's case, the shot exploded his eye, leaving him with a gaping hole where it used to be along with multiple internal head injuries. Of the wiretaps released by the media of police involved discussing the case, one stood out for its levity and colonial imagery of a hunt: "Now that there are cameras everywhere, [. . .] we can't play anymore, it's over." Had article 24 passed, those videos would be inadmissible or impossible to film.

But there is also the indifference to, acceptance of, or complicity with these practices by fellow law enforcers, their superiors, and ultimately the French state, all of whom enable them. At a press conference in 2017 focused on cases of police violence in France, an attorney involved in another case, discussed ahead, addressed these points and specifically the trauma of the "ceremony of degradation": "If the police can do this; if they can search, grope, and sexually assault minors over the years and bring them back to the police station outside of any formal procedure, it is because they are allowed to do so at the very least . . . so all these practices, which have publicly taken place in plain sight for years on minors, can thrive because there is at least the silence and the culpable inaction of their superiors . . . either instructions were given or those practices were tolerated." Police violence is a reasoned and measured cause to run to the detriment of French society.

Human Rights Watch, which has been monitoring France on these issues for at least twenty years, reports in their 2012 study, *"The Roots of Humiliation": Abusive Identity Checks in France*, that the "ceremony" carries the real "threat of criminal sanction add[ing] a coercive dimension to identity checks."[36] This includes a reflexive reaction, as occurred with Zecler and so many others, that is, the automatic impulse to simply protect oneself from violence. Police have interpreted self-protection as failing to comply on some level, such as "refusal to cooperate," "insulting an officer" (*outrage*), and "assaulting an officer" (*rébellion*), all serious crimes.[37] At times, the "ceremony" serves to provoke people during identity checks to justify the violence rained down upon them, including should they react out of pain. Jean-Uriel's case is instructive in this regard, one of far too many documented by Human Rights Watch in their sobering 2020 report titled *"They Talk to Us Like We're Dogs": Abusive Police Stops in France*, which shows continuities and the self-same patterns of abusive policing reported in their earlier studies. Jean-Uriel's encounter with the "ceremony" also illustrates that police violence does not discriminate by age. The forty-one-year-old who lived in Northern France (l'Oise) recounted having been racially profiled during the COVID-19 lockdown in 2020 and stopped by the police on his doorstep in front of his two-year old. "It was profiling because the officers turned back to target me, the street was full of people and I was the only Black person . . . and I have long hair and dreadlocks, so I tick several boxes." To pull him away from his door, one of the police seized him by the collar, causing Jean-Uriel to "*react [ ] by lifting his left arm*—he thought the officer was going to hit him—the others tackled him to the ground, where he says they put handcuffs on one of his ankles." He was detained ten hours at the police station and charged with "resisting authority." Jean-Uriel's take down and having his ankles "shackled" to a bench in the lobby evokes Lamine's capture. It was, Jean-Uriel stated, "reminiscent of slavery, of France's colonial past, of how they treated the slaves in the Antilles . . . at the police station." Many would agree. In keeping with the rituals of the "ceremony," Jean-Uriel reported that the officer added racist insult to injury: "We see negros like you every day and you're not the first or the last."[38]

"OUR KIDS": NO ANGELS, NO HUMANITY

When speaking about the youth in his care, Corentin, like others, refers to them as "our kids" (*nos gosses*), which is not simply a term of endearment but also a recognition that they, as a result of empire-making and its legacies, are children of the French Republic. But they have been treated over generations with indifference, as social pariahs, and not full-fledged French people (*à part entier*) only *à part*, excluded. During an interview in 2017, I asked him about the indifference among the mainstream public to police violence against "our kids," to use his term. Corentin invoked in response something that I have often heard in France and in the United States as a rationalization of police brutality: "You know, people generalize about our kids, but let's be honest; we have young people in our neighborhoods who are really problematic. Let's face it, some of them are no angels. But all police officers are not angels too, so you can't generalize. But people who tend to generalize about kids from the *banlieue* [the outer cities], don't when it comes to other kids [read: white and upper class]." Corentin's remark, "our kids are no angels," flows from hegemonic discourses that hold these children of the republic and inferiorized groups more broadly to a different standard. Consequently, "our kids" must be exemplary, supergood, unimpeachable, above reproach, and certainly never visibly angry, if they are to deserve (not necessarily receive) basic humane treatment from law enforcers and in the society writ large. That they are "not always angels" sets the bar for humane treatment at a level that "our kids" could never attain by dint of their racialization and discriminatory collective beliefs and practices that result from it. Such politics of respectability, as scholar-activist Brittney Cooper reminds us, has never been a formula for the recognition of inferiorized people's humanity or "dignity," when what is considered "respectable," or *bien élevé* (well-mannered or well-bred), is always already racialized in these struggles to determine "who it is [im]possible or [in]appropriate or [in]valuable to be" in a society.[39] "Our kids" understand well the politics of belonging and identity and therefore opt to run.

I was first introduced to the logic of fleeing the French police when conducting fieldwork in 2006 in the epicenter of the 2005 revolts, the town of Clichy-sous-Bois, with Maboula Soumahoro, whom I have known for many years. We were there to listen and learn from Siyakha Traoré about what happened on October 27, the day his younger brother Bouna died at the age of fifteen alongside his seventeen-year-old friend, Zyed Benna. I recall my own bitterness over the many media stories about the number of buildings and cars burned or destroyed during the uprisings, precipitated by Bouna's and Zyed's deaths. Precious little attention was focused, however, on those stolen lives and the loved ones crushed with grief in the wake. Although Siyakha graciously agreed to speak with us, he wore his heartbreak on his face. Sensitive to his loss, the last thing we wanted was to have him relive what happened, but in answering my principal question, he could not avoid that terrain. I wanted Siyakha to help us, and especially people outside of France, understand why Bouna and Zyed would run from the police when they had been doing nothing wrong. Siyakha was accompanied by a family friend, a spokesperson in the neighborhood, who actually did most of the talking; with them were a couple of boys, one of whom was Muhittin Altun (then seventeen years old) who had been with Bouna and Zyed at that fateful moment when the two mistook a transformer in a power substation for a safe hiding place from the police. Tragically, it was not. Massive volts of electricity claimed their lives while Muhittin, the survivor, suffered multiple injuries from serious burns as well as untold emotional trauma, to which I attributed his reluctance to speak. Even so, we felt his moral support.

As they recounted, it was late afternoon during Ramadan when Bouna, Zyed, Muhittin, and a group of their friends were returning home after playing soccer in Clichy-sous-Bois, where they lived in Seine-Saint-Denis. Though their area is located just 24 kilometers from the Eiffel Tower, in terms of socioeconomic disparities, it is more like 24 light-years. While they were en route, someone called the police upon seeing these youngsters supposedly prowling about a construction site, either fearing for their safety or, as some believed, thinking the youths were up to no good. Upon merely seeing the police car, the boys flew into a panic and fled in multiple directions from the police. The events that followed came to be known as the "Clichy Affair." The families' attorneys detail what happened next in their book, *L'Affaire Clichy: Morts pour rien* (*Dead for Nothing*). Their account corroborates what the entourage shared during the interview and captures key aspects of the "ceremony" that fuel a logic of running:

> They are in a hurry to go home because it is almost time to break the daily fast. They are hungry and thirsty because they have not eaten nor drunk anything since the morning. They need to be, and they want to be, at home on time. Their parents and families are strict. They must not be late. And, should they be stopped by police, they will have to show their ID, but they are coming back from playing sports and *don't have their identity papers with them*. They are *minors*. This means *a control*, or even an administrative *detention for one to four hours at the police station*, and their parents would have to pick them up. The whole evening would be ruined. (emphases mine)[40]

Fearing strict parents, however, is not why they ran. "They were actually running away from the police," continue their attorneys—from, more accurately, the "ceremony of degradation." The fear was real, so real, that in a panic state, the boys scaled the fence of a power station unaware of signs and the warnings they screamed: "Stop! Electricity is stronger than you!" "Stop! Don't Risk Your Life!" Once inside, they ran zigzagging about and straight into a high voltage transformer. "Electrocuted, they die instantly," confirm their attorneys. Around 6:00 p.m., there was an electrical outage. Siyakha was getting dressed at that moment to go buy bread for dinner; his younger brother would not make it home to share that meal.[41]

   Their deaths did not unleash unbridled riots, as described in the media, but instead a calculated intergenerational reckoning against their conditions of racial oppression and inequality of which policing brutalities were symptomatic. Beyond the stark facts provided by their lawyers, Siyakha and his friend poignantly described what drives "our kids" to run, which remains as true then as now: "Today, the identity checks are more physical," said Siyakha, but before finishing his thought, his friend quickly chimed in:

> Today we're faced with a type of police that inspires fear. It's always the same people who do identity checks, sometimes several on the same day. . . . When it's bad, they insult you and make all kinds of insinuations. They speak to you disrespectfully, and you wind up at the police station, if you don't have your papers. So, kids grow up with an obsessive fear of the police . . . [frustrated and agitated, he continued:] This story didn't start on October 27,

2005! Not that specific date, no! To understand why they ran, you need to go back five years, even six, seven or ten years back because in Bouna and Zyed's minds, they already knew how things go down: people taken to the police station for no reason, others beaten up. To really know what happened on October 27, you have to understand what they were thinking, and what they've already experienced in their lives.

This "obsessive fear" and knowing "how things go down" did not begin on that day. These *bavures policières* ("slipups" or "errors"), the French expression used largely in the media for misconduct and brutality, cover a wide swath of time and include legendary cases well before 2005, notably Malik Oussekine (killed in 1986) and Makomé M'Bowolé (killed in 1993). M'Bowolé's shooting and interrogation at the police station and Oussekine's beating to death by riot police would inspire the 1995 cult film classic *La Haine* (*Hatred*). Mathieu Kassovitz unapologetically critiques vertical and horizontal oppressions operating in mind-numbing outer cities, where violence (police-driven and blighted, neglected neighborhoods) breeds hate. Although *Hatred* was the first widely received and acclaimed film to focus this way on the French outer cities, as Laila Amine writes, "images from Kassovitz's iconic film *Hatred* have [also] played a crucial role in fixing ideas of racialized bodies as out of place in central Paris and linking the graffiti to banlieue vandalism," bodies always already criminalized.[42] In 1994, Amnesty International (AI) released a chilling report titled *France: Shootings, Killings and Alleged Ill-Treatment by Law Enforcement Officers*.[43] Among the many cases cited is the killing of seventeen-year-old M'Bowolé at a police precinct in the 18th arrondissement of Paris where "the inhabitants complain of incessant police identity checks and generally insensitive policing."[44] To contextualize this case, AI reported that between 1993 and 1994, there was a pattern of "reckless use of force" among law enforcers indicative of the "ceremony of degradation." Then as now, "alleged physical and sexual abuse is often accompanied by specifically racist insults as well as general verbal abuse" directed largely at people of "non-European ethnic origin, people whose ethnic origin lies in the Maghreb countries, the Middle East and Central and West Africa."[45] Unlike in *Hatred*, officer Pascal Compain had been ordered to end the over two-hour interrogation of M'Bowolé but apparently persisted in an attempt to force a confession from the youngster. A heated exchange reportedly ensued, during which Compain claimed that M'Bowolé "verbally threatened the officer who then took his handgun from a drawer and placed it against M'Bowolé's temple," he said, "to frighten him."[46] Instead, he shot M'Bowolé at pointblank range, killing him on the spot, reported AI.

It is unclear if the teenager was handcuffed at the time. What was the heinous crime that M'Bowolé and two of his friends allegedly committed, one of whom was also a minor? They allegedly stole cigarettes from a tobacco shop, something they had denied. For those of us in the United States, this case rings eerily familiar, recalling Michael Brown (killed in Ferguson, Missouri, in 2014, at the age of eighteen by Darren Wilson) and his alleged theft of cigarillos from a convenience store before he was gunned down. Brown needed no weapon. He *was* the weapon, according to an armed Wilson, who claimed to have felt threatened and feared the size of Michael's racialized body, as was also said about Lamine. The courts ruled M'Bowolé's killing "involuntary manslaughter"—in other words, an accident, one of many "accidents" or lethal shootings of unarmed young men of color in France around that time by the French police. Although Charles Pasqua, the right-wing hard-liner and twice interior minister (1986 and 1993) would suspend the officers, it was widely reported that the police felt protected by Pasqua's "law and order" politics. Nevertheless, human rights groups and surviving families decried what they saw as the license of police to use greater force and operate with impunity granted by a right-wing, anti-immigrant government. As in 2005 and subsequently, M'Bowolé's killing ignited revolts in France, but the scary truth of Amnesty International's report is that it could have been written yesterday.

Malik Oussekine's cause of death remains in dispute.[47] Witnesses described how baton-wielding motorcycle police (*voltigeurs*), under Pasqua's ministry, savagely clubbed anyone believed to be involved in massive student protests that took place concurrently with pro-immigration mobilizations in which people of color became visible prey.[48] The official cause of death was attributed to a heart attack and renal failure associated with a preexisting condition, but witnesses reported that Oussekine, who was leaving a jazz club in the Latin Quarter of Paris, was chased by three *voltigeurs* who cornered and mercilessly beat him in the lobby of a building where he sought refuge. On the twentieth anniversary of his death, the City of Paris placed a memorial stone on the sidewalk in front of the building where he was killed, but it does little to settle the debate. It reads: "In memory of Malik Oussekine, a 22-year-old student, beaten to death during the demonstration of December 6, 1986." Beaten to death by whom? The plaque doesn't say. Admission by omission of this kind only provides cover for the violence and killings perpetrated by the unidentified police. Insult is added again to injury by locating the plaque not on the building's facade but underfoot where dogs relieve themselves and where people carelessly and indifferently walk upon it, as I have seen.

Plaque in memory of Malik Oussekine.
Photos by Trica Keaton.

For Bouna, Zyed, and Muhittin, transcriptions of police radio communications from that evening show one officer saying: "If they enter the site, there's not much hope they'll make it out alive." Nothing was apparently said or acted upon to stop them from entering the power station, the consequences of which the police were clearly aware. Those officers were eventually charged with failing to render assistance to a person in danger, as French law requires. Failing to do so is a crime. Ten years after the boys' deaths, in 2015, the French courts acquitted the officers in a final ruling, only to reinforce what police violence already makes plain in everyday French society.

ON VIOLENCE, ON POLICE VIOLENCE

In this context, the sights and sonics of the police, police vehicles, and sirens operate as a type of first warning system, alerting those targeted that it is time to flee a predictable "excess of cruelty" at the hands of the police. Citing Étienne Balibar, Fassin further writes of cruelty and brutality as an effect of power from which pleasure derives, that is, the "enjoyment of hitting or humiliating a defenseless individual is both a characteristic of the officers involved (though obviously, not all are), and a fact that needs to be understood (well beyond the ranks of the police)."[49] Following this insight, psychologists Phillip Goff et al. argue that "dehumanization," an essential ingredient of police violence, "is a method by which individuals and social groups are targeted for cruelty, social degradation, and state-sanctioned violence."[50] Indeed, as Weber averred long ago, the state successfully claims the "the monopoly of the legitimate use of physical force within a given territory," and the spokesperson for this monopoly on the "'right' to use violence," as affirms Fanon, is the "police officer" but "only to the extent to that the state permits it," concludes Weber.[51] Permit it, the French state surely does. A law enforcer may interpret "forcing suspects to the ground, and subjecting them to painful armlocks, throat compressions, suffocation and beatings" as legitimate force or a "right to use violence."[52] From the standpoint of the viewing public and individuals on the receiving end, what they may see, film, and experience directly or indirectly is a legitimate reason to run, even as running triggers that "right" and/or can and does result in death.

Police violence, however broadly or narrowly conceived, is a multiscalar issue in many societies. It manifests not only as a physical attack on the body but also as an insidious violation of the psyche. Violence itself, following anthropologists Nancy Scheper-Hughes and Philippe Bourgois' analysis of the concept, entails "assaults on the personhood, dignity, sense of worth or value of the victim" and their surviving families, which also offers important insight into why everyday antiblackness and racism are apprehended as violence by people subjected to them.[53] The police in France are civil servants and thus are extensions and representatives of that state, which renders police violence ultimately state hegemonic violence, reflecting (coercive) complicity with a taken-for-granted world. Keeping with these scholars who gesture to Fanon, we can argue that this violence is destructively reproductive and generative of what it inflicts, which, in the hands of the dehumanized or animalized, for Fanon, becomes redirected at that which embodies the French state: its policing forces. In other words, for Fanon, violence served becomes violence returned as a condition for liberation, not an end unto itself, and liberatory uprisings against oppression are a well-established French tradition whose clear historical analogues are the French and Haitian revolutions. With every Molotov—popularly called in other contexts "the grenade of the poor"—and every car or building burned, those oppressed assert, at the same time, their humanity, meditates Fanon, who further writes that "they know they are not animals. And at the very moment when they discover their humanity, they begin to sharpen their weapons to secure their victory."[54] For "our kids," rebelling against state violence in this framing becomes a path to rehumanization, securing *human* rights, expressing racialized solidarity, and, specifically in this context, refusing institutionalized police violence.

Just as *Hatred* brought these everyday issues to the French mainstream and to an international audience through the cinematic power of storytelling, the French post-2005 banlieue cinematic genre, with its autobiographic bent, carries the torch forward about "the realities of a part of French society that had previously been either ignored or reductively represented by outsiders," writes Dominic Thomas in his analysis of this France in film and literature.[55] Award-winning successor films, such as Houda Benyamina's *Divines* (2016) and Ladj Ly's *Les Misérables* (2019), are noteworthy in this context, Ly's in particular for its raw depiction of revanchism that results when youth stop fleeing the French police and their "ceremony." Ly's film is informed by its namesake, Victor Hugo's 1862 quintessential historical novel about the wretchedness of class dispossession and the injustices of penal law in nineteenth-century France. But more than Hugo, Ly channels Fanon's classic *Wretched of the Earth*, a prescient analysis of the dehumanizing consequences of white settler colonization on the colonized who are represented by outer-city youth in his film. As Fanon writes, they are "dominated but not domesticated" yet "made to feel inferior, but by no means convinced of [that] inferiority," and so they "patiently wait [ ] for the colonist to let down its guard and then jump."[56] Ly's formidable and spectacular denouement runs with this idea as both a warning and signpost for the French state ("the colonist") when portraying fed-up outer-city boys (the "dominated but not domesticated") who have sharpened their weapons and refuse, this time, to run. Instead, they plan and wait for the opportune moment to turn the tables on their police perpetrators, making them instead their prey.

Trapped in the bowels of a public housing tenement, wounded, and blinded by smoke and gas from a pitched battle, three police officers desperately search for an exit from the melee. These police reflect race representations in French society, and, as practitioners of the "ceremony," disrupt neat ideas and dualities about "good" and "bad" cops in terms of race. There is a b/Black conformist who is nonthreatening to power structures and goes along to get along; a white-appearing cop whose inferiorized Spanish or Portuguese immigrant origins make him the butt of bigoted slurs from the narcissist w/White, presumably "authentic" Frenchman (*français, français*), whose slurs and especially his violent treatment of "our kids" confirm him as a racist and completely unsympathetic character.

The desperate pleas of these trapped policemen fall on ears long deafened by police violence. Not a single person in the building offers safe haven to the three whose only exit is blocked by an armed brigade of "our kids," standing their ground. Through the mayhem, a blackened boy named Issa emerges as the film's protagonist, who is "no angel." Ly positions Issa on the landing of a stairwell that looks down upon the cornered police in distress. He is wearing a hoodie, a trigger for law enforcers, that barely conceals his swollen black eyes and other facial injuries sustained earlier in the film when these cops had attempted to arrest Issa for stealing a lion cub from a nearby circus in the area. Things quickly escalate when Issa's friends come to his rescue, knowing "how things go down," should Issa be caught. Instead of running, they opt to fight back, using rusted cans, rocks, bottles, anything they could find, eventually wresting from the b/Black policeman his pepper spray that they use on him this time. Angered and unable to see yet brandishing a flash ball gun, he "accidentally" shoots a handcuffed Issa in the face, as he tried to escape, and knocks him out cold. In the film, the white-appearing, Spanish/ Portuguese-origin cop assumes the white saviorist role when seeking to render aid to the boy but ultimately complies with his colleagues' attempt to cover up their crime. On that day in the stairwell, the two face off. Issa holds a Molotov with a burning wick, and the saviorist cop points his gun squarely at the boy, imploring him to drop his weapon. With a look of glacial hatred on his already distorted face, Issa contemplates his next move, as the camera fades to black. The ending is not resolved for the viewers, but the lack of resolution only heightens the effect of drawing us into not the vicariousness of everyday racism but instead the vicariousness of vengeance and payback. As in actual revolts, Ly captures that releasing effect about which Fanon warns, from being on the receiving end of everyday oppression that finally finds expression, like a released pressure valve, when it is returned to its most immediate maker, the police who embody vertical oppression. However, violence served also has a way of rebounding, as Césaire reminds us through his boomerang effect concept, whereby greater oppression and the dehumanization of self become the price of that ticket. In the end, Ly leaves France on the edge of a precipice where we could all be easily pushed over or uncertain which way to turn.

During a symposium on police violence that I co-organized in 2021, a French activist was asked pointedly about the hate that abusive policing reproduces. He responded: "When I organize debates sometimes between young people and police officers, you can feel that dialogue is possible, that things can be said . . . you can tell that most of these young people don't have hatred in their hearts. But, at the same time, I am extremely worried because for all of our struggles, for all of our victories from legal battles, well, it doesn't really change our government. And, at the end of the day, the police are systematically protected, so at a certain point, you wonder about a violent blowback; sometimes I, you can hear it, in the things people say, particularly from young people who are tired of a particular police unit's violence and want to respond to it, so we try to calm them down to gain some time . . . but there is a real concern; I'm worried. I'm worried that one day, they will take it out on a cop or kill a policeman because the anger is there, and sometimes the violence [that they experience] is truly terrible." This "patriarchal power" in France, in the words of Rigouste, is "fundamentally male violence, conceived and implemented by a vast majority of white males committed to the preservation of the social order."[57] Police violence is systemic, argues advocacy groups discussed in section II of this chapter, and the French case is "paradigmatic" of state repression, exercised on the most at-risk people to sustain a "social order," argues Fassin, which also sustains a preference for racial sameness whether the government is left or right wing.[58] Spectacularized arrests of vulnerable people may indeed yield symbolic value in the media, but the social cost is legitimizing that monopoly of violence and thus the "power to exert power in unlawful ways, to deploy illegal practices they would never consider deploying in other contexts," in the words of Fassin.[59] In the everyday, however, what makes police violence dangerous for the society is not its brutality but more its tolerance, acceptability, and routineness, so that it becomes normal to treat "our kids" outside the codes of ethics and law: "Officers sometimes affirm that giving a good slap to a teenager who has committed a minor offense (done without fear) has a pedagogical value," observes Fassin, but it does rebound against its maker on the streets and in the courts.[60]

SECTION II

"Il faut se battre!" ("You Have to Fight!"): Racial Profiling, Strategic Litigation, and Accountability

––––––––––

Make no mistake: police targets and their families are not passive victims, nor do they subscribe to a victimhood mentality. They have been, however, victimized in the pure sense of the term, that is, repeatedly subjected to callous indifference and the aforementioned cruelty in a system where, in the words of an attorney who spoke at the police violence press conference in 2017: "these abuses are known and have been tolerated by authorities." As some young people run from police violence, others have unrelentingly fought back over the years and on multiple, imbricated fronts. *Il faut se battre*! ("You have to fight!") was an expression that I heard often in response to the question of what to do about these issues. Fighting back has manifested itself in a variety of ways, including social scientific studies, protests, the arts, sports, social media, and various other means that have drawn police violence from the shadows into light with the aim of effecting legislative reform. But fighting back is difficult in a raceblind state that denies and/or ignores the existence of the most common features of the "ceremony," namely, racial profiling and its institutionalized nature. Although changing, racial profiling in France is commonly termed in public discourse *un contrôle au faciès*, a raceless construct that uses "appearances," physical traits and/or clothing, as the basis or factor in discriminatory identity controls or stops by French police. However, "appearances" also operates as code for race and/as ethnicity, which are the primary grounds used by French police in racial profiling that initiates the "ceremony of degradation." I prefer to retain the French word, "identity control," as it connotes having power over someone's very identity, which captures this practice better than "stop" or "check," the English translations.

Owing to the gravity of the problem in France, a group of diverse activists, grassroots and civil society organizations, and attorneys have formed a consortium in the battle against police violence and racial profiling. Among the consortium's members are individuals such as Omer Mas Capitolin, founder of Community House for Supportive Development; attorney Slim Ben Achour; Lanna Hollo, senior legal officer with Open Society Justice Initiative; and participants from international NGOs, such as Human Rights Watch. They aim to expose and attack the problem strategically in the French courts, which has resulted in cautious "victories," culminating in 2020 with the first-ever class action lawsuit in France against not only individual police officers but also the French state for racial profiling and discriminatory identity controls. In their communiqué about the class action, the consortium explains why policing practices implicate the government: "The French State, represented by the Prime Minister, the Ministers of the Interior and of Justice . . . are responsible for the planning and implementation of policing strategy."[61] Because the French legislature defines class action narrowly, "what we have is more class action *à la française*," as an interviewee involved in these cases calls it, which means that "we bring a lawsuit on behalf of a plurality of plaintiffs so that their cases are examined in the same suit and not in x different ones." The difference and lynchpin are race and/as ethnicity, the very thing from which race-blind republicanism retreats. While it is not a class action à la the United States, Slim Ben Achour, the lead defense attorney in many of these cases, acknowledges that the landmark *Floyd v. City of New York et al.* informed their strategy. *Floyd et al.* charged that the New York Police Department (NYPD) engaged in patterns of racial profiling and unconstitutional stop and frisks that targeted thousands people racialized-as-black and brown in New York.[62] In 2013, a federal judge issued a historic ruling against the NYPD and the city. From 2012 to 2020, Ben Achour and his team have brought to trial two groundbreaking cases, which made possible the aforementioned class action suit with others in the offing. Building off strategies and lessons learned, these cases have resulted in landmark rulings that have shed light on the normalization of police violence and underdiscussed but known violations, such as the sexual assault of boys and young men during identity controls and arrests. What follows derives from a variety of interactions with members of the advocacy team whom I have interviewed off and on since 2015, various data sources about cases highlighted, and a highly instructive press conference called by the legal team to which I was invited in 2017. As one lawyer involved in these cases put it after a favorable ruling and the hope it inspired: "Our clients have started to take their rights seriously . . . and they take their basic rights very seriously now."

On April 11, 2012, the same day that the US special prosecutor in the Trayvon Martin case issued a second-degree murder charge against George Zimmerman, someone I call Ousmane and twelve other individuals, on the other side of the pond, filed what would be a watershed lawsuit against the French state for racial profiling. Ousmane and I met in 2015 at an event focused on that topic where he was a featured speaker. After his panel, I approached him, briefly introduced myself, and explained my interest in interviewing him in relation to my research on *la discrimination anti-noire* in France. Hearing that description caused his eyebrow to raise, something I would see again, seemingly in bemusement or perhaps curiosity. A couple of weeks later, I interviewed Ousmane in his neighborhood at his insistence because, as he would later confess, he presumed that I, an American, had never visited what he called "the real France, *le 93*," the administrative number for Seine-Saint-Denis. On a warm summer's day, I met Ousmane just outside the metro, and we strolled to a nearby park for the interview. During our conversation, I disabused him of his presumption when discussing my previous research in *le 93*, causing that familiar rise of the brow and him to grin slightly, in an expression of pleasant surprise, it seemed this time. As with all interviewees, I asked Ousmane to introduce himself to me and highlight whatever he thought was most important about himself. "I'm Muslim, practicing, French, and *n/Noir*, so totally French," he said facetiously, knowing that anti-immigrant and anti-Muslim identity politics would cast him as anything but French. He also made no distinction between an upper- or lower-case understandings of *n/Noir*, when I asked him if it bothered him being called as such. He said no because, as this twenty-something young man put it: "It's obvious; I'm *n/Noir*," but then went on to describe how "black" is associated with "everything that's negative in the collective imagination in France." Ousmane's responses also offer some insight into b/Black diasporic identity politics during that period, as discussed in the introduction, whereby ascribed, political, claimed, or desired b/Blackness is subject to temporalities and geographies.

Ousmane spoke in a concise, contemplative manner, and seemed careful of his word choice, at times sticking to just the bare facts, no window-dressing, and an economy of words when describing his identity control. While the tragic loss of a loved one is a powerful motiving factor in pursuing a lawsuit, the fact that his younger siblings witnessed and were traumatized by his public degradation propelled Ousmane. The vicarious effect made that control one control too many. "I would never have filed a complaint if my sisters were not there. //Why not?// Because I'm an activist; because I teach my sisters certain things; because I'm the elder and their role model, and they, they're younger . . . it marked them . . . they were afraid; they were also angry, and I, I always told them that they have to defend themselves, to fight back. If I let them get away with it, what message would I be sending? I couldn't; I had to do something."

When describing what happened that day, Ousmane explained that he had been visiting his parents, and to convey the relevancy of racialized space to the "ceremony," he added, unsolicited: "My parents live in an HLM [public housing]," he said, pointing to a large housing complex across the way from where we were seated, "and so do I." After the visit, he was out walking with his sisters, and along the way, Ousmane noticed several police officers entering the area. No big deal, he thought, since they were permanent fixtures in his neighborhood, so he paid them scant attention; he was also preoccupied with trying to catch up with his little sisters who had gotten ahead of him, he said. Ousmane continued to describe the lead-up to his control, offering another unsolicited detail of having worn a hoodie that he pulled over his head because it was cold out. Through these revelations, Ousmane was both providing the scaffolding to the "ceremony" and the all-too-common subtext or pretext for his stop—his neighborhood, skin color, clothing (hoodies being associated with urban youth culture)—signifiers that provoke racial profiling. The association of hoodies, policing, and violence still elicits strong emotions for those of us who recall Trayvon Martin's murder at the age of 17 in 2012.

"Suddenly," he went on to say, "a policeman grabbed my arm and took me to the side. //Your sisters didn't see anything at that moment?// My sisters were looking at me. They saw what was happening, but they didn't understand. I said to myself that it was just a misunderstanding and that each of us would go our separate ways." Not likely, for the ceremony had already begun. Ousmane continued: "I said to him [the officer], 'What are you doing?' He didn't answer. I repeated, 'What are you doing?' He said 'Police!'" Ousmane emphasized, again unsolicited, that he spoke respectfully to the police officer who, in his authoritarian, elevated tone, might as well have said "obey," a word actually used by some officers when controlling targeted youth. "Obey" is typically preceded by "shut up and . . . ." Noncompliance typically means elevated violence. Next, Ousmane described being shoved face forward against a wall, still with no explanation, so he turned toward the policeman once more to ask why he had been stopped. Showing him his taser, the policeman screamed as if talking to a recalcitrant animal: "Police, you want me to taser you?!" That Ousmane was also disrespectfully addressed in the informal *tu* during the "ceremony," was "just the minimum," he said, when compared to the threat of being electroshocked. For me and undoubtedly for anyone familiar with the case, that moment in Ousmane's control conjures Texas State Trooper Brian T. Encinia's vicious threat, spewed at Sandra Bland during a 2015 pretextual traffic stop: "I will light you up!" Three days later, an otherwise healthy Bland, a Black woman, was found hanged in her cell, her death officially ruled a suicide. Meanwhile, Trayvon's killer, George Zimmerman, attempted in 2019 to sue the Martin family for $100 million in damages, alleging false evidence and other conspiratorial claims, as if getting away with killing their child was not enough.[63]

"I see how things are getting out of hand," Ousmane told me, "and at that point you have two options. Either you react, and they charge you with contempt and resisting arrest [*outrage et rébellion*], or you do things intelligently." For Ousmane, at that moment in front of his distraught sisters and to protect them from further harm, "intelligently" meant "obeying," no matter how painful or unjust, so that he might live to fight the battle another way, on another day. At times, Ousmane described his control in a seemingly disembodied way, as though he were watching and analyzing in his mind's eye what he had experienced. He knew his treatment was unjustified but seemed to be searching for some indicator or insight that might shed light on the police's behavior toward him. Though he had been stopped before, particularly when he was younger, he somehow expected to be treated differently, he confessed, as someone who was university educated, "well raised," and a respected and respectable person in his community. Racial profiling, however, rendered Ousmane's self-perception meaningless, because what is seen, to return to Fanon and Stuart Hall, is just the "minimal self," not a person but an overdetermined blackened body, transmogrified by the very contextual cues that he had already shared. After he recounted his experience, I noted that he had not highlighted the type of physical abuse that is often part of these accounts, so I asked Ousmane, a small-framed man, if he had been hurt by the policeman whom he described as *costaud* (strong, burly, or husky). He looked at me dead in the eye and, in stark terms, replied coldly: "He grabbed me by the arm; he slammed me against a wall; he threatened to taser me; he beat me. And still, I said to myself that it's really incredible to react that way." He added that it was "a real violation," and when he threatened to file a complaint, the officer, perhaps confident that nothing would be done, told him go ahead, returned his ID, and shooed him off. The next day, he did file the complaint. But when he asked if he would be notified about the outcome, he was told that the matter would be handled internally. "Merci, au revoir," Ousmane said, and then contacted the association *Stop le Contrôle au Faciès*, which had launched a massive multimedia campaign against police identity controls in France about which I have written elsewhere.[64]

Similarly, Corentin minced no words when discussing the emotional injustice of repetitive, unjustified, and abusive identity controls that have become so normalized in the society to which he, youth in his care, and I have been subjected:

Some think these identity controls are a banal act that lasts 5 minutes and then it's over, or people say: "But if you've done nothing wrong, then you have nothing to worry about," blah, blah, blah. But why are these identity controls problematic? In fact, they are terribly problematic for us, and when I say "us," I mean people with the color that I have. It's like what [James] Baldwin said, it's a kind of distortion of reality. Think about it. You live in a capital city like Paris where you can meet people from all walks of life and have positive, nice interactions with them. But then baf! One day, you cross a street like everyone else, and the police tell you that you're not an individual like other people, that your color makes it so. And this sort of thing, this violence, this ceremony, happens. It's degrading; it's humiliating, and most of the time these controls aren't even justified.

In 2021, Corentin returned to this point without missing a beat since little has significantly changed. He described the checks as "totally twisted," adding that "today in a capital city like Paris, if you don't clean up your dog's droppings on the sidewalk, you get a fine; if you park your car badly, you get a fine, and it's documented, written up. But in Paris, in the capital, if you're nonwhite and you're stopped by the police . . . you can be sequestered for hours or a whole day at the police station, and after 24 hrs, they simply say to you, get out! There are no traces, no elements, no documents, no written documents. . . . Imagine if you're stopped during your lunch break, you can't prove to your employer that you weren't out drinking with your friends but were stopped for an identity control! . . . So there's a dynamic, for me, as a French person that I experience, a feeling of being a second-class citizen. And it seems that no one recognizes that I have a certain dignity or what it means to be subjected constantly to these controls as a citizen who's constantly controlled by the police."

The lack of police documentation about illegal police controls, the lack of transparency over the number of complaints filed, and the lack of follow-up with complainants have been decried by attorneys and other civil society organizations for some time.[65] However, according to the French criminal code, the police can legally carry out identity checks in cases of flagrante delicto (when one is in the act of committing a crime), when there is a threat to public safety, or when ordered to do so by public prosecutors.[66] Law enforcers must justify what motivated the control, but in reality, the police in France can and do stop just about anyone, anywhere. They can and do search their person and their personal belongings to confirm someone's identity "with no requirement that these stops be based on a reasonable suspicion of involvement in crime or illegal activities," reports Human Rights Watch, nor are they under any obligation to explain the reason for the stop.[67] It is perhaps the Open Society Justice Initiative that best sums up the direct and indirect vicarious violence of police identity controls in their insightful 2021 guide on police stops and the law, *Challenging Ethnic Profiling in Europe*: "Police stops that may appear to majority populations as innocent and brief interruptions of the daily routine—worth the sacrifice for the sake of more safety and security—can cause tremendous fear, trauma, and humiliation to ethnic, racial, and religious minorities."[68] And, as noted in the introduction, a wide body of research shows that racism and discrimination are serious public and personal health threats. These observations from diverse authorities further reinforce the idea that blackened French people are unprotected "national minorities," as discussed in the chapter, "The Choice of Ignorance."

Ousmane and the twelve others would have their day in court. On March 24, 2015, the Court of Appeals in Paris issued a ruling that held the state liable, but, in only five of the cases, the perpetrators were ordered to pay the victims for "emotional damages" (i.e., *réparation de leur préjudice moral*).[69] The decision was appealed and sent to France's highest civil appeals court, the Court of Cassation, which, four years later, issued a landmark ruling that definitively held the French state accountable for "discriminatory identity controls," arguing that "an identity check based on physical characteristics associated with a real or supposed origin, without any prior objective justification, is discriminatory: it is a serious offence which renders the State liable."[70] Nevertheless, the Court of Cassation determined that not every case presented met that standard, leaving the others to appeal the decision at the European Court of Human Rights. In addition to the European Court of Human Rights, a wide range of watch groups continue to identify racial and/as ethnic profiling by law enforcement as violations of international human rights law, among them authorities at the United Nations and the European Convention on Human Rights.[71] The importance of the ruling condemning the French state extends beyond these cases. The Court also determined that nondiscrimination law applied to policing in France, as it did in other sectors (i.e., housing and employment), as the litigants argued. Consequently, writes the Open Society Justice Initiative about this case, the ruling shifted the burden of proof onto the state, which now had to demonstrate that "the difference in treatment [by the police] is justified by objective factors."[72] Racial profiling, by definition, does not meet that standard and is unlawful. Despite or perhaps because of what happened to him, Ousmane, like many others, said he's not anti-police; to the contrary: "We need the police, but we are in a country where we don't like our police . . . we don't trust them, and it's not normal not to like the police because these people are supposed to protect us." This point was not lost in the French Human Rights Defender's 2017 report: "This distrust of the police also extends to the justice system."[73]

POLICE VIOLENCE AS SEXUAL ASSAULT: HUMILIATE TO CASTRATE

Strategic litigation has also drawn increased legal attention to cases of sexual assault (*des agressions sexuelles*) against boys and young men by the police. The beating and rape-by-police-baton of twenty-two-year-old Théo Luhaka in February 2017 catapulted this intergenerational dimension of the "ceremony of degradation" into the mainstream. Sociologist Fabien Jobard captures what Théo suffered and, as Ousmane did in his interview with me, sets the context as explanatory of the violence:

On 2 February 2017, a police brigade was patrolling in a town in Seine-St-Denis that was marked by intense drug trafficking. The brigade (one of those touted by the minister in 2010, when he explained that he did not want to see any more police officers "in shirtsleeves") stopped and searched some young men, placing them against a wall, hands flat, legs apart. When one of the young men was slapped by an officer, Theo Luhaka, a 21-year-old black man, stepped in, causing the other officers to intervene. They pinned him to the ground and one of the police officers proceeded to violate the young man's anus with his extendable baton, causing a ten-centimeter-long internal injury with irreversible medical consequences. The incident was recorded by the town's CCTV cameras and the images were broadcast on the internet. This generated an intense emotional response from the public and brought forward numerous accounts of similar behavior in housing estates in the banlieues.[74]

As reported in the media, Bruno Beschizza, "the rightwing mayor of Aulnay-sous-Bois," a former police officer, "described Theo as a 'respectable' young man who came from a respectable family, which had been 'psychologically destroyed' by what had happened."[75] Had Beschizza not deemed him "respectable" would that mean that this inhumane violation was justifiable on some level for "our kids"? For me, this case recalls the violence in 1997 suffered by Abner Louima whom New York City police tortured and sexually assaulted after wrongfully arresting him outside a nightclub where a fight had erupted. Policeman Justin Volpe mistakenly believed that Louima had punched him during the melee. A sadistic beating followed, including kicking a cuffed Louima in the testicles. At the precinct, Volpe sodomized Louima with a wooden broom or plunger handle while others stood by. So severe were his injuries that he needed several major surgeries.

Théo's case, and the broader issues that it exposes, produced anxieties and defensiveness in France among nonbelievers, including among French people whom I know personally. For them, this type of police assault is isolated or exceptional, even as COVID confinement brought from the shadows other sexual abuses hidden from public view, notably alarming cases of incest and other forms of domestic violence. These floodgates are opening wider in France thanks to the Me Too movement. The young people in Corentin's care, his colleagues, and a wide variety of advocacy groups would also beg to differ about this invisibilized horror, designed to terrorize and castrate boys and young men, violence that operates as a silent killer attached to masculinist notions of shame. "With Théo's, there was video," said Corentin during an interview, "but there're other cases like that. There was the little [name redacted] just before Théo. Nobody talked about it because he didn't have a video. . . . Now, in the neighborhood, young people are taught to use their phones. They have the right to film identity controls in France; we have the right to film this kind of thing." The comprehensive security bill, discussed in section I of this chapter, stood, however, to curb or penalize this "right."

During an interview in 2018, Corentin described how he became aware of the issue of sexual assault during a reunion at his center, ironically focused on improving police-youth relations. One day, a fifteen-year-old, whom I will call Amir, arrived at the center for a meeting "super angry," said Corentin. Imitating the boy's agitated voice, Corentin repeated what he said: "I've had it! I'll kill one! I'm going to kill one; I'm going to kill him! I'll kill him!" The boy went on to tell Corentin and other boys in the group what happened, but Corentin noticed that Amir's type of assault was something known among other boys who frequented his center. While subjected to a hail of racist insults by a small gang of police, Corentin recounted further what Amir shared, imitating his angered tone: "They put their fingers up your butt; they dig a finger up your ass all the time!" Corentin shared what Amir had said about the police "touch[ing] your genitals," adding in his own words: "You have policemen who take their time; they slip their gloves on in a very ceremonial way . . . and they bend down to see if the kid has an erection," so that "our kids" are made to question their masculinity. For Corentin and advocates in their case, these acts are not just humiliating. They are pure violence. Corentin conveyed how difficult it was for these boys to pursue a lawsuit that required them to publicly reveal what they had kept hidden from their families and tried to bury deep inside, internalizing the shame that belongs to the perpetrators: "Unfortunately, they don't dare talk about it because it's not easy for a young guy to tell you, 'I was groped from behind by a police officer.'"

When experiencing these cases vicariously, I am taken back to Stuart Hall's keen insights on the white gaze and racism as a denial of sexualized desire in Isaac Julien's 1995 film, *Frantz Fanon: Black Skin, White Masks*. Projecting depravity onto the victim to justify brutal treatment and conceal and/or deny that desire—"which is in the gaze itself," states Hall—results in ever increasing acts of violence against that which is secretly yearned for but publicly demonized. If we take this as a historical continuity traced to the rape of enslaved and colonized blackened people whose skin color denoted evil and perversion, historian William Cohen's insight about seventeenth- and eighteenth-century European travelers to Africa is instructive. "Unmarried European males, most of them young and away from home for long stretches of time," writes Cohen, "may have projected their own sexual fantasies onto the Africans, especially the women."[76]

A study by Human Rights Watch echoes similar misconduct described by adolescent boys in Corentin's care that they shared with their attorneys; the study details alarming racial profiling and police violence inflicted on children as young as ten years old. For instance, one eighteen-year-old in Strasbourg recounted his experience with the "ceremony" this way to Human Rights Watch researchers: "They said 'simple stop.' Hands against the car for the pat-down. They focus on the buttocks, legs, genitals. It was embarrassing. . . . I think it's because of how I look. It's profiling. I'm Black [capital theirs], tall." Another conveyed a similar story when he was out delivering food on his motorbike:

They took my phone to see if it was stolen, they threw it on the ground. . . . They called me a *sale connard* [dirty asshole]. . . . It was just insults, provocations. I asked for the stop form. They said, "you can just go complain to your momma or you can go to the police station." They took my arms . . . put me up against the wall. Without gloves, they frisked me everywhere.[77]

These assaults are often performed in a public space and without consent, both of which are illegal. As Human Rights Watch further reports, the most despised abusive practices centered on the "so-called security pat-downs that include touching genitalia and buttocks, leading to abusive recourse to this measure."[78]

Abusive stops are a type of "perfect crime," to borrow an expression from an interviewee, in that victims of color are rarely believed or taken seriously, or they go under-reported, as discussed in the chapter, "The Choice of Ignorance." What's more, the French Defender of Rights (*Le Défenseur des Droits*) underscored the lack of a paper trail, that is, "the lack of a traceability system for [identity] checks," which means there is no evidence and no way of knowing the scale of a problem, compounded by the lack of ethno-racial statistics. All are great obstacles to accountability. Fabien Jobard and Jacques de Maillard reinforce this point in their analysis of police identity controls in France, noting that available data are often scattered and rarely was there follow-up action after ID controls, which are mostly "invisible within the police organization itself." They argue further that "the authorities have no administrative tracking of the number of stops and how they are distributed, either among agents and units, or in space and time."[79] The bottom line is that enforced public policies are needed for monitoring identity controls and mechanisms outside the state's purview for investigating abusive policing.

In the name of crime prevention, profiling is permitted and commonly used by the police in many countries where categories based on perceived ethno-racial origins, religion, and nationality are allowed to be considered when stopping individuals. However, "they cannot use any of these characteristics as the *sole or main criterion* to stop the individual [emphasis mine]," according to the European Union Agency for Fundamental Rights, as this would be tantamount to "racial profiling, which constitutes direct discrimination and is unlawful."[80] And yet, this occurs every day in a raceblind France.

When discussing this research, and as a Black American, I inevitably encounter people who insist that "things are not as bad in France" compared to "your country." Such commentary ends up minimizing life-and-death issues in French society by citing the high rates of police killings and shootings of people racialized as black and brown in the United States, which indeed surpasses France. In fact, sociologist Jerome Karabel dubbed US police shootings "the other capital punishment," and Frank Edwards et al. write in their study on the role of "race/ethnicity" in deaths involving the police in the United States that "police kill, on average, 2.8 men per day" and that 8% of all homicides between 2012 and 2018 were due to policing killings.[81] These scholars further found that "police homicide risk" is greater than what is officially reported and that, while place dependent, "Black and Latino men are at higher risk for death than are White men" from the police. In 2020, over 1,000 people were shot and killed by the police in the United States, according to the *Washington Post* Police Shootings Database, and annually police have shot and killed about that same number since 2015, when the database was launched to address the issue of under-reported data.[82] Although Black Americans represent less than 13% of the population, they "are killed by police at more than twice the rate of White Americans; Hispanic Americans are also killed by police at a disproportionate rate," at almost twice the rate of w/White Americans. Other data sources show that victims are over 95% male, and over half are between the ages of 20 and 40 years old.[83] Fine-tuning that point, data from the Mapping Police Violence database show that in 2020, of the 1,127 people killed by police, 28% were b/Black. In other words, these data across time continually show that "Black people were more likely to be killed by police, more likely to be unarmed and less likely to be threatening someone when killed" in the United States.[84] There is also little accountability for killings by police. Between 2013 and 2020, 93.3% of police killings resulted in no charges, according to the findings of Mapping Police Violence.[85]

In contrast, publicly available data in France are scarce and limited owing to the inability to generate ethno-racial statistics; but in the same vein as the Mapping Police Violence and *Washington Post* databases, investigative journalists Ivan du Roy and Ludo Simbille have curated and analyzed an instructive site that documents police violence in France between 1977 and 2020. This forty-three-year period is significant in that it captures dramatic economic recessions and skyrocketing unemployment that followed post–World War II economic prosperity (1945–1975—*Les Trente Glorieuses*). Increasingly during this period, right-wing politicians would link "postcolonial" immigration with citizenship, unemployment, labor competition, national identity, and national security, issues on which Jean-Marie Le Pen of the extreme-right National Front Party would build his base in the 1980s, alongside instrumentalizing French republicanism in the name of an unstated but implied white nativism.[86] The persistent effects of that period would eventually pave the way for another extreme-right presidential hopeful Éric Zemmour to whom I return in the coda.

Although Roy and Simbille note "a peak in lethal interventions" when Pasqua was minister of the interior, party affiliation was not determinant. In 2001, under Socialist Lionel Jospin, they also register a peak in fatalities and, since 2014 under (nominally) Socialist Manuel Valls, they note that "the number of lethal police interventions remains exceptionally high, with over 20 deaths each year," and over thirty in 2017 under the center-right Macron administration.[87] Over this timespan, these researchers also note a "hardening" of practices and behaviors by law enforcement, resulting in "the multiplication of serious injuries and mutilations among demonstrators" protesting police violence.[88] Thus, between 1977 and 2020 in France, this database shows that "746 people have died following an intervention by the police of which 78 were caused by off-duty officers," and 57% of those shot and killed were unarmed.[89] Moreover, 60% were killed by gunfire; 12% by asphyxiation, often involving controversial immobilization or compression methods. Half of the recorded victims were less than 26 years old, and 92% of them male. The recurring victim profile in France, according to these researchers, is "a young man under 26 years of age, having an African or North African sounding name who lives in a working-class neighborhood on the outskirts of a city like Paris, Lyon or Marseille."[90] Often left underexamined are the killings of women in France, who number 51 of the 746, all ages combined; these data also register 11 fatalities among children and 71 among adolescents between the ages 13 and 17 years old. Roy and Simbille also note that 297 lost their life "while fleeing from law enforcement," and 199 deaths occurred following an arrest. Indeed, from a US perspective, these numbers suggest that "things" are not as bad in France as on the other side of the pond. Still, each figure represents a person, a loved one, and so while kill rates differ dramatically, the difference is clearly one of degree, not kind. Cases like George Floyd and Black Lives Matter mobilizations resonated so deeply in France and internationally largely for that reason.

Racist policing and abuses within a highly militarized police force cannot be decoupled from the effects of zero-tolerance, law-and-order politics and policies in France, which during the 1990s were actually imported from the United States with lasting effects, as has shown sociologist Loïc Wacquant.[92] Yet, these policies and ideologies underpinning them are never identified in "divisive ideas" discourse, though they are precisely that. These measures resulted in a shift from community-based to results-oriented policing with an emphasis on revenue generation, performance, productivity, and measurable outcomes. Law-and-order neoliberal discourses and practices would, by the early 2000s, flourish under then conservative minister of the interior and later president, Nicolas Sarkozy, who, ironically, in March 2021, would be convicted of corruption and influence peddling in France. As political scientists Jacques de Maillard and Mathieu Zagrodzki write: "The police, particularly the commissaires, were to be evaluated—and compensated—based on their numbers. Pitting this new, data-based approach to policing against community policing, which he [Sarkozy] deemed soft, inefficient, and excessively 'social' . . . making arrests were instead to be prioritized."[93] The politics of numbers (*politique du chiffre*), decried by many police officers, serve to convey not only that the police are doing their job but also that the level of force applied reflects the quality of their performance.[94]

For instance, in March 2019, during the "great national debate" to address and/or appease predominantly white-appearing Yellow Vest protesters, President Macron denounced the expression "police violence" and its existence in France, which many of these protesters experienced firsthand during their revolt. Shortly

Facing page, top: Black Lives Matter protest in Paris, June 6, 2020. Photo: Samuel Boivin/ NurPhoto via Getty Images.

Facing page, bottom: A protestor wears a T-shirt on which "Justice for Adama Traoré" is written, while holding a placard reading *Ni Pute Ni Soumises* ("Neither Whore Nor Submissive") in the Face of Police Violence, June 6, 2020."[91] Photo: Geoffroy Van Der Hasselt/AFP/Getty Images.

thereafter, UN Commissioner for Human Rights Michelle Bachelet called for "an urgent and thorough investigation of all reported cases of excessive use of force," citing France among the violators, the only country of the Global North which found itself in the company of Sudan, Zimbabwe, and Haiti on these issues.[95] The resolution, adopted by the Human Rights Council on June 19, 2020, would address that question in terms of the specificity and resurgence of antiblack racist ideologies and violence "against Africans and people of African descent," examined in the chapter, "The Choice of Ignorance." This resolution also stipulates the need to protect African-descended people from "excessive use of force and other human rights violations by law enforcement officers."[96] Similarly, the council initiated an "urgent debate" on "racially inspired human rights violations, systemic racism, police brutality and violence against peaceful protests."[97] During an interview in December 2020 with *Brut*, a French digital media platform popular with young people, President Macron would find himself eating his words when confronted by the beating of Michel Zecler shortly before that interview.[98]

PATHOLOGIZE TO JUSTIFY SYSTEMIC POLICE VIOLENCE

Fundamental to police violence in France, as elsewhere, is the practice of pathologizing and demonizing those targeted to justify brutality. As the spokesperson for Lives Stolen, Ramata, Lamine's older sister, has shouldered the emotional burden of reframing her brother's story against damaging media, police, and state medical examiners' narratives of events. Some media reported that "Lamine Dieng had violently hit his girlfriend" that night and was found by the arresting officer in a crisis state.[99] At the same time, the police reportedly described Lamine as possessing "great physical power" and invoked his body size as a source of fear and threat to justify their use of excessive force in ways that recall again Darren Wilson's representations of Michael Brown.[100] Then, there was the issue of cause of death in Lamine's case, which the state initially attributed to cardiac arrest due to an overdose of cocaine, cannabis, and alcohol. Independent medical examiners would later refute this assertion. Though it was unsubstantiated, Lamine was portrayed as a woman-beating drug user with all the pathological and racialized connotations that this representation harbors. Pathologizing in this context defines always already racialized suitable enemies as abnormal or deviant, indeed problems, like a disease, to be managed, controlled, and eradicated. If left unchecked, they risk infecting all of society, per this reasoning, for which the police wrongly become the cure or, as UN consultant Dominique Day puts it, "problem solvers."[101] The insidiousness in the French case is that raceblind republicanism simultaneously denies race and antiblackness as animating forces in police violence and relies on broad structural complicity in order for it to operate as efficiently as it does.[102]

During the 2020 summer uprisings, the media dubbed Adama Traoré the "French George Floyd," owing to the striking resemblances in their killings, and later similarities in disputes about the causes of his death. Adama's elder sister Assa Traoré has become such a tireless champion against police violence in France that in December 2020 *Time* magazine named her a "Guardian of the Year" in recognition of her "fight for racial justice."[103]

On July 19, 2016, on his twenty-fourth birthday, Adama died in police custody after fleeing an identity control. Assa describes this tragic moment in her book, *Lettre à Adama* (*Letter to Adama*): "Because you didn't go to the city hall to get your identity card. Because you were planning to celebrate your birthday that evening. Because you don't want to find yourself in police custody as always happens when a young person doesn't have his papers. This time, no, not for so little."[104] Moments before, Adama was with his brother Bagui in the Parisian suburb of Beaumont-sur-Oise when they were stopped for an ID control by the police, who had been searching for Bagui, allegedly related to another crime. Not having his identity papers on him, Adama ran. Predictably, as the Traoré family's demands for truth and justice grew, so did representations in the media about the brothers' prior arrests and jail time that wound up demonizing the entire family. They were also pathologized by long-standing stereotypes of African families (e.g., polygamy, numerous children, poverty) in French society. In March 2021, after a nearly five-year-long battle to determine the cause of Adama's death, independent experts weighed in and upended several contradictory medical reports and theses put forth between 2016 and 2020 by the state's medical examiners.[105] An alcohol-induced heart attack, other intoxicants, a preexisting heart condition, heat stroke from running from the police during a heat wave, and other preexisting health issues were causes of death, according to the state. In short, he supposedly died by accident or from natural causes. In 2021, independent experts determined that Adama Traoré's death was "linked to a mechanical traumatic asphyxia syndrome caused by a blockage of thoracic and abdominal breathing *in the aftermath of a ventral plating*, aggravated by hypoxemia due to exertion [emphasis mine]."[106] In the words of an established sociologist in France with whom I corresponded about this outcome via email in February 2021,

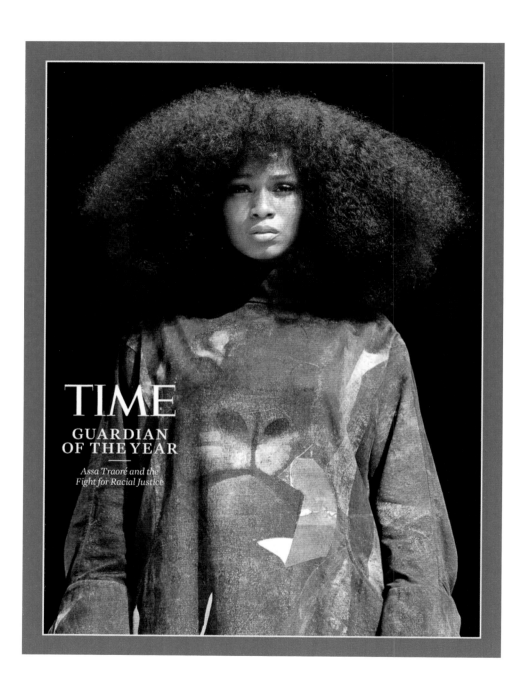

Assa Traoré, *Time* Guardian of the Year, 2020.
Photo: Kenny Germé.

the translation is this: "Yeah, we won't contradict other causes alleged in earlier examinations (preexisting medical conditions) and being overheated, but being pinned down by the weight of three cops could not have failed to aggravate things. Splits the difference but is a shade better than that because it does challenge police accounts that deny being pinned down was a cause at all." In other words, Adama could not breathe, and police involvement was a preexisting condition. It is all very familiar. As with George Floyd, sickle cell disease was supposedly one of Adama's preexisting or underlying health conditions.

In 2021, *New York Times* investigative journalists examined thousands of records over a twenty-five-year period in the United States connected to in-custody deaths of Black people in which sickle cell trait had been invoked as contributing to or being the cause of death.[107] This misdirection relies on long-debunked but ever-active ideas rooted in scientific racism, that is, the belief that "sickle cell anemia is a black genetic disease and therefore proves that race is a genetic category . . . [and that] sickle cell was uniquely inherent in 'Negro blood,'" writes sociologist Dorothy Roberts.[108] This becomes another way to convey that black inferiority is encoded in the genes. Far from a "black disease," sickle cell provides resistance to or protection from malaria, which is found in many regions outside the continent of Africa, the cradle of the so-called "black race," which is largely immune. In the words of evolutionary biologist Joseph Graves and biological anthropologist Alan Goodman: "The bottom line: continent or race does not explain sickle cell trait, but evolution does beautifully."[109]

Citing Simon Dyson, a British researcher who analyzes in-custody deaths attributed to sickle cell, the *New York Times* journalists state that "the cases follow a well-established pattern in which the trait is listed alongside other conditions, like high blood pressure or drug use, to create doubt about the role of law enforcement" as causal in the death. Among the many examples documented by these reporters, they also uncovered that "in roughly two-thirds of the cases, the person who died had been forcefully restrained by the authorities, pepper-sprayed or shocked with stun guns . . . the determinations on sickle cell trait often created enough doubt for officers to avert criminal or civil penalties," even when signs of brutality were present on the body.[110] This is also familiar. Indeed, principal investigators Nicholas Shapiro and Terence Keel from the Carceral Ecologies Lab and the BioCritical Studies Lab respectively found in their study of "jail deaths" in the United States that "that the majority of Black and Latinx men are not dying from 'natural causes' but from the actions of jail deputies and carceral staff," which include physical violence, abuse of people suffering mental illness, and/or medical negligence.[111] Medical authorities concluded that police custody deaths that are attributed to natural causes in which sickle cell is identified as contributory or the cause itself—instead of oxygen-depriving restraining techniques—should be closely scrutinized. The trait has been used as a default in many cases of b/Black people dying in police custody in the United States, revealing an alarming, nationwide pattern. The extent to which this pattern exists in France and beyond is an area ripe for research, but hindered by prohibitions around ethno-racial statistics and thereby data deficiencies. As reported in diverse media, the state's medical examiners' assessment of the disease as potentially causal in Adama's case raises similar questions and concerns.

These medical and legal gymnastics come across, then, less as fact-finding than exonerating the police and reinforcing the belief that the French judicial system operates not in the interests of minoritized targets of police violence but as a deterrent to seeking justice. Pathologizing and demonizing representations achieve their end, however. As sociologist Laurent Bonelli clarifies, "The authorities could stigmatize them and the press smugly reveal possible prior convictions [or sensationalized accusations], creating doubt about what had happened and strengthening the police version of events."[112] Having "priors" or previous run-ins with the law connects the logic of running with the politics of policing, which then brands racialized individuals with criminality, possibly for life. In this context, priors are inscribed in a broader social dynamic of entrenched environmental and economic disparities born of structural racism that shapes life chances and life choices. Sociologists Jason Smith and David Merolla's study on the effects of crime and racial stigma associated with a past criminal history is insightful for the French context.[113] Their research showed a "consistent effect of criminal history" in that people, particularly with "high racial prejudice," deemed police violence justified in the United States against b/Black people with previous criminal records, records that carry an enduring stain of guilt. Amine Bentounsi's case captures this point. "Delinquent," "criminal," "repeat recidivist," "armed robber," and "fugitive" were terms commonly used in the media, and thereby the courtroom of public opinion, to portray Amine. This discourse simultaneously served to *explain* the officer's anger and justification for shooting the twenty-eight-year-old in the back and *explain away* that killing to the public. Media reports from the trial highlight that Amine was running away with his back to the police shooter, as confirmed by the ballistic report and the autopsy. But officer Damien Saboundjian maintained that he was defending himself and that Amine aimed a gun at him, so he fired, though no eyewitnesses backed up his version.[114] However, one of his colleagues initially supported Saboundjian's self-defense claim but later admitted to lying. Self-defense peppered with "alternative facts" is a frequent response from police-perpetrators, and they often get off using this defense, so much so that this claim reinforces the idea that the police system serves and protects officers, not the people, by defending their framing (in both senses) of victims and events. This time, however, no one corroborated Saboundjian's narrative, apparently causing a presiding judge to remark that "there is one thing on which all the witnesses agree with you. You were livid at the time of the facts. You were conscious of having done something serious," and lied to cover it up.[115] In 2017, five years after killing Amine, Saboundjian was convicted of assault without premeditation, given a five-year suspended sentence, and was not removed from duty. Still, his conviction is at least part of the public record, and he has a life sentence of another kind. He has to carry Amine's blood on his hands for life, though a life sentence that offers little consolation for Amine's loved ones.

Space precludes discussing in depth the multitude of cases of police violence documented by advocates and activists over the years. I conclude, however, with what became known as the "12th arrondissement affair" because it encapsulates all aspects of police violence explored in this chapter. This includes what sociologist Magda Boutros calls identity "control-evictions" in this neighborhood that targeted those whom police officially designated in databases and police logs as "undesirables," code for race and socioeconomic status.[116] On matters of accountability, this case also illuminates how those institutionalized violations surpass the behaviors of individual police officers and come to indict an entire chain of authority. Building on strategies and lessons from Ousmane's case, the same advocacy group would provide the legal means for fighting back. Later, they would be backed by "a foundational and historic decision," in the words of Slim Ben Achour, issued in 2020 by Jacques Toubon, then French Human Rights Defender, who recognized and denounced the "systemic" nature of racial profiling. Toubon's declaration, as Ben Achour asserts, was watershed: "This is the first time that a state authority, such as the Human Rights Defender, has recognized a discriminatory *system*, and this within the police force. This decision highlights collective responsibility, which can be decisive in battles to stop discriminatory harassment as well as institutional discrimination that many young people suffer from the police [emphasis mine]."[117]

Between 2013 and 2015, seventeen young people, aged 11 to 18, reported having been repeatedly subjected to nearly every expression of the "ceremony," barring physical death, by police in the 12th district of Paris and in a neighborhood undergoing gentrification at the time. Toubon noted in his declaration that "all describe themselves as black or Arab or were perceived as such."[118] In 2015, they filed a joint lawsuit in the criminal courts against eleven police in that arrondissement, and, in 2019, a civil case against the state for those offenses. In 2018, three of the eleven police were convicted for "aggravated assault" but given suspended prison sentences and fines, while in 2020, the state was found guilty of "gross negligence" in the affair. All are under appeal, as I write. The offenses fell broadly into three overlapping categories: sexual assault during "security pat-downs"; illegal detentions at the police station and/or what attorneys called "sequestration," a type of kidnapping; and "racial discrimination." As one attorney stated at a press conference when describing the case: "It's not just any child to whom they do this," in foregrounding the racial aspect.[119] Beatings, racist insults (e.g., filthy black/*sale noir*; you monkey/*espèce de singe*, and more), and destruction of personal property (usually cell phones) were also documented in the investigation. Retaliation also occurred in the form of preying on these youths in other ways, such as levying fines (*verbalisation*) as high as 150 euros against youth for a supposed minor offense, though "our clients did absolutely nothing," said another attorney.

During the investigation, the police invoked at times ridiculous justifications for their actions that left me wondering if they were being facetious. For instance, frisking someone for reasonable suspicion of a weapon is one thing; repeatedly touching the same boys' genitalia and digging into the cracks of their butts or elsewhere for a supposedly concealed knife conjures an altogether different image of police. This is particularly true for those involved in this case who were nicknamed after a predatory animal, "tigers," in reference to the insignia on their uniforms. Humiliation, emasculation, domination, and submission were counter-motives advanced by attorneys and advocacy groups involved in the case. That these youths were known to the police—they were repeatedly profiled and controlled—discredited the justification given for stopping "our kids" in the first place for identify verifications, which strengthened instead claims of racial profiling with nefarious intent. Admittedly, I did not quite understand what was meant in this context by "sequestration." An attorney filled in the gaps: "Without any justification or verification of their identity," the supposed rationale for the stop, these young people would be taken to the police station and held. "So they grabbed children, kept them for a few hours at the police station and released them without any reason . . . imagine what was going on in that child's mind . . . and the family. In France, in the middle of Paris, we can take children off the street, make them disappear and then reappear."[120] He went on to say that dictatorial regimes work that way, not democracies. No traceability but a license to abuse authority is once more a perfect crime.

The perfect crime involved practices embraced by the police force that were based on the self-same vicious circular logic of framing and officially categorizing targets as "undesirables" to justify racial profiling in abusive identity checks. Aggressive policing tactics were used to evict "undesirables" from public space in *their* gentrifying neighborhood, supposedly in response to complaints from some gentrifiers who equated kids hanging out with trouble and probable crime.[121] As Toubon writes further, it was always the same young people who were targeted and designated with this "particularly stigmatizing term," which was also reserved for Romani people and the unhoused, implying that all are dregs of society. The repetitiveness and significant number of violations alleged, occurring over an extended period of time and involving the same officers, raised the question of whether orders from their superiors played a role, as Boutros notes in her insightful ethnography of this case.[122] The officer claimed that they were following orders in practicing these evictions that amount to "broken widows" policing in which otherwise lawful conduct in public (e.g., hanging out with friends, listening to music, eating, drinking, sleeping) is criminalized and, if left unchecked, supposedly opens the door to actual or/and greater crime. Punctuating the point, an attorney added, "they were instructed [by their superiors] to clear the streets of undesirables; okay, it's not written anywhere that undesirables means b/Blacks and Arabs, but you don't have to say it," because racial profiling illustrated it to be so.[123]

The gravity of the racialized category, "undesirable," in a category-raceblind France should not be minimized, even as it seems less offensive than other racist insults uncovered in this case or other racialized categories used by police. Just as racist police violence targeting African-descended people has a history, so too does this term, as Jennifer Boittin and Lanna Hollo observe: "At one time, undesirables were Algerians," asserts Hollo, "undesirables were Jews. Undesirables today are young Black and Arab men in poor neighbourhoods."[124] In the documentary about this case by Marc Ball, *Police, Illégitime Violence* (*Police: Illegitimate Violence*), anti-discrimination attorney Slim Ben Achour makes no bones about his views of this seemingly deracialized term in the French context: "It is a term noted and assumed totally by police officers . . . this term does not exist in the penal code . . . so we have this absolutely monstrous notion, *monstrous*, of a citizen, that they consider future citizens, children, our children, as undesirable!"[125] Here, Ben Achour's observation recalls Fanon's reflection about the cause being the effect: You are racialized, thus pathologized, because you are undesirable. You are undesirable because you are racialized, thus pathologized, the "enemy of [French] values," writes Fanon.[126]

For families who have lost loved ones and those horribly preyed upon, the victories in these cases may seem pyrrhic. Nothing brings back stolen lives or compensates for what "our kids" have suffered needlessly, even as I write. Without the state officially and specifically addressing the issue of racism and race in policing, any reforms put forth will fail to see the forest for the trees. Still, these cases of fighting back illustrate several salient points to current and future prey, the public, and the police, points that effectively put the French state on notice. Each case and victory, even if appealed and no matter how seemingly small, becomes a crack in the armor that traditionally protects the police. Perhaps more importantly, they signify that even those written off or vilified have rights—including the right to equality that is free of race-based discrimination—in life as in death, and that people will fight back no matter how long it takes. What's more, those rights can be defended, if not through the French courts then through the European ones, and if not through criminal law then through civil proceedings. And these outcomes also show, despite entrenched beliefs and evidence to the contrary, that the French state can be held accountable when its police force violates those rights. Finally, every court case exposing police violence in France gnaws at raceblind republicanism's negation of race and proves fatuous and impractical its promulgated tenets of equality through invisibility in a multiracialized French society where power, status, and resources have been racially drawn. What these cases also make plain is that French laws and public policies must address disparate impact, inequality, and treatment through *visibility*, that is, rendering visible racism *with* race, indeed antiblackness *with* people who have been racialized-as-black, and their everyday consequences on the ground.[127]

UNIVERSALIZE TO PANTHEONIZE: SCRIPTING JOSEPHINE BAKER

On November 24, 2021, I returned to the Antoine where this journey began. This time, I was with another dear friend and mentor whom I will call William, an established social scientist who immigrated to France nearly fifty years ago, and someone I had not seen since the outbreak of COVID-19. Having discussed my research with him over the years, I wanted to show him where the incident in the prologue that precipitated this book occurred. A great deal has changed since then. The omnipresence of a mutating virus, the "new normal" of mask-wearing, and vaccination passport (*le passe sanitaire*) checks were now common rituals, though neither fully embraced nor enforced in Paris, as elsewhere. However, little seemed to have changed at the Antoine seven years later, except the terrace where Moussa and I had originally sat on that warm August night. On this occasion it was winterized: enclosed in plastic panels that obstructed the view but not the cold air seeping into what had essentially become the smokers' chamber. As nonsmokers, and no lovers of frigid temperatures, we opted to sit indoors where the heat also freely flowed. This time, thankfully, no unruly patrons or police interrupted our conversation, but I was still almost the only b/Black person in the bistro, the other an employee, so two down from four in 2014. That evening, however, broader social politics in France weighed heavily on my reunion and discussion, which drew into the same orbit the extreme-right presidential hopeful Éric Zemmour and the pantheonization of Josephine Baker that illustrate in a variety of ways the fallacies, contradictions, and seductive power of universalist raceblind republicanism that I explore in this book.

The presidential primaries were in full swing, with the candidacy of Éric Zemmour still undeclared. In their *New York Times* opinion piece, Mitchell Abidor and Miguel Lago describe Zemmour as a new face of old bigotry in France, specifying that "the great irony is that Mr. Zemmour, twice convicted of inciting racial hatred and discrimination, is a Jew—a member of the very community once targeted by the racists whose traditions he inherits and invokes. He has updated France's oldest hatred for a new era," or has repackaged the same anti-immigration, grand replacement, and misogynistic discourses while using the Left's and Right's rhetoric against them.[1] We have seen this before. At the same time, he plays up his North African Jewish ancestry and plays on universalist republicanism to undercut claims that he and his platform spew racism, sexism, and foment other schisms through various -isms. William observed that Zemmour has purposely run his campaign so far to the right that he even outflanks Marine Le Pen, who sharpened her political chops on territory originally staked out by her father, Jean-Marie Le Pen, and now claimed by Zemmour. In many ways, he is both symbolic and an effect of the licensing of authoritarian populism, neo-fascism, and extremism that rely on historical revisionism and a negating of past-present racism that preserves white power structures and safeguards racial sameness under the banner of universalism. In this framing, antiracism, the exposure of those structures, is branded the enemy of French universalism; racism, an invention of its victims, and charges of racism and racial discrimination, become badges of honor to be worn with pride. Even as Zemmour is old wine in a different bottle, his message still pairs well with same raw red meat.[2]

"And what does a Zemmour say about France, then?" I asked William, particularly in the wake of the 2020 Summer of Reckoning. An astute social critic and political scientist in another life, he first looked off into the distance, then turned toward me and said: "It says something very ugly about France." William went on to say that "Zemmour's candidacy is, obviously, pure poison, possibly one of the ugliest things I've seen in French politics to date. He's powerfully promoted by TV, radio, and even the book industry—the last time I was at Charles de Gaulle airport, his stuff was all over a whole table." To this, he added that "he's overtly racist in a very targeted way, and he's allowed to get away with it, more than the (ex)-National Front. . . . But listen, compared to twenty years ago, there are more movements and associations, of very different sorts, that study, critique, denounce, and oppose many of the horrors, including the everyday ones, described in your book, and I think this trend appears genuinely to upset the authorities, so this leads me to believe that these movements, fragmented though they may be, must be doing something right!" Indeed, they are! This includes challenging prevailing universalist republican doxa and orthodoxy not only in terms of public discourse but also public policy, which not only upsets but frightens those longing for sameness. At the same time, this climate says something "very ugly" and quite dangerous about the unprotected status of people racialized and minoritized in French society, and only sounds louder alarms raised in the *Trajectories and Origins Survey* (*TeO*) on diversity and discrimination in France and by the European Union that I address in the chapter, "The Choice of Ignorance."

While the Zemmour phenomena preoccupied the media, the induction of Josephine Baker (1906–1975) into the Panthéon on November 30, 2021, brought to bear other ironies and contradictions for me personally and in relation to what I have called raceblind republicanism in these pages. I had mixed emotions about attending the ceremony, with it coming on the heels of viewing the Di Rosa paintings at the National Assembly the previous week and an interview that morning with a politician involved in the removal of the *Au Nègre Joyeux* business sign. My thoughts also drifted to a discussion the next day with Corentin, introduced in the chapter on police violence, about his group's latest action against excessive fines levied on youth targeted by the police, what he referred to as "an extra weapon in their arsenal for racial profiling." Those moments, coupled with all that I have witnessed over the years and documented in this book, were not far from my mind as I sat in the audience, reflecting on my own privileged positioning as a Black American woman and scholar in France at this event, during a pandemic no less, who *could* travel and conduct research for which French colleagues and friends in France were being denounced. This too was familiar. But, if I am being totally honest, the ceremony was moving and captured, through visual storytelling, including extraordinary projections of key moments in Baker's life onto the facade of the Panthéon, why she deserved this crown from her country where she is known and celebrated more than in the United States.

Baker was "fascinating and unsettling," as Bennetta Jules-Rosette writes in her richly and meticulously documented study *Josephine Baker in Art and Life: The Icon and the Image*, and defied prevailing expectations of respectability.[3] Indeed, Baker, this multilayered individual, was not without complication and controversy, as diverse scholars illuminate further in their respective analyses of the different facets and phases of her life.[4] For Baker, like my mom and countless other women inferiorized racially and subjected to soul-killing intersectional oppression, im/migration was an escape hatch, one that also shaped life choices and life chances

Images of Josephine Baker projected onto
the Panthéon monument, November 30,
2021. Photo: Thibault Camus/POOL/AFP
via Getty.

Josephine Baker induction outside the
Panthéon. Photos: Trica Keaton.

for the good and the bad, choices they may not have countenanced in another world. Settlement elsewhere is not only a symbol of desperation and deprivation but also an expression of agency and risk-taking that involved nonetheless life-and-death decision-making. How to earn money; where to stay; whom to trust; how to feed your children; whom to love—all were part and parcel. Yet, despite and perhaps because of unimaginable obstacles, Baker and such women learned to turn very bitter lemons into sweet lemonade. I do not begrudge the Bakers of the world their success. Rather, I condemn the structures and lived realities of racism and racialized discrimination that set them flowing. I also condemn those in France who would instrumentalize "African American expatriation" to score political points and finger-wag at antiracism activists and advocates battling these issues in order to deny or minimize homegrown racism, be it antiblackness, anti-immigration, anti-Muslimism, anti-Romani, anti-Semitism . . . I could go on. Fanon long recognized that racism otherizes and inferiorizes to the benefit of its maker, so he is worth repeating at this moment when fascist discourse has crept into the mainstream: "When you hear someone insulting a Jew, pay attention; he is talking about you."[5]

Baker was not merely an expatriate but also an *im/migrant*—and let's reclaim and resignify that word—who settled in France and became, on that day in November, the first b/Black woman so honored by the French state. But this same state officially negates b/Black life and chooses to reject b/Black identities in the name and because of a failed universalism that has not achieved equality or inclusion through ethno-racial invisibility. To the contrary, state policies and practices have engendered instead the very identities that raceblind republicanism seeks to disappear while re-narrating as anything but race-based the lived experiences that accompany those understandings.

President Macron's tribute to Baker seemed heartfelt, but in order to pantheonize her, he also had to universalize her *à la française* through raceblindness, which meant unwitnessing her b/Black identity and thereby missing the significance of the antiblackness that made her identity salient in the United States *and* France where she was also racialized-as-black and treated accordingly. More could be said about her lived experience of antiblackness in France and about the causes of her immigration to Monaco, her final resting place. Even as Macron acknowledged the racism and specifically the *nègre* (his word) imagery and representations that she mocked and reinforced in her performance, his representation of, for instance, her multiple marriages and upbringing ironically racialized and performed a similar labor. "Her cause was that of universalism," stated Macron—whose universalism?—adding that Baker placed equality for all before individual identity, and that being American and French outweighed a b/Black identity in her battles for equality and dignity.[6] This message was not only about Baker but was also interpreted by many as no veiled message to activists and scholars asserting b/Black and plural identities in battling for equality and human dignity in France. In some ways, this read of Baker reminds me of people who say, "I don't see color, differences, race, or 'b/Black' people," which is another way of saying "I don't see (or have to see) racism and antiblackness," for doing so means having to address it. "This is somewhat like the legendary monster that couldn't see you if you couldn't see it," shared another dear friend and colleague in 2021 about French universalist raceblindness; "all you had to do in defense was close your eyes and it would disappear, powerless." Yet the beast is still there.

The pantheonization and universalization of Baker also raises a number of other questions, among them the selection of Baker among the universe of possibilities and the timing of her induction. Why not honor her on the date in 1937, as reported on France 24, on which she married French industrialist Jean Lion, through whom she gained French citizenship?[7] And what was the motivation driving her induction? That this honor occurred during a presidential election cycle when heavy vote-courting takes place and in a context of heightened white supremacist ideology caused none too few raised eyebrows. Whatever the motivation, some felt that honoring Baker was more political strategy, "another way to say, 'Oh see, we're not so racist,'" said a French politician whom I interviewed while in Paris for the induction, which again relies on harnessing the African American expatriate narrative to misdirect. One sure effect of Baker's pantheonization was the interpellative zero-sum trap that it sets up over who should have been the first, making anyone who asks an obvious, valid question—Why not an "Indigenous" b/Black French woman?—appear on the one hand petty or a hater, and on the other hand antiblack. Indeed, why not, for instance, "La Mulâtresse Solitude" (ca. 1772–1802), a heroine in anti-slavery insurrections in Guadeloupe who came to symbolize unsung, unnamed, and enslaved blackened women worldwide, or why not, as people are rightly asking, Baker's contemporary, Paulette Nardal (1896–1985), the award-winning French intellectual, writer, professor, and activist, among other recognitions? Nardal, as Brent Edwards further writes, "became the most important connection between the 'Harlem Renaissance' writers and the Francophone university students who would become the core of the Negritude movement."[8]

Paulette Nardal. Wikipedia Commons.

As Maryse Condé reminds us, Nardal, through her varied trailblazing socio-cultural undertakings, writings, international collaborations, and activism, "was trying to impose the idea of a black presence in Paris at a time when 'black' was equated with savagery, brutality, pure force and nothing intellectual at all."[9] If one criterion for entering the Panthéon is loving France, as Macron stated in his praise of Baker, then there is no better expression of love of country than holding it to the very principles it claims to hold dear, as Nardal and countless other peoples of French coloniality have done. It is the epitomic expression of French values. If political strategy or opportunism were motivating forces, then what could be more strategic, no less during a period when the media and enthusiasts aggrandize and spectacularize Zemmour in the wake of the 2020 Summer of Reckoning, than honoring Solitude, Nardal, or, more radically, all three? "We should claim it [Baker's induction]," continued the same politician. "It is a result of the woke movement in France, to claim it and say yes to Josephine Baker, a b/Black *migrant* woman, even as so many others could be celebrated. . . . We should say yes to Josephine but also to the others who were fighting against racism. Keep in mind that the same [France] that is celebrating Josephine Baker because of her resistance work and antiracist work is also demonizing and criminalizing actual, living antiracist b/Black and migrant women."

Meanwhile, on the other side of town, the arsenal of police violence expands to include fines or "non-contact fines" in conjunction with racial profiling, meaning law enforcers can issues tickets without physical contact or identity checks thanks to surveillance technologies. Used under the pretext of identifying people who violated COVID confinements, these fines serve to drive out the "undesirables" from public space by hitting their wallets instead of their bodies.[10] For anti-police violence advocates and activists, such as Corentin, these fines are predatory, repetitive, and used to harass and/or retaliate against the same people already preyed upon by the police, namely youth of predominately African descent. It is a weapon and violence from which they cannot run. "These fines are a strategy of repression that target those who lack a voice in the dominant mainstream media," Corentin said. "Some young people have received dozens of fines each that regularly increase and reach as high as 10,000 or 15,000€, creating a debt for the family," he added.

At the conclusion of his speech, President Macron passionately stated: "My France is Josephine," and *La France* is also Paulette, as well as all blackened peoples on French shores who are "here" because France was "there." This includes "our kids" who flee to their death or/and are maimed by police violence in a country where law enforcement is shown to vote more far-right than the rest of the voting population.[11] And, it is families and individuals who confront daily what France officially denies and thereby allows to fester, in this case antiblackness in the everyday and other ways in the society. These ills are the actual threat to French principles, values, and the nation-state, and if left unaddressed will continue to tear apart not only France but everywhere they reside.

Nota bene: Today, June 19, 2022, I write from Paris, France, days after attending a memorial for my friend and mentor Tyler Stovall, a distinguished Black historian whose work long challenged conventional notions of raceblindness in French society. In the United States, it is Juneteenth, a federal holiday that commemorates the date when the last enslaved Black people on those shores were finally informed of their freedom, over two years after the signing of the Emancipation Proclamation. Meanwhile, in France, the media exploded with the results of the legislative elections: "The National Rally [RN]," the former extreme right National Front (FN) party "makes a historic breakthrough in the National Assembly," reported the public outlet *France Info*. "In 2017, only 8 FN elected officials had managed to win. They would be 89 in 2022."[12] This extreme is the mainstream and the struggle continues. Forward ever, backward never.

ACKNOWLEDGMENTS

This book was a long time in the making but well worth the journey, even through tremendous adversity that ultimately strengthened my resolve to stay the course. There have been many along the way without whom this book would be impossible. First and foremost, I can never acknowledge enough my mother and her pearls of wisdom. She would say, when I needed to hear it the most: "You've not been brought this far, Trica, just to fail." Thank you dear mom!

I am especially indebted to the many activists, advocacy groups, and people who shared over the years not only their stories, pain, and suffering but also their strength and determination to fight back against formidable obstacles, often at great risk and peril.

I am eternally grateful to Roy Jensen and other cherished people who generously read early iterations of the manuscript, chapters, or sections—even when their time was extremely limited—and whose indispensable feedback and/or encouragements to persevere were unparalleled. In this regard, I am profoundly indebted to James (Jim) Cohen, Emily Hopkins, and Deborah King, alongside Charlotte Bacon, Kimberly Juanita Brown, Michael Chaney, William Cheng, Mamadou Diouf, N. Bruce Duthu, Philomena Essed, Dienke (D.G.) Hondius, Sue Peabody, Stephen Small, Richard Wright, Melinda Herron, Karen Lindo, and last but not least, Tyler Stovall. In November 2021, shortly before his passing, Tyler, a distinguished historian and former dean of the Graduate School of Arts and Sciences at Fordham University, told me that he had reviewed my manuscript for the MIT Press. His keen insights, thought, and wisdom sharpened my analysis and scholarship in general, making his final words and observations about this book even more precious and invaluable. Tyler was a dear friend, more a big brother, since very early in my career, and I was very fortunate to collaborate with him on many projects over the years. While we were unable to complete this last one before his heartbreaking passing, I take comfort in knowing that it will happen in his honor. His reach was far and wide, so he will live on through so many of us, and for me, there would be no Afro/Black Paris and Afro/Black French Studies without Tyler Stovall. You left us far too soon.

I lack sufficient words to express my thanks to Victoria Hindley, my acquisitions editor at the MIT Press, and her colleagues, especially Judith Feldmann and Gabriela Bueno Gibbs, for their swift attention to this book and generous support throughout its production. Victoria's early belief in this project and sensitivity to its content, as well as her professional integrity and kindness toward me, are immeasurable. I am fortunate to be one of her authors. Our meeting was thanks to the Leslie Center for the Humanities at Dartmouth College's publishing series, and I am elated that they facilitated that introduction.

I would also like to express my appreciation and thanks to the many friends and colleagues at Dartmouth College who have shown me exceptional kindness and support and with whom I have had life-affirming opportunities to work collaboratively on a range of events. My specific thanks to the Dean's Office and Matt Delmont for providing resources toward this book's publication. They have been a sure and steady reminder that even during difficult times, there are a thousand beautiful things awaiting us, sometimes right before our very eyes. Over the years, I have also been very fortunate to have amazing students in my Afro/Black Paris and France courses whose creative, spirited engagement with the material and brilliant analyses were not lost in these pages.

Among the institutions that were directly instrumental to this project, I wish to thank the Rockefeller Foundation Bellagio Center Residency Program that afforded me needed time in a breathtaking setting to think through an early version of the chapter, "*Au Nègre Joyeux* and Friends," and my thanks to Deborah Willis, Cheryl Finley, and *Nka Journal for African Art* for publishing it. I also wish to thank researchers at Amnesty International, Human Rights Watch, the European Parliament Anti-Racism and Diversity Intergroup, the European Union Agency for Fundamental Rights, the Council of Europe, and those who made possible the *Trajectories and Origins* (*TeO*) survey on population diversity in France, for their invaluable data and opportunities to exchange ideas over these issues.

I also benefited greatly from the generosity, kindness, and wisdom of other individuals and friends along the way, often since very early in this journey and perhaps without them even realizing it. They include Vanessa Agard-Jones, Kpedetin Mariquian Ahouansou, Laila Amine, Jacqueline Andall, Kehinde Andrews, Aminkeng Atabong, Vilna Bashi Treitler, Jean Beaman, Slim Ben Achour, Erik Bleich, Richard Blint, Jennifer Boittin, Isabelle Boni-Claverie, Magda Boutros, Rashida Braggs, Julia Browne, Marcus Bruce, Joanne and David Burke, Velma Bury, Tina Campt, Joy Calico, Fred Constant, Margo Crawford, Kimberlé Crenshaw, Jeanette

Demeestère, Celina de Sá, Rokhaya Diallo, Manthia Diawara, Tara Dickman, Kévi Donat, Samba Doucouré, Brent Edwards, Fatima El Tayeb, Nathalie Etoké, Iolanda Évora, Sarah Fila-Bakabadio, Éric and Didier Fassin, Crystal Fleming, Roderick Ferguson, Franck Freitas-Ekué, Vera Grant, Kaiama Glover, Lewis Gordon, Farah Griffin, Nicole Grégoire, Dell Hamilton, Véronique Hélénon, Denise Herd, Lanna Hollo, Wendy Johnson, Nikki Jones, Annette Joseph-Gabriel, Ebun Joseph, Bennetta Jules-Rosette, Ousmane Kane, Florence Ladd, Jake Lamar, Jane Landers, Carolyn Lilly, Omer Mas Capitolin, Michael McEachrane, Laurie McIntosh, Dena Montague, Mathias Moschel, Pap Ndiaye, Mame-Fatou Niang, Kwame Nimako, Ifeoma Kiddoe Nwankwo, Lucius Outlaw, Euzhan Palcy, Alexis Peskine, Christy Pichichero, Laurella Rinçons, Daniel Sabbagh, Patrick Simon, Maya Smith, Maboula Soumahoro, Hortense Spillers, Stephen Steinberg, Judith Sunderland, Ula Taylor, Vanessa Thompson, Dominic Thomas, Louis-Georges Tin, Kira Thurman, Françoise Vergès, Nadège Veldwachter, Fatimata Wane-Sagna, Gloria Wekker, Monique Wells, Elisa Joy White, France Winddance Twine, Deborah Willis, Michelle Wright, and Brune Biebuyck, director of Reid Hall and her staff, especially Krista Faurie, for always providing me with a "home" while in Paris, and my research assistants, Kalia Hunter, Lobna Jbeniani, and Maya Velez, especially for navigating vicariously the material on police violence. If I have forgotten anyone, my apologies; it was not intentional.

As I concluded this book, a number of devastating losses occurred in addition to Tyler Stovall, towering individuals whose thought, praxis of antiracism, and capacity to speak truth to power enriched and empowered countless others, notably Archbishop Desmond Tutu, Sidney Poitier, Lani Guinier, bell hooks, Charles Mills, and Greg Tate.

Because death, violence, and grief were such a part of the making of this book, it often felt like I was deep within what Iyanla Vanzant calls "the valley," but, as she astutely reminds us, there is value, too, in that experience. There is a quote attributed to bell hooks that seems appropriate not only here but also for people fighting injustice everywhere, which is worth repeating over and over again: "Sometimes people try to destroy you, precisely because they recognize your power—not because they don't see it, but because they see it, and they don't want it to exist."

Finally, I am forever grateful to Frantz Fanon and Philomena Essed. Simply put, this book is here because you were thankfully there.

APPENDIX

FRAMING EVERYDAY ANTIBLACKNESS IN A RACEBLIND FRANCE

"Antiblackness" and "antiblack" were not concepts or words that were in vogue in France when I formally began research for this book in 2014, nor was self-identifying as *n/Noir.e.s* generally embraced, despite a resurgence of *Noir.e.s* subjectivity and activism in the wake of the 2005 revolts. Instead, I encountered at times varying strategies of race and *noir* avoidance among diverse people who privileged certain euphemisms, such as the English term *black*, over the French word *noir* to describe oneself and others. This "black/*noir*" duality, a dying but distinctive identity discourse in France, was not lost on tweeters responding to *Libération*'s hashtag in 2015. "#YouKnowYoureblackInFranceWhen . . . tweeted one, "when you're called 'black' so much [as if] mentioning your existence is a problem." Or, as an interviewee put it back then, "when they call you *la BLACK* because they don't know or remember your name." *Noir* dodging in everyday parlance included referring to b/Black people as *les Afros*, invoking origins, and/or describing people without mentioning color because, in the words of an interviewee who echoed others, "*noir* sounds racist." In 2017, a young woman in her mid-twenties recounted one of several personal experiences with *noir* avoidance this way: "There's this thing about describing people. It's really quite interesting, and I do it myself sometimes. When you're discussing someone you don't know, and he's black, you avoid saying he's black; it's really quite interesting; you discuss everything about this person except the fact that he's black." She then offered a personal example of her complicity with this practice when arranging a meeting with friends of a friend, someone she had never met: "I told them I would be wearing bright lipstick and described my clothes," she said laughingly while admitting that it would have been easier to say that she was *n/Noire*. When discussing this young woman's example with a university graduate, he reiterated the "*noir* is racist" perspective when explaining *noir* avoidance: "It's really frowned on here, and when you use it, you feel like people think you're a racist. That's why we use substitutes; it's less violent on the ear [pauses]. It [*noir*] brings up the darkest thoughts in people's minds." My point is that interviewees and others whom

I met during this research were not always comfortable with my use of *noir* and were occasionally uncertain what I meant by the term *anti-noir* in reference to discrimination and racism. Even so, many understood the combination of *anti* + *noir* and demonstrated their comprehension through accounts of direct and vicarious experiences, the latter discussed ahead.[1] In the course of explaining my research to a self-identified *n/Noir* medical professional and activist in his mid-forties before a formal interview in 2016, I asked him whether he understood what I meant by antiblack discrimination and racism in French society. Initially, he like others, spoke of employment, educational, and residential disparities, but he also was quite vocal about the impossibility of knowing the magnitude of these problems given the prohibitions on ethno-racial statistics in France, something he referred to as "the perfect crime." Then, he went on to described what he called "low-intensity racism or discrimination," that is, "the racism or discrimination that *les n/Noir.e.s* in France encounter while doing banal or ordinary things," he said, "for example at the supermarket, at the bank, while walking down the street, at work, at the university, in the metro or bus, in a group; when reading a newspaper or magazine with certain descriptions or representations. It's that feeling when you see African nannies with white children, so it's the discrimination or racism you can't see when you are on the other side of the fence." He also spoke strongly about the ingrained nature of these violations, likening them to a disease spreading through the social body with "devastating consequences for your entire life." In short, he defined everyday antiblack discrimination and racism through lived experience, as did others whom I interviewed, and similarly, the experiences he recounted were not single incidences but were encountered "all the time." Through the force of repetition, this reality had a shaping effect on people's awareness and grasp of misconduct and mistreatment for no other reason than existing-while-b/Black.

In this section of the appendix, my aim is to make conceptual and contextual sense of a lived experience that a dogmatic raceblind republicanism prohibits, through my primary thinking companions—Frantz Fanon and Philomena Essed—whose thought elucidates my framing of everyday antiblackness in terms of racialization-as-black inferiority. Philomena Essed's theories and analysis of everyday racism in the context of ideological and state-driven racelessness remain as timely and evocative as when first introduced. By "everyday racism," Essed refers to "a process in which socialized racist notions are integrated into everyday practices and thereby actualize and reinforce underlying racial and ethnic relations," structured by power asymmetries and expressed in institutional practices (e.g., systematically hiring blackened and brown bodies to police bodies similarly perceived).[2] What's more, and perhaps more revealing of the damage caused by this formation, "racist practices themselves become familiar, repetitive, and part of the 'normal' routine in daily life," thus largely unquestioned and/or acquiesced to in the society, including among those targeted. Racial profiling and police identity controls in France are exemplar as well as examples of visual culture examined in this book. Everyday racism, as she further writes, consists not of singular acts but exists "in the plural form, as a complex of mutually related, cumulative practices, and situations . . . that activate the whole pattern of injustices of which it is part."[3]

To unpack what lies at the core of antiblackness itself and its material expression as discrimination and racism in French daily life, I turned to Frantz Fanon's meditations on antiblack racialization, which, over seventy years later, demonstrate that Fanon remains our contemporary interlocutor and one of the most incisive thinkers of the past century. His thought is an essential reference for any analysis of antiblackness in French society precisely because he diagnosed not only the fraudulence of universalist raceblind republicanism but also its lasting, multiscalar effects. Moreover, he fundamentally understood and demonstrated through his own narrative the destructive, alienating force of black racialization in the service of dehumanization. Fanon "points to the seriousness of blackness," writes Lewis Gordon, as he "developed a profound social-existential analysis of anti-black racism," by placing in stark relief "its materiality in the world of negrèphobia, where the black is treated as pure surface, reduced exteriority, a thing, in other words, without an inside, an inner life, or a point of view."[4] Still, it is impossible to ignore the patriarchy in Fanon's writing, similar to other progressive critical thinkers of and before his day. bell hooks, similar to Gayatri Spivak, interrogates this critical "blind spot" and is worth citing at length:

There has never been a moment when reading Freire that I have not remained aware of not only the sexism of the language but the way he (like other progressive Third World political leaders, intellectuals, critical thinkers such as Fanon, Memmi, etc.) constructs a phallocentric paradigm of liberation—wherein freedom and the experience of patriarchal manhood are always linked as though they are one and the same. For me this is always a source of anguish for it represents a blind spot in the vision of men who have profound insight. And yet, I never wish to see a critique of this blind spot overshadow anyone's (and feminists' in particular) capacity to learn from the insights.[5]

I could not agree more.

The opening of chapter 5, "The Lived Experience of the Noir," in *Black Skin, White Masks* (*BSWM*) captures Gordon's insight. Indeed, it is here where the content and substance of this quotidian force crystalizes as absolute alienation, rooted in the coloniality that separated blackened people from humanity, an alienation experienced through a socially transmitted fearful gaze. The cries of a w/White child—the embodiment of innocence and ultimately humanity—interpellate not Fanon but "an object among other objects" when the child vomits out: "*Regarde* [look at] *le nègre*! . . . *Maman un nègre*! . . . I'm afraid."[6] "Dirty *nègre*," or simply, "Look, a *nègre*!," seeks and destroys. This fabulation of a reappearing past offers no existence save that which racism "fixes" into racialized black inferiority, projected outward by a gaze masquerading as a worldview. This unnatural yet naturalized separation amounts to a disfigured presence and normative absence in which presence is ultimately a form of absence, following Gordon on Fanon.[7] Even as this blackened condition fosters despair, it compels and hails a consciousness that is indispensable on the long road to dis-alienation, freedom from the chains of racialized thought toward constituting a liberated "Human." "To become *nègre* is to die as a human," writes philosopher Ronald Judy, an insight to retain in those chapters where this entity rears its ugly head, but is resignified into a discourse of refusal, including a refusal of raceblindness, boldly articulated as *Noir.e.x.s.*[8]

LIVED EXPERIENCE AND ANTIBLACKNESS IN THE EVERYDAY

Lived experience lies at the heart of my project and constitutes the through line and connective tissue joining Fanon's thought on racialized black inferiority with Essed's concept of everyday racism, both of which inform my approach. The coalescence of their thought in this way illuminates a path for understanding and exposing the personal, direct, indirect, and systemic movement of everyday antiblackness, camouflaged by hegemonic raceblind ideology. My aim, however, is not to retread or review scholarly ground already well-laid by critical scholars of Fanonian thought and everyday racism, too numerous to name here. I lay anchor in chapter 5 also because that is where Fanon poses a fundamental question that I raise in this book. "How," as Ronald Judy writes, "can the existence of the Black . . . be properly understood" when pathologized and constituted antithetically vis-à-vis racialized whiteness that claims exclusive rights on universality and supremacy as an inherent, normative fact? As demonstrated in this book, lived experience in this framing is a sociohistorical and temporal process through which those subjected to antiblackness gain intersubjective awareness and comprehension of this dehumanized black condition, of being reified into something less-than. In keeping with Fanon and Essed, this process entails being rendered a "problem" from within and without, in which culture assumes the labor of race. At the same time, this dimension invokes an unmistakable Du Boisian double consciousness that extends beyond US boarders, that is, the peculiar sense of "twoness" from life within the "veil" that produces "second sight" or again multiple, intersectional jeopardies shaping consciousness, following sociologist Deborah King. It is, then, that peculiar capacity to see oneself and the world through the categories and representations that white supremacy created only to recognize those entities as artificial, unnatural, but very much determinant of one's life chances.

Nearly fifty years later, Fanon would theorize "two frames of reference" or a dual consciousness but with a distinctly French twist. Socialization in the French model promulgates raceless "one-ness" or *E pluribus unum* (i.e., out of many, one), but it is packaged with a colorline that materializes in daily life through practices of *négrification* or an "epidermalization of inferiority," to cite Fanon, affixed to constructs of culture and civilization. With its dialectical dimension in mind, sociologist Paget Henry explains that "double consciousness results from the [black] subject having to exist for a self-consciousness that racialized itself as white" by antithesis, but whose whiteness is absurd without black racialization.[9] B/black inferiority, observes Michelle Wright in her analysis of racial subjectivity in Fanonian thought, "is the result not of objective observation but instead of the need for self-definition. In order to posit itself as civilized, advanced, and superior, Western discourse must endlessly reify Africa and the Black as its binary opposite."[10]

What Fanon identifies in *BSWM*, then, as "epidermalization" and its attendant destructive effects inheres in what he later terms "racialization" in *The Wretched of the Earth*, which concerns not only racial category formation but fundamentally black race-making "under white domination" whose endgame is social death.[11] Some credit Fanon with having trailblazed the concept of racialization in his analysis of colonial racism's aggregation of diverse African peoples into a racial category, indeed into a "race."[12] Over the years, the concept of racialization has been the object of debate among scholars, as sociologists Karim Murji and John Solomos assert in their insightful volume, *Racialization: Studies in Theory and Practice*. For some, this notion is a proxy concept for any "race-inflected social situation," and thus is diluted to the point of being meaningless, or suffers from "a distinct lack of clarity about who and what is doing the racializing."[13] However, in raceblind European countries in which the social reality and relevancy of race and specifically antiblackness are contested, I find that the concept of racialization elucidates how "race-thinking operates," that is, "the processes by which racial meanings are attached to particular issues [or people]—often treated as social problems," and how race is central to how these so-called problems are defined and apprehended.[14] On matters of antiblackness, this insight is evocative of the very question posed by W. E. B. Du Bois at the opening of the *Souls of Black Folk*—"How does it feel to be a problem?"—which Essed theorizes as "problematization" (discussed ahead) in analyzing everyday antiblack racism which, through Fanonian thought, emerges at those explicit and implicit "Look, a *nègre!*" moments or, in this case, a response to: "You know you're black in France when. . . ."

Essential to my framing is the importance and validity that Fanon and Essed also accord to the perspectives of b/Black people against invalidating voices and forces, none more so than raceblind ideology itself. Fanon's very example *in* and *as* chapter 5, if not the entirety of *BSWM* as an autobiographical response essay to French antiblackness, saliently exemplifies this point. This "descent into hell and a road out of hell," writes Gordon, is where Fanon "asserts his full humanity through producing his theory, the theory issued from this experience and deeply rooted in it."[15] Essed similarly documents this dimension based on revealing findings from careful, intensive interviewing of b/Black women, which includes having cataloged over 2,000 experiences in one individual's case alone of the existence of denied everyday racism against the grain of a Dutch discourses of "tolerance." These lived experiences, as illustrated in this book, occur in the "everyday," which refers to "a familiar world, a practical world, a world of practices we are socialized with" to negotiate the fact of antiblackness on the ground.[16]

RACEBLIND RACISM AND CULTURE

In the 1980s and 1990s, Essed introduced the concept of everyday racism in her groundbreaking comparative study of b/Black Surinamese women in the Netherlands and b/Black American women in the United States to theorize and expose how racism is incorporated into ordinary practices. Through that study, Essed not only shared the experiences of these women during a time when little had been written about racism in the Netherlands from the perspective of b/Black women. Her meticulous analysis of the "smaller and bigger day-to-day violations of the civil rights . . .

humanity and . . . dignity" of her informants' oft-aggressively disregarded claims of racism also demonstrated more broadly how these violations pervaded the daily routine of ethno-racialized groups in ways that showed "regular patterns," ranging from hiring/firing practices to who is granted authority over the "formulation of academic theories."[17] Similarly, her analysis of her informants' "comprehension" of everyday racism revealed coherence, uniformity, consistency, and commonalities with respect to recurring experiences, situations, and perpetrators that were institutional and driven by ideologies of racism. Examples run the gamut in the French context, from more common instances, as in seemingly mundane language and expressions, such as using "black" in English instead of the French word *noir*, or recurring questions in work or educational settings, such as the proverbial "Where are you *from*, from?" which asks not one's provenance but questions belonging; to more extreme examples, as in the case of police custody brutality and killings. Even as those targeted are neither defenseless nor passive in the face of everyday antiblack indignities and violence, as Essed observes, they may lack a "comprehensive and theoretical framework [or language] for explaining these experiences" in an environment where the social prohibition of race and/as color is potent.[18] Reactions to the concept of "anti-*noir*" captured this aspect for me and "race" more broadly, particularly when such concepts are attributed to importations from the United States.

In European cultures and countries where the denial of racism and tabooing of race have been formidable means for gainsaying the lived experience of antiblackness, Essed's framing, then as now, brings into sharp relief how racism operates as a conflict-sustaining ideology of "racial domination and oppression" that has been historically drawn and socioeconomically and politically sustained across time and space. In harmony with Fanon, racism, argues Essed, "denotes the definitive attribution of *inferiority* to a particular racial/ethnic group [emphasis mine]," which, when invisibilized, sustains an existing order while turning the inferiorized into problems of their own design.[19] On this point, what Essed identifies as interlocked and interdependent processes of everyday racism find fertile ground in French society (as elsewhere), that is, (ascriptive) problematization; marginalization, including rigid exclusions; and repression, which encompasses humiliation, containment, and state-driven violence. All labor to keep those inferiorized by race in their supposed place by controlling their inclusion and social mobility in society. These processes are abetted by practices of pathologizing, a subprocess of problematization, which relies on a certain "tolerance of racism," and/or indifference, as illustrated throughout this book.[20]

Indeed, problematization is fundamentally how everyday racism, and specifically everyday antiblack racism and discrimination, manifests where these formations thrive; it occurs through a dynamic interaction between the idea that "Blacks *have problems* (biological and cultural)," argues Essed, which is used to explain "the attribution that they *create* problems [emphasis in the original]" and consequently *are* problems for society, for which marginalization and repression become socially accepted responses.[21] By definition, this is the quintessential "negro/*nègre* question," diagnosed and demystified by Du Bois and Fanon, which is played out every day in the French outer cities. The unintended effect, however, is that a society's naturalized pathologies become exposed in the process through the very act of abnormalizing peoples always already cast in terms of deficiencies. Invisibilizing blackened people and thereby concealing antiblackness in the name of equality only to make those people unprotected "national minorities," antiblack visual culture, and policing practices, as examined in this book, say a great deal more about France than those individuals who have been pathologized by institutionalized practices. The reversal of the gaze onto its makers invokes the very question about the actual source of pathology that Fanon raised: "How does an oppressing people behave?"

Thus, Fanon moves us to the structures and uses of culture as mechanisms through which racism (antiblack and otherwise) operates and materializes as "cultural racism," which also finds expression as French universalist raceblind republicanism. In his provocative essay "Racism and Culture," delivered in 1956 at the First International Congress of Black Writers and Artists in Paris, one of the most important meetings of b/Black male intellectuals of that era, Fanon elucidates that dynamic and the concept of cultural racism in terms of "the systematized oppression of people," defined by "the doctrine of cultural hierarchy" in which "ways of life" become biologized and occupy the space held by biology.[22] Racism, writes Fanon, "has had to renew itself, to adapt itself, to change its appearance," and adds that "this racism that aspires to be rational, individual, genotypically and phenotypically determined, becomes transformed into cultural racism. The object of racism is no longer the individual man but a certain form of existing."[23]

Non-Western cultural "ways of life" and values, exemplified by, for instance, "language, dress, technique, are devalued"[24] in a consistent and documented pattern of exploitation that becomes justified in culturalist, racist terms, as demonstrated by Fanon and Essed. Moreover, performances of "pseudo-respect" or politeness mask "contempt" and allow for the appearance of being nonracist, or again tolerant.

An actress in her forties whom I interviewed captured this thought when sharing that her long-term w/White companion "loved Africans," but continually chastised her for her "Afro" clothing styles and for congregating with the few b/Black people in the room at predominantly white social gatherings, saying to her on more than one occasion, *Que ça fait ghetto* ("It's so ghetto"). She added snidely: "One person, okay, but two or three, that's ghetto." The reverse, however, is simply the norm. She, like others, also described over the years incidents of being warmly greeted at restaurants when with w/White friends, but when returning to the same place with b/Black friends, being seated in the back, away from other diners, or somewhere out of sight entirely, if allowed to enter at all. I have experienced this type of reception myself, which is usually prefaced by the proverbial gatekeeping device: "Do you have a reservation?" And, when made, the reservation is "surprisingly" nowhere to be found.

Étienne Balibar invokes Fanonian "cultural racism" in a raceblind France as "racism without races," which, in this study and framing, is more "antiblackness without b/Blacks." As Balibar writes, the dominant idea is "not biological heredity but the insurmountability of cultural differences, a racism which, at first sight, does not postulate the superiority of certain groups or peoples in relation others but 'only' the harmfulness of abolishing frontiers (including the construction of 'Frenchness'), the incompatibility of life-styles and traditions," coupled with the fear of replacement.[25] Sociologist Eduardo Bonilla-Silva conceptualizes this phenomenon in the United States as "color-blind racism," which posits that life chances and mobility become explained and apprehended less in terms of racism in a post–civil rights era and more as presumed cultural deficiencies and pathologies of "minorities." Expressions such as "I don't see color, only people" or "failure to take personal responsibility" are indicative of this "frame that relies on culturally based arguments such as 'Mexicans do not put much emphasis on education' or 'blacks have too many babies' to explain the standing of minorities in society."[26] What differs between the French and US frames is the animating force of French universalist raceblindness, which negates reified racial existence altogether; what is similar is the ignoring and obscuring of the legacies and effects of centuries of racism and race that lawmakers on both sides of the pond seek to legislate out of existence, including banning the word "race" itself from French law. In France, who could forget the law of February 23, 2005, which was introduced just months after the 2005 revolts. This law would have required schools to teach only the positive aspects of colonialism in French national education, where the subject was barely entertained and certainly not in its full truth.[27]

It is worth noting as well that pathologizing is not only the attribution of cultural pathology or deviance, argues Essed, it is also a way to disqualify and invalidate pushback by racism's targets and their claims of racism or racial discrimination in the society. Race-neutral responses to claims of everyday racism and antiblackness, include identifying targets as overemotional, or oversensitive, or, more classically, claiming that "it could have happened to anyone."[28] Here, I am reminded of the many times when I was mistaken for the cleaning person or simply not considered a resident at a place for foreign researchers where I typically stay when doing research in Paris. The housekeeping staff is made up of only African-descended women, and I am often the only Black researcher during my stay. On one memorable occasion, I was returning to the residence after having worked out at a local gym and was wearing baggy sweats and a T-shirt. As I arrived at the front door, a middle-aged, white-appearing resident was having difficulty using the door code. Not yet seeing me, she began banging heavily on the door and was clearly frustrated by the situation. Standing by her side at that point, I asked her in French if I could help, but before I could add that I lived there, she screamed: "I can't get in; you people are never around when we need you!" To which I replied forcefully in English, "I live here!" She froze, then began to apologize profusely. I opened the door with the code, and she walked in contritely after me. Then, there were the many occasions at night when my very presence at the door transformed into "pure surface" or "reduced exteriority," when another resident arrived at the same time.[29] This was usually accompanied by fearful looks and social distancing of another kind in which the person would step far away from me and the door until I entered the door code, thereby proving that I legitimately lived there. When I shared the screaming resident story later with a Caribbean scholar in his sixties, he gave that classic response—"It could have happened to anyone"—but when I gave other examples of what had become a recurring issue, he asked whether I had been dressed a particular way. When that failed, as I have often been mistaken for a custodial person and/or secretary at the residence, he conceded that "my color" spoke louder than my ID card or door code about how I was perceived.

POINT OF VIEW AND VICARIOUS EXPERIENCE

In formulating my framing of everyday and other way antiblackness, I was also drawn to Fanon and Essed for the empirical value that they place not only on the perspective of people racialized-as-black but also their grasp of the lived experience of antiblackness, directly and vicariously. Essed writes plainly that everyday racism is in fact "racism from the point of view of people of color, defined by those who experience it."[30] In this way, valuable knowledge and data derive from testimonials (i.e. "stories" or "verbal reconstructions") that show how their experiences "fit into a coherent system of oppression, control, and legitimation," as saliently illustrated by police violence. And, through the recurrence and patterns unveiled in differing situations, these accounts provide the "grounds for the belief that racism permeates everyday life, in a systematic and cumulative way," argues Essed.[31] The point of view of blackened people is all the more instructive in raceblind geographies where silences and taboos prevail around race-relevant issues, as these accounts tell us important information and details about the "what, where, and how" of racial injustice as well as how targets, in turn, problematize those sites. "Comprehension" is a word that Essed uses deliberately to underscore its role as deliberative and not reducible to simple "common sense" or "taken-for-granted assumptions."[32] Comprehension of racism, argues Essed, "is acquired through deliberate problematization of social reality," which necessitates having a general knowledge of how racism and norms of a society operate in order to recognize when they have been breached. It encompasses understanding racism according to what individuals already have experienced or learned about their societies, as illustrated for instance by the logic of youth running from the French police. Strategies to invalidate those claims, argues Essed, also presume "that people lack that understanding."[33]

These accounts are highly reflective and undergirded by years of experience that has necessitated the critical questioning and assessing of race-relevant events in white-dominated and controlled spaces, often over the course of a person's life, in order to live in society and avoid racial violence. Through its autobiographical form, the entirety of chapter 5 in *BSWM* is its own testimonial, indeed Fanon's entire rumination on antiblackness, which, similar to verbal reconstructions, shows how b/Black people, like other inferiorized groups, are intentionally analyzing from their own and others' experiences how they are defined and treated in a society. In doing so, they reveal that they have developed and/or are sharpening and deploying a "racial literacy," following sociologist France Winndance Twine's notion discussed in the methods ahead, which includes strategizing and assesses risks and consequences associated with discriminatory or racist treatment. This aspect is exemplified in calls to generate ethno-racial statistics in the interest of antidiscrimination and the increasing use of the French and European courts to battle racist slurs/insults (*injures racistes*) and abusive policing by advocacy groups. Indeed, the details of these accounts also exemplify having acquired "knowledge of dominant or subcultural codes of behavior" and expectations that come into sharp view when those codes are threatened or presumptively violated. These accounts, particularly in a raceblind context, become powerful evidence of life from people officially unseen or mis-seen, and their recurrence also reinforces the understanding that rules and justice function differently for inferiorized peoples, in accordance with how groups are racialized in the society, even when that racialization is denied.

A final dimension of my framing that I wish to highlight in this section concerns the vicarious experience of antiblackness, foregrounded by Essed. Indeed, a great deal of racism and racialized discrimination is experienced "through friends, family members, and other Blacks, through the media, and cognitively, through their general knowledge of racism in the system," as she argues.[34] Vicarious experience is understood intersectionally and in terms of identifying with other targets of racism or through the experiences of others.[35] A key informant for Essed, Rosa N., captures well the former when interrogating the "pseudo-respect/politeness" of "specific Whites" who deem her respectable thus acceptable because she is a physician. When elaborating on her experiences, Rosa N. interestingly channeled Fanon: "when they intimidate another Black because he is 'just' a worker, they are doing it to you too," she said to Essed.[36] In this book, this aspect is acutely exemplified through the experiences of Muslim boys racialized-as-arab and black in the French outer cities who are routinely targeted by abusive policing. The Twitterstorm created by *Libé*'s hashtag #YouKnowYoureblackInFranceWhen . . . that I revisit in in the chapter similarly titled and specifically the b/Black nanny phenomenon are examples of the many ways in which I explore vicarious antiblackness and its effects in this book. At the same time, I also acknowledge that books of this nature are not without their own vicarious effects. Antiblackness and racial injustice hurt and enrage, whether directly or through others. This tension is ever present in these pages.

The Fanonian/Essedian frame allows, then, for an unflinching critique of antiblackness that, on the one hand, exposes the futility of state-driven racelessness in multiracialized yet raceblind geographies when state actors fail to deliver this fruit. This results precisely in what the raceblind state seeks to avoid, community formation, consciousness, and revolt in terms of race. On the other hand, this frame lays bare both an ingrained preference for racial sameness, as does it expose the anger, frustrations, revulsion, alienation, and emotional injustice suffered from antiblackness and racism in a raceblind context, an expression of violence that is "invisible to the dominant group but overwhelmingly present in the everyday experiences of non-dominant groups."[37] Sociologist Juliette Sméralda drives this point home in her lucid 2015 foreword to *BSWM* when discussing that book's ongoing significance. Similar to Fanon's brilliant essay, my framing and the cases in this book also aim "especially to inform those who would never have the opportunity to experience '*le racisme de peau*' ('skin color racism'—in effect, antiblackness) nor comprehend how destructive it is" in b/Black people's daily lives.[38]

METHODS

What is antiblackness? What forms does it take in this raceblind geography? How is it generated and why does it persist? What is its specificity? How do French people racialized-as-black understand and respond to antiblackness in their daily lives? What are the material consequences of raceblind republicanism not only for b/Black and other racially minoritized groups but also for those seeking to document statistically these issues in France? Exploring and attempting to understand everyday antiblackness in a raceblind France from the perspective of b/Black French people necessitated a triangulated multimethodological approach that involved various data sources. Among them were archival material, multimedia, social media, participant observation at events, policy analysis, shadowing, virtual research to access relevant forums and participants cut off by the COVID-19 pandemic, and more centrally interviews in seeking to grasp antiblackness from the perspective of b/Black French people in mainland France. For this project, I conducted formal research from 2014 to 2019 in Paris and other regions in the south of France during intermittent stays, lasting from two weeks to a year, though I incorporate relevant issues prior to that timeframe and after, from 2020 to 2021, which have been debated in the media and other forums. In some ways, this journey began with my earliest incursions into mainland France as a Black American women, where my lived experiences and research over the years on matters of race and racism have resulted in an ever-evolving questioning of the issues raised in this book, issues I confront directly and indirectly in a society with a powerful and alluring Black American expatriation narrative. That questioning has led to my involvement in the organization and development of a variety of events, conferences, writings, study away programs, and the development of a growing field of Afro/Black French Studies that also inform this work.

Because b/Black French people are not officially recognized as a category or social group, their direct accounts or testimonies of lived experience were essential to this research and a core data source. In total, I formally interviewed 79 people between the ages of 20 and 65 from various walks of life, including activists, actors and others involved in the French film industry, advocates, artists, attorneys, community organizers, scholars, security guards, and everyday people from a variety of professions in sessions that lasted two to three hours, with follow-ups when necessary and possible. Some of my participants were people whom I had come to know from previous research and travels to France; others I found through snowball sampling or events in which I participated or attended. Interviews occurred in cafés, people's homes, offices, rooms in community centers, the Mitterrand Library, museums, via social media, and at times in my office and home. I met participants anywhere they felt comfortable. I used nondirective interviewing to encourage my participants to speak openly about their experiences, as well as directive interviewing in which I incorporate relevant anonymized excerpts from other interviews or related material, such as *Libé*'s hashtag or other news items, to probe more deeply the themes that emerged. As an outsider, this aspect allowed me also to explore difficult topics by sharing what others had already said on the matter, particularly around sensitive issues such as police brutality. That I am a Black woman also allowed some people to speak more openly who assumed shared experiences; but the American aspect could be a magnet for opposition on these issues. I was at times cast as a trafficker of US race ideas, well in advance of the current backlash.[39] I memorably recall a black student who aggressively came up to me after overhearing me discuss my research during a coffee break at a conference in 2015 to tell me that France did not have "those problems." When I asked, "What problems?" She whispered, "race," and basically said that France is not the United States before abruptly leaving and then giving me glacial glares during the rest of the conference. She was not the first nor the last to accuse of me this.

These testimonies provided, nonetheless, valuable knowledge and data that show how these lived experiences fit into a broader system of power asymmetries and a "coherent system of oppression, control, and legitimation" that reveals how antiblackness pervades everyday life, to return to Essed.[40] Although her study of everyday racism among interracial couples occurred in a race-conscious Britain, sociologist France Winddance Twine's notion of "racial literacy" is also insightful in this context. Twine defines "racial literacy" as "a set of conceptual tools and analytical skills . . . a reading practice, a way of perceiving and responding to the racial climate and racial structures that individuals encounter daily."[41] In some ways, I have witnessed the development of that racial literacy in France in the afterlife of the 2005 uprisings, among, for instance, ordinary people asserting a *n/Noir.e.s* identity, and I have also encountered silence, hesitancy, and rejection of the words *race* and *noir* in public settings. Raceblind republicanism remains powerful.

The lack of ethno-racialized data is a constant limitation when doing research of this nature in France. Another obstacle occurred when attempting to directly interview boys and young men about sensitive issues, such as sexual assault during identity controls or stop and frisks by certain French police. My professional positioning, gender, age, and nationality were factors that inhibited young people who were understandably reluctant to speak to me about such sensitive issues, even when I was invited into intimate circles by trusted people. Similarly, there were times that interviewing someone about violence that they or their family had suffered would inflict more harm than further any good that might come from such a method. In those instances, I also turned to other sources, such as relevant films, interviewees' own writings, media reports, recordings of events, and the like, when available. People have shed tears in my presence, as have I in private and when writing this book because of what I have seen and/or learned. Being sensitive to that difficulty without reproducing harm was/is an ever-present concern. The people in these pages are not data but *people*, to whom I am grateful for their time and stories, which will hopefully engender positive change and raise consciousness among those who, to return to Sméralda, do not themselves experience, understand, or recognize antiblackness.

NOTES

PROLOGUE

1. Throughout this book, all names have been changed or anonymized.

2. Throughout this book, I write "b/Black" (racialized and politicized discourses). I return to this point in the introduction.

3. Stuart Hall, "Minimal Selves," in *Identity: The Real Me*, ed. Homi Bhabha and Lisa Appignanesi (London: Institute of Contemporary Arts, 1987), 2; Katherine McKittrick, *Demonic Grounds: Black Women and The Cartographies Of Struggle* (Minneapolis: University of Minnesota Press, 2006), 76–78, Kindle.

4. McKittrick, *Demonic Grounds*, 61–62.

5. On this issue and the creation of eco-friendly public toilets, see Dan Bilefsky, "Paris Turns to Flower-Growing Toilet to Fight Public Urination," *New York Times*, February 2, 2017, https:// www.nytimes.com/2017/02/02/world/europe/paris-turns-to-flower-growing-toilet-to-fight -public-urination.html.

6. Lewis Gordon, *Bad Faith and Antiblack Racism* (New York: Humanity Books, 1999), 102.

7. Nirmal Puwar, *Space Invaders: Race, Gender and Bodies Out of Place* (London: Bloomsbury Academic, 2004), 55.

8. Frantz Fanon, *Black Skin, White Masks* (New York: Grove Atlantic, 1967), 95–96, Kindle. For the French version: *Peau Noire Masques Blancs* (Paris: Seuil, 1952), 113.

9. William Cheng, *Loving Music Until It Hurts* (Oxford: Oxford University Press, 2019), 66.

10. Human Rights Watch, "'Like Living in Hell': Police Abuses against Child and Adult Migrants in Calais," July 26, 2017, https://www.hrw.org/report/2017/07/26/living-hell/police -abuses-against-child-and-adult-migrants-calais.

11. See also the bittersweet memoir by Manthia Diawara, *We Won't Budge: An African Exile in the World* (New York: Basic Books, 2004), for earlier critiques of racism in France.

12. bell hooks, cited in Janet Mock, *Redefining Realness: My Path to Womanhood, Identity, Love & So Much More* (New York: Atria Books, 2014), Kindle.

INTRODUCTION

1. Nadine Morano, interviewed by Yann Moix, in the program "On n'est pas couché," France 2, September 26, 2015. This incident went viral and is found on many sites on the internet and social media. See for instance, France Info, September 27, 2015, https://www.francetvinfo .fr/economie/medias/video-on-n-est-pas-couche-nadine-morano-parle-de-race-blanche-et

-provoque-la-polemique_1102045.html. In her defense, Morano attributes her statement to one made in 1959 by the founder of the Fifth (and present) Republic, Charles de Gaulle. What observers found shocking is her espousing explicitly ideas of race and white supremacy that are ironically at odds with the very principles and values of the French Republic.

2. Jérémie Gauthier, "Le contrôle au faciès devant les juges. Entretien avec Slim Ben Achour," *La Vie des idées*, February 2, 2018, https://laviedesidees.fr/Le-controle-au-facies-devant-les-juges.html.

3. "C'est quoi être noir(e) en France, au quotidien? Racontez-nous," *Libération*, July, 1, 2015, https://www.liberation.fr/societe/2015/07/01/c-est-quoi-etre-noire-en-france-au-quotidien-racontez-nous_1340838. My formulation, "race *and/as* color, ethnicity," serves to signify that the entity following "as" also functions as a race proxy in France. What I'm calling official raceblindness in France is often periodized in relation to the Shoah and scientific racism during the Nazi/Vichy era. In the post–World War II era, the UN issued a number of declarations and conventions, refuting scientific racism and created UNESCO in 1945 whose 1950 *Statement on Race* declared there was no scientific basis for race. This statement would create a firestorm of controversy in the US where Jim and Jane Crow segregation was in full force. In France, with its living memories of Nazism, this Statement and others during the 1950s and '60s, discrediting scientific racism, were integral to banning constructs of race as biology in the French Constitution. These ideas persisted under French and European colonial rule. Aimé Césaire's *Discourse on Colonialism* remains one of the most lucid rejoinders of this double standard, examined further in the chapter, "The Choice of Ignorance." See also Tyler Stovall, "The Color behind the Lines: Racial Violence in France during the Great War," *American Historical Review* 103, no. 3 (1998), 737–769.

4. I am grateful to the field of Disability Studies for reminding us of the negative connotations attached to blindness. My use aligns with Fanon's understanding of a hegemonic ideology that drives the *unseeing* of blackened life and racism in France. Riffing off James Baldwin's title, *The Evidence of Things Unseen*, what I present, then, is the evidence of people misseen who are also "thingified," in Aimé Césaire's sense, thus dehumanized and treated as disposable.

5. The survey dates were between 2008 and 2009. Cris Beauchemin, Christelle Hamel, and Patrick Simon, *Trajectoires et origines: Enquête sur la diversité des populations en France—TeO1* (Paris: INED/INSEE, 2015), 448. The results from the long-awaited study, *Trajectoires et Origines 2* (*TeO2*) were not yet released at the writing of this book. See Ined and Insee, May 30, 2022, https://www.insee.fr/fr/information/4172158.

6. Beauchemin et al., "Les discriminations: Une question de minorités visibles," *Population Sociétés* 466, no. 1 (2010).

7. In this book, I use "arab" in lower case or "arabianized" to designate an imposed racialized and amalgamated identity discourse that eclipses a long history of black Africanity and other peoples in those regions (i.e., the Imazighen). The word "Arab" is also a site of contestation, an identity discourse claimed by people racialized-as-black who may not be apprehended or perceived as "Arab." For a historical context, see, for instance, Chouki El Hamel, *Black Morocco: A History of Slavery, Race, and Islam* (Cambridge: Cambridge University Press, 2013).

8. Défenseur des droits, *Enquête sur l'accès aux droits: Relations police/population, le cas des contrôles*, January 2017, https://www.defenseurdesdroits.fr/sites/default/files/atoms/files /enquete-relations-police-population-final2-11012017.pdf.

9. Solène Brun and Patrick Simon, "L'invisibilité des minorités dans les chiffres du Coronavirus: Le détour par la Seine-Saint-Denis," in *Inégalités ethno-raciales et pandémie de coronavirus*, ed. Solène Brun and Patrick Simon, May 19, 2020, http://icmigrations.fr/2020 /05/15/defacto-019-05/.

10. The Department of Seine-Saint-Denis, *Baromètre des discriminations en Seine Saint Denis* by Harris Interactive, 2019, http://www.maisonegalitefemmeshommes.fr/ressource/711/514 -barometre-des-discriminations-en-seine-saint-denis.htm via http://www.maisonegalite femmeshommes.fr.

11. For the population figure of 4–5%, see *TeO1* and Ndiaye, *La Condition Noire* (Paris: Calmann-Lévy, 2008), Kindle. I have also written about these issues in Trica Keaton, "Racial Profiling and the 'French Exception,'" *French Cultural Studies* (2013) and Keaton, "The Politics of Race-Blindness: (Anti)blackness and Category Blindness in Contemporary France," *Du Bois Review: Social Science Research on Race* (2010).

12. Audrey Célestine and Sarah Fila-Bakabadio, "Introduction," *African and Black Diaspora: An International Journal* 10, no. 1 (2017): 3. Also see Célestine, *La fabrique des identités: L'encadrement politique des minorités caribéennes à Paris et New York* (Paris: Editions Karthala, 2018) and Fila-Bakabadio, *Africa on My Mind: Histoire sociale de l'afrocentrisme aux États-Unis* (Paris: Les Indes savantes, 2016); cf. Claude Ribbe, *Les Nègres de la République* (Monaco: Éditions Alphée, 2007).

13. *Libération*, "C'est quoi être noir(e) en France, au quotidien ? Racontez-nous," July, 1, 2015, https://www.liberation.fr/societe/2015/07/01/c-est-quoi-etre-noire-en-france-au-quotidien -racontez-nous_1340838. For tweets cited in this book from the hashtag, see *Libération* (@libe). "#TuSaisQueTesNoirEnFranceQuand," Twitter.com, July 1, 2015, https://www .liberation.fr/societe/2015/07/01/c-est-quoi-etre-noire-en-france-au-quotidien-racontez-nous _1340838/ and https://twitter.com/libe/status/616217032045031425.

14. I have opted not to cite direct interview sources in the endnotes to avoid redundancies and owing to word count limitations. I have instead contextualized them within the body of the book.

15. Pap Ndiaye, *La Condition Noire*, 17, Kindle.

16. Mae Ngai, *Impossible Subjects: Illegal Aliens and the Making of Modern America* (Princeton, NJ: Princeton University Press, 2004), xxiv, Kindle.

17. kihana miraya ross, "Call It What It Is: Anti-blackness," *New York Times*, June 4, 2020, https:// www.nytimes.com/2020/06/04/opinion/george-floyd-anti-blackness.html.

18. Frantz Fanon, *Black Skin, White Masks* (New York: Grove Press), 89–92. French Version from Editions Seuil, 107–108. My understanding of white supremacy here is not only the belief in inherent white superiority but a global structure that is "*itself*," emphasizes Mills, "a political system [and] particular power structure of formal or informal rule, socioeconomic privilege [thus advantage], and norms for the differential distribution of material wealth and opportunities, benefits and burdens, rights and duties." Charles Mills, *The Racial Contract* (Ithaca: Cornell University Press, 1997), Kindle. See Charles Mills, *Blackness Visible:*

Essays on Philosophy and Race (Ithaca: Cornell Paperbacks, 1998). See also Crystal Fleming, *Resurrecting Slavery: Racial Legacies and White Supremacy in France* (Philadelphia: Temple University Press, 2017) and Stephen Steinberg, "The Whiteness of Race Knowledge: Charles Mills Throws Down the Gauntlet," *Ethnic and Racial Studies* 41, no. 3 (2018): 541–550.

19. Tyler Stovall, *White Freedom* (Princeton, NJ: Princeton University Press), 191, Kindle.

20. Moon-Kie Jung and João Costa Vargas, eds., *Antiblackness* (Durham, NC: Duke University Press, 2021), 6, Kindle; Charles Mills, *The Racial Contract* (Ithaca: Cornell University Press, 1997), Kindle. "Racial Contract" for Mills refers to "the contract between those categorized as white over the nonwhites, who are thus the objects rather than subjects."

21. Mills, *Racial Contract.* His complete thought is: "On matters related to race, the Racial Contract prescribes for its signatories an inverted epistemology, an epistemology of ignorance, a particular pattern of localized and global cognitive dysfunctions (which are psychologically and socially functional), producing the ironic outcome that [some] whites will in general be unable to understand the world they themselves have made. Part of what it means to be constructed as 'white' (the metamorphosis of the sociopolitical contract), part of what it requires to achieve Whiteness, successfully to become a white person . . . is a cognitive model that precludes self-transparency and genuine understanding of social realities. To a significant extent, then, white signatories will live in an invented delusional world, a racial fantasyland, a 'consensual hallucination.'"

22. Gloria Wekker, *White Innocence: Paradoxes of Colonialism and Race* (Durham, NC: Duke University Press), 17.

23. In addition to readings by Kimberlé Crenshaw and other authors of CRT, see Kimberlé Williams Crenshaw, Luke Charles Harris, Daniel Martinez HoSang, and George Lipsitz, eds., *Seeing Race Again: Countering Colorblindness across the Disciplines* (Berkeley: University of California Press, 2019).

24. See also Jennifer Boittin, *Colonial Metropolis: The Urban Grounds of Anti-imperialism and Feminism in Interwar Paris* (Lincoln: University of Nebraska Press, 2010), 93, who also notes another silent dimension to belonging during the interwar years, namely that "Antilleans had been French citizens since the abolition of slavery in 1848 and were distinctive in the long-standing guarantee of citizenship. West Africans from the Four communes of Senegal (Dakar, Saint Louis, Rufisque, and Gorée) had also considered themselves citizens since that date. And indeed, ever since . . . the latter were distinguished from all other Africans. But their status as citizens was repeatedly questioned and openly challenged by various French courts, ministers, and governors until World War I." Cf. Mamadou Diouf, *Histoire du Sénégal: Le modèle islamo-wolof et ses périphéries* (Paris: Maisonneuve et Larose, 2001); Silyane Larcher, *L'autre citoyen: L'idéal républicain et les Antilles après l'esclavage* (Paris: Armand Colin, 2014), Kindle.

25. Mills, "The Illumination of Blackness," in *Antiblackness*, ed. Moon-Kie Jung and João Costa Vargas (Durham, NC: Duke University Press, 2021), 35.

26. Fatima El-Tayeb, *European Others: Queering Ethnicity in Postnational Europe* (Minneapolis: University of Minnesota Press, 2011), 263, Kindle. Also see chapter 6 in Stephen Small, *Decolonizing the Mind: 20 Questions and Answers on Black Europe* (The Hague: Amrit Publishers, 2018). See Elisa Joy White, *Modernity, Freedom, and the African Diaspora: Dublin, New Orleans, Paris* (Bloomington: Indiana University Press, 2012) and Michael McEachrane, ed.,

Afro-Nordic Landscapes: Equality and Race in Northern Europe (London: Routledge Press, 2016).

27. I have written elsewhere on this issue. See Trica Keaton, "'Black (American) Paris' and the 'Other France': The Race Question and Questioning Solidarity," in *Black Europe and the African Diaspora*, ed. Darlene Clark Hine, Trica Keaton, and Stephen Small (Urbana: University of Illinois Press, 2009). See also Michel Fabre, *La Rive Noire de Harlem à la Seine* (Paris: Lieu Commun, 1986); Roi Ottley, *No Green Pastures* (New York: Charles Scribner's Sons, 1951); Tyler Stovall, *Paris Noir: African Americans in the City of Light* (Boston: Houghton Mifflin, 1996); and Bennetta Jules-Rosette, *Black Paris: The African Writer's Landscape* (Urbana: University of Illinois Press, 1998).

28. I became aware of this exchange when being interviewed by Benoît Morenne, then reporter for the *Wall Street Journal* on June 15, 2020. See James McAuley (@jameskmcauley), https://twitter.com/jameskmcauley/status/1271468385193340930; Gérard Araud (@GerardAraud), June 12, 2020, https://twitter.com/GerardAraud/status/1271634234231357440.

29. Linda Alcoff, "Afterword: The Black/White Binary and Antiblack Racism," *Critical Philosophy of Race* 1, no. 1 (2013): 122), http://dog.org/10.5325/critphilrace.1.1.0121. See also Lewis Gordon, *Bad Faith and Antiblack Racism* (New York: Humanity Books, 1999).

30. Frantz Fanon, *Toward the African Revolution* (New York: Grove Press, 1969), 17, 21; Gordon, *Anti-black Racism*, 104.

31. Philomena Essed, *Understanding Everyday Racism: An Interdisciplinary Theory* (Newbury Park, CA: Sage Publications, 1991); *Everday Racism: Reports from Women in Two Cultures* (Claremont, CA: Hunter House, 1990); "Everyday Racism," in *Encyclopedia of Race and Racism*, ed. John Hartwell Moore (New York: Macmillan).

32. Essed, *Understanding Everyday Racism*, 288.

33. Other scholars have made similar arguments in relation to "colorblindness" in the United States. See, for instance, Patricia Williams, *Seeing a Color-Blind Future: The Paradox of Race* (New York: Farrar, Straus and Giroux, 2001); Kimberlé Crenshaw et al., eds., *Seeing Race Again*; Eduardo Bonilla-Silva, *Racism without Racists: Color-blind Racism and the Persistence of Racial Inequality in the United States* (Lanham, MD: Rowman & Littlefield, 2010); and David Goldberg, *Are We All Postracial Yet?* (Cambridge: Polity Press, 2015).

34. Mills, "The Illumination of Blackness," 35.

35. The literature is too vast to cite here. See Centers for Disease Control and Prevention, "Media Statement from CDC Director Rochelle P. Walensky, MD, MPH, on Racism and Health," in which Walensky declares racism "a serious public heath threat," April 8, 2021, https://www.cdc.gov/media/releases/2021/s0408-racism-health.html. See also David R. Williams's extensive body of research on social influences affecting poor health, including his work measuring everyday discrimination: David R. Williams, "Measuring Discrimination Resource," June 2016, https://scholar.harvard.edu/files/davidrwilliams/files/measuring_discrimination_resource_june_2016.pdf; T. T. Lewis, C. D. Cogburn, and D. R. Williams, "Self-Reported Experiences of Discrimination and Health: Scientific Advances, Ongoing Controversies, and Emerging Issues," *Annual Review of Clinical Psychology* 11 (2015): 407–440; as well as Zaneta Thayer and Christopher Kuzawa, "Ethnic Discrimination Predicts Poor Self-Rated Health and Cortisol in Pregnancy: Insights from New Zealand," *Social Science*

& *Medicine* 128 (2015): 36–42. In the French context, see Solène Brun and Patrick Simon, "L'invisibilité des minorités dans les chiffres du Coronavirus: Le détour par la Seine-Saint-Denis," in *Inégalités ethno-raciales et pandémie de coronavirus*, eds. Solène Brun and Patrick Simon, May 19, 2020, http://icmigrations.fr/2020/05/15/defacto-019-05/.

36. Philomena Essed and David Theo Goldberg, "Cloning Cultures: The Social Injustices of Sameness," *Ethnic and Racial Studies* 25, no. 6 (2002): 1070.

37. Essed and Goldberg, 1070; Jennifer Anne Boittin, *Undesirable: Passionate Mobility and Women's Defiance of French Colonial Policing, 1919–1952* (Chicago: University of Chicago Press, 2022).

38. Essed and Goldberg, 1074.

39. Essed and Goldberg, 1074.

40. Crystal Fleming makes a similar argument about gaslighting in "On the Illegibility of French Antiblackness: Notes from an African American Critic," in *Antiblackness*, ed. Moon-Kie Jung and João Costa Vargas (Durham, NC: Duke University Press, 2021).

41. Jean-Louis Borloo, *Vivre ensemble, vivre en grand la République, pour une réconciliation nationale*, April, 2018, 7, https://www.vie-publique.fr/rapport/37321-vivre-ensemble-vivre-en-grand-pour-une-reconciliation-nationale.

42. Borloo, *Vivre ensemble*.

43. Borloo, *Vivre ensemble*.

44. Christina Sharpe, *In the Wake: On Blackness and Being* (Durham, NC: Duke University Press, 2016), Kindle.

45. See the forthcoming book by Nicole Grégoire, Sarah Fila-Bakabadio, and Jacinthe Mazzoc-chetti, *Black Studies in Europe: Questioning the Politics of Knowledge* (Evanston, IL: Northwestern University Press).

46. Anonymous, email to author, August 8, 2021.

47. Nathalie Etoké, *Afro Diasporic French Identities*, directed by Etoké (Movimiento, 2011).

48. Pierre Boulle, "François Bernier and the Origins of the Modern Concept of Race," in *The Color of Liberty: Histories of Race in France*, ed. Sue Peabody and Tyler Stovall (Durham, NC: Duke University Press, 2003), 13, 15.

49. Geraldine Heng, *The Invention of Race in the European Middle Ages* (Cambridge: Cambridge University Press, 2018), 16–17, Kindle. See also Trica Keaton, "Race," in *Keywords for African American Studies*, ed. Erica Edwards, Roderick Ferguson, and Jeffrey Ogbar (New York: NYU Press, 2018).

50. Achille Mbembe, *Critique of Black Reason* (Durham, NC: Duke University Press, 2017), 40. This English translation of *Critique de la raison nègre* uses "Blacks," but the French term "*n/Nègres*" is more appropriate in this context. For an analysis of the translation of *nègre* and its semantic rehabilitation, particularly during the interwar period, see Brent Edwards, *The Practice of Diaspora: Literature, Translation, and the Rise of Black Internationalism* (Cambridge, MA: Harvard University Press, 2003). On antiblack sentiment and color prejudice also see David Goldberg, "Racism, Color Symbolism, and Color Prejudice," in *The Origins of Racism in the West*, ed. Miriam Eliav-Feldon, Benjamin Isaac, and Joseph Ziegler (Cambridge: Cambridge University Press, 2009).

51. Cedric J. Robinson, *Black Marxism* (Chapel Hill: University of North Carolina Press, 1983), Kindle.

52. Robinson, *Black Marxism*.

53. Heng, *The Invention of Race*, Kindle.

54. Heng, *The Invention of Race*, Kindle.

55. Heng, *The Invention of Race*; see also Thomas Gossett, *Race: The History of an Idea in America Book* (New York: Oxford University Press, 1997).

56. William Cohen, *The French Encounter with Africans: White Response to Blacks, 1530–1880* (Bloomington: Indiana University Press, 2003), 14.

57. Heng, *The Invention of Race*, Kindle.

58. Heng, *The Invention of Race*, Kindle.

59. Suzanne Conklin Akbari, *Idols in the East: European Representations of Islam and the Orient, 1100–1450* (Ithaca: Cornell University Press, 2012), 194. Mills also explores these points, citing Debra Higgs Strickland and others in terms of "the symbolic equation of black with spiritual darkness, implying the concomitant equivalence of white with spiritual enlightenment," and role of blackness in the dehumanization of Ethiopians. Mills, "The Illumination of Blackness," Kindle.

60. Frank M. Snowden Jr., *Before Color Prejudice* (Cambridge, MA: Harvard University Press, 1983), 63.

61. Snowden, 63.

62. Snowden, 83, 84.

63. Michel Pastoureau, *Black: The History of a Color* (Princeton, NJ: Princeton University Press, 2008), 21, 27.

64. David M. Goldenberg, *The Curse of Ham: Race and Slavery in Early Judaism, Christianity, and Islam* (Princeton, NJ: Princeton University Press, 2005), 137–138, Kindle.

65. Toni Morrison, *Playing in the Dark*: *Whiteness and the Literary Imagination* (New York: Vintage Books, 1993), 49, Kindle.

66. Robert Stam and Ella Shohat, *Race in Translation: Culture Wars around the Postcolonial Atlantic* (New York: NYU Press, 2012), 246, Kindle. On this point and following Foucault, sociologist Nacira Guénif-Souilamas and the authors analyze further these dynamics in terms of governmentality located on the politicized and racialized body that has been produced, managed, and controlled through statist institution, finding that "the normative biopolitics that shape citizenship and subcitizenship in postcolonial France, regulat[e] the bodies and behavior of the children of immigrants of color. While the dominant discourse assumes a general freedom of self-invention for all people, the marginalized are made to feel incarcerated in their own bodies, held back by the invisible barrier that separates off those who lack 'civilizational legitimacy'" (256, Kindle).

67. Toni Morrison, interview by Charlie Rose May 7, 1993, PBS, https://archive.org/details/Charlie-Rose-1993-05-07.

68. Kate Lowe, "Introduction: The Black African Presence in Renaissance Europe," in *Black Africans in Renaissance Europe*, ed. T. F. Earle and Kate Lowe (Cambridge: Cambridge University Press, 2005), 19.

69. Lowe, 20.

70. Jim Cohen, "Postcolonial Colonialism: French Struggles Against Ethnic-Racial Discrimination and the Emerging 'Postcolonial' Critique of the Republican Model of Citizenship," *Situations: Project of the Radical Imagination*, no. 1 (2007): 110.

71. Lorelle Semley, *To Be Free and French: Citizenship in France's Atlantic Empire* (Cambridge: Cambridge University Press, 2017), Kindle.

72. Larcher, *L'autre citoyen*. See also Laurent Dubois, *A Colony of Citizens: Revolution and Slave Emancipation in the French Caribbean, 1787–1804* (Chapel Hill: University of North Carolina Press, 2004), for an illuminating analysis of how the colonized in the French Caribbean made claims to universalism in order to challenge imperial institutions; that is, peoples in whom those in authority held little confidence in their capacity to appreciate universal rights.

73. Tyler Stovall, "The Color behind the Lines," 766.

74. Pierre Bourdieu, "Deux impérialismes de l'universel," in *L'Amérique des Français*, ed. C. Fauré and T. Bishop (Paris: Editions François Bourin, 1992), 150.

75. Robert Stam and Ella Shohat, *Race in Translation: Culture Wars around the Postcolonial Atlantic* (New York: NYU Press, 2012), 114–115, Kindle.

76. Lewis Gordon, "Black Existence in Philosophy of Culture," *Diogenes* 59, no. 3–4 (2013): 96. See also Emmanuel Eze, ed., *Race and the Enlightenment: A Reader* (Malden, MA: Blackwell, 2003).

77. Catherine Raissiguier, *Reinventing the Republic: Gender, Migration, and Citizenship in France* (Stanford, CA: Stanford University Press, 2010), 1.

78. Michael Omi and Howard Winant, *Racial Formation in the United States from 1960s to the 1990s* (New York: Routledge, 1994), 67.

79. David Scott, "The Re-enchantment of Humanism: An Interview with Sylvia Wynter," *Small Axe*, no. 8 (September 2000): 159.

80. Tyler Stovall, *Transnational France: The Modern History of a Universal Nation* (New York: Routledge, 2015), 233, Kindle.

81. See also Sankar Muthu, *Enlightenment against Empire* (Princeton, NJ: Princeton University, 2003), for how eighteenth-century thought more broadly was comprised of multiple Enlightenments, strains that included a commitment to universal principles. See also Stovall, *White Freedom*.

82. Stovall, *Transnational France*, Kindle.

83. Jean Beaman, *Citizen Outsider: Children of North African Immigrants in France* (Berkeley: University of California Press, 2017), 23.

84. Aimé Césaire, *Discourse on Colonialism* (New York: Monthly Review Press, [1950]/2000), 3.

85. For analyses of the Thorez letter, see Robin D. G. Kelley's foreword to the 2000 edition of Césaire, *Discourse on Colonialism*; Brent Edwards, "Introduction: Césaire in 1956," *Social Text* 103, no. 2 (Summer 2010).

86. Keith Walker, *Countermodernism and Francophone Literary Culture* (Durham, NC: Duke University Press, 1999), Kindle.

87. Walker, *Countermodernism*, 15, Kindle.

88. Barnor Hesse, "Im/plausible Deniability: Racism's Conceptual Double Bind," *Social Identities* 10, no. 1 (2004): 20.

89. See Julien Suaudeau and Mame-Fatou Niang, *Universalisme* (Paris: Anamosa, 2022), for similar arguments. What they term pseudo-universalism, informed by Césarian thought, amounts to *la raison coloniale* (colonial logic or reasoning), they maintain, which has not disappeared from society and operates not in the service of humanity but labors as an ideology that sustains racialized hierarchies and power asymmetries, necessitating "an antiracist universalism," as a countervailing force or response. See also Trica Keaton, "Racial Profiling and the 'French Exception.'"

90. Michelle Wright, *Physics of Blackness: Beyond the Middle Passage Epistemology* (Minneapolis: University of Minnesota Press, 2015), 4, Kindle. See also Manning Marable and Vanessa Agard-Jones, eds., *Transnational Blackness: Navigating the Global Color Line* (New York: Palgrave Macmillan, 2008).

91. Wright, *Physics of Blackness*, Kindle.

92. Philomena Essed, "A Brief ABC on Black Europe," in *Invisible Visible Minority: Confronting Afrophobia and Advancing Equality for People of African Descent and Black Europeans in Europe*, ed. The European Network Against Racism (ENAR) (Brussels: ENAR, 2014), 59.

93. Craig Calhoun, "Social Theory and the Politics of Identity," in *Social Theory and the Politics of Identity*, ed. Craig Calhoun (Malden, MA: Blackwell, 2003), 21.

94. Bennetta Jules-Rosette, "Identity Discourses and Diasporic Aesthetics in Black Paris: Community Formation and the Translation of Culture," *Diaspora* 9, no. 1 (2000): 40.

95. Dipesh Chakrabarty, *Provincializing Europe: Postcolonial Thought and Historical Difference* (Princeton, Princeton University Press, 2000), 100.

96. W. E. B. Du Bois, "That Capital 'N,'" *The Crisis*, February 11, 1916, 184. All subsequent references from Du Bois in this context are from this article.

97. Ronald A. T. Judy, "Fanon's Body of Black Experience," in *Fanon: A Critical Reader*, ed. Lewis R. Gordon et al. (Oxford: Blackwell , 1996), 54.

98. Juliette Sméralda, "Foreword" to Frantz Fanon, *Peau noire, masques blancs* (Montréal: Kiyikaat Editions, 2015), 25.

99. Deborah King, "Multiple Jeopardy, Multiple Consciousness: The Context of a Black Feminist Ideology," *Signs: Journal of Women in Culture and Society* 14, no. 1 (1988): 42–43.

100. Kwame Anthony Appiah, "The Case for Capitalizing the B in Black," *Atlantic*, June 18, 2020, https://www.theatlantic.com/ideas/archive/2020/06/time-to-capitalize-blackand-white /613159/; Nell Irvin Painter, "Opinion: Why 'White' Should Be Capitalized, Too," *Washington Post*, July 22, 2020, https://www.washingtonpost.com/opinions/2020/07/22/why-white -should-be-capitalized/.

101. David Lanham and Amy Liu, "Not Just a Typographical Change: Why Brookings Is Capitalizing Black," Brookings Institute, September 23, 2019, https://www.brookings.edu/research /brookingscapitalizesblack/.

102. Essed, *Understanding*, 160.

1. Patrick Simon, "The Choice of Ignorance: The Debate on Ethnic and Racial Statistics in France," in *Social Statistics and Ethnic Diversity*, ed. Patrick Simon, Victor Piché, and Amélie Gagnon (Heidelberg, NY: Springer, 2015), 66.

2. United Nations Committee on the Elimination of Racial Discrimination (CERD), *International Convention on the Elimination of All Forms of Racial Discrimination*: Twentieth to Twenty-first Periodic Reports/France, May 23, 2013, https://docstore.ohchr.org/SelfServices/FilesHandler.ashx?enc=6QkG1d%2FPPRiCAqhKb7yhsrYJhxxpxgI0H2gkhVJfP3Oppc lynyY4%2B9fZQPa%2F98eISN3H6XAkWm%2BJXv7%2B89VzXmmMJj8V%2BMA%2FTg MEEmvUzeqwmijhjNFrodeuzBj92%2F6l.

3. European Union Agency for Fundamental Rights (FRA), *Second European Union Minorities and Discrimination Survey (EU-MIDIS II): Being Black in the EU* (Luxembourg: Publications Office of the European Union, 2018), 7.

4. In this chapter, I am using "national minority" as it is used by the Council of Europe and related EU agencies. Comprised of 47 member states and 27 EU countries, including France, the Council of Europe describes itself as the "continent's leading human rights organization" whose agenda includes the protection of national minorities through its Framework Convention for the Protection of National Minorities (FCNM). The council does not define "national minority," as there is no agreed upon definition among member states, which means that it is at the discretion of the states to comply with international law and principles set out in the FCNM. France has neither signed nor ratified the FCNM to date. Council of Europe, *Factsheet on the Framework Convention for the Protection of National Minorities*, https://www.coe.int/en/web/minorities/fcnm-factsheet.

5. Following the release of the European Union Agency for Fundamental Rights (FRA)'s 2021 report, titled *Equality in the EU 20 years on from the Initial Implementation of the Equality Directives*, I asked a principal investigator which countries in the EU collect data on race and ethnicity beyond those typically documented, such as the UK, who responded: "Ireland is collecting data on ethnicity on a regular basis; Malta is going to add racial and ethnic origin among other relevant characteristics to the census; Hungary, Slovakia, Bulgaria, Czechia, Romania collect information about ethnicity (nationality) etc. mainly related to their national minorities such as the Roma; the Baltic States have also information on nationality (Russian minorities etc.)." This person added that "one has to carefully look at each country" and noted that developments are on the horizon at the EU-level, including new legislation envisioned "for the future censuses (2031) which will look at ethnic and racial origin among others." However, convincing member states is the hurdle. Email to author, September 2, 2021.

6. Lilla Farkas, *Data Collection in the Field of Ethnicity: Analysis and Comparative Review of Equality Data Collection Practices in the European Union* (European Commission, 2017), 16.

7. Farkas, *Data Collection*, 16.

8. For more on antiracism legislation in France and the EU, see Erik Bleich, *Race Politics in Britain and France: Ideas and Policymaking since the 1960s* (Cambridge: Cambridge University Press, 2003/2012), and Terri Givens and Rhonda Evans Case, *Legislating Equality* (Oxford: Oxford University Press, 2014).

9. Michael Gomez, *Reversing Sail: A History of the African Diaspora* (Cambridge: Cambridge University Press, 2008/2020); Crystal Fleming, *Resurrecting Slavery: Racial Legacies and White Supremacy in France* (Philadelphia: Temple University Press, 2017).

10. Michel Wieviorka, "Should France Collect Race Statistics" (paper presented at the National Debates on Race Statistics: Towards an International Comparison," Fondation Maison des sciences de l'homme and Columbia University, New York, 2011), https://halshs.archives-ouvertes.fr/halshs-00677217/document.

11. Trica Keaton, "The Politics of Race-Blindness: (Anti)blackness and Category Blindness in Contemporary France," *Du Bois Review: Social Science Research on Race* 7, no. 1 (2010): 103–131. Cited in this article are a variety sources about this debate.

12. United Nations, "International Decade for People of African Descent 2015–2024," https://www.un.org/en/observances/decade-people-african-descent, accessed April 14, 2022.

13. European Union Agency for Fundamental Rights (FRA), *Being Black in the EU*, 8, 3. For France and the UK, the sample included people from the overseas departments and territories.

14. FRA, *Second European Union Minorities and Discrimination Survey (EU-MIDIS II): Technical Report* (Luxembourg: Publications Office of the European Union, 2017), 7.

15. FRA, *Subgroup on Equality Data*, https://fra.europa.eu/en/project/2019/subgroup-equality-data; the European Commission, *Communication from the Commission to the European Parliament, the Council, the European Economic and Social Committee and the Committee of the Regions: A Union of Equality: EU Anti-racism Action Plan 2020–25* (Brussels: European Union, 2020), 1, 16.

16. United Nations International Convention on the Elimination of All Forms of Racial Discrimination (CERD), *Reports Submitted by States Parties under Article 9 of the Convention* (CERD/C/FRA/20–21, 2013), 4. Anonymous, email message to author, Wednesday, August 25, 2021.

17. FRA, *Being Black in the EU*, 8. Many civil society organizations expressed concerns about the omission of Spain from this survey, given the countries historical significance to the African diaspora and present realities on the ground. For more on those limitations, see FRA, *Technical Report*, 14–15. One principal investigator communicated that a number of factors precluded including Spain in its sample, such as data limitations and the inability to analyze trends. In an upcoming report, b/Black populations in Spain will be included.

18. FRA, *Being Black in the EU*, 15.

19. Michael O'Flaherty, "Foreword," *Being Black in the EU*, 3.

20. Défenseur des droits, *Enquête sur l'accès aux droits: Relations police/population, le cas des contrôles* (Paris: Défenseur des droits, République Française, 2017).

21. Solène Brun and Patrick Simon, "L'invisibilité des minorités dans les chiffres du Coronavirus: Le détour par la Seine-Saint-Denis," in *Inégalités ethno-raciales et pandémie de coronavirus*, ed. Solène Brun and Patrick Simon, May 19, 2020, http://icmigrations.fr/2020/05/15/defacto-019-05/.

22. Brun and Simon, "L'invisibilité des minorités."

23. Brun and Simon, "L'invisibilité des minorités."

24. Pap Ndiaye, *La Condition Noire* (Paris: Calmann-Lévy, 2008), Kindle.

25. Ndiaye, *La Condition.*

26. Ndiaye, *La Condition.*

27. FRA, *Being Black*, 14.

28. FRA, *Equality in the EU*, 7, and FRA, *Second European Union Minorities and Discrimination Survey (EU-MIDIS II)*, 10, 13.

29. Maya Angela Smith, *Senegal Abroad: Linguistic Borders, Racial Formations, and Diasporic Imaginaries* (Madison: University of Wisconsin Press, 2019).

30. FRA, *Equality in the EU 20 Years on from the Initial Implementation of the Equality Directives* (Luxembourg: Publications Office of the European Union, 2021), 7, drawn from *EU-MIDIS II*, 13. Although FRA shows anti-Asian discrimination and racism, these groups are not similarly included in tables and such statements.

31. Giovanni Picker, *Racial Cities Governance and the Segregation of Romani People in Urban Europe* (New York: Routledge, 2019).

32. FRA, *EU-MIDIS II*, 10, 3.

33. FRA, *Being Black*, 67.

34. FRA, *Equality in the EU*, 19.

35. FRA, *Equality in the EU*, 50. For more on the European Council and Parliament Directives on gender equality, see Directive 2004/113/EC; Directive 86/613/EC; Directive 2006/54/EC; and Directive 2010/41/EU.

36. FRA, *Equality in the EU*, 50.

37. European Network Against Racism (ENAR), "What's the Existing EU Legislation on Racist Crime?," https://www.enar-eu.org/Frequently-asked-questions-1004.

38. FRA, *Equality in the EU 20 Years on from the Initial Implementation of the Equality Directives* (Luxembourg: Publications Office of the European Union, 2021), 6. The European Commission functions as an executive branch of the EU and forms and informs EU laws and policies among other activities. The term "racial origin," for the commission, "does not imply an acceptance of theories that attempt to determine the existence of separate human races." The European Commission, *A Union of Equality: EU Anti-Racism Action Plan 2020–2025* (Belgium: European Commission, 2020), 1. See also FRA, *Being Black in the EU*, 10.

39. Lilla Farkas, *Data Collection in the Field of Ethnicity: Analysis and Comparative Review of Equality Data Collection Practices in the European Union* (European Commission, 2017), 16.

40. The 1978 Data Protection Law, notably article 8, prohibits collecting directly or indirectly personal information pertaining to "racial or ethnic origins," political, philosophical, or religious opinions or beliefs, among other characteristics. Rare exceptions are determined by the CNIL on a case-by-case basis. For an instructive analysis of this law and its implications for *TeO* researchers, see François Héran, "Preface," in *Trajectoires et origines: Enquête sur la diversité des populations en France*, under the direction of Cris Beauchemin, Christelle Hamel, and Patrick Simon (Paris: INED, 2016), 7–16.

41. This meeting took place at FRA headquarters in Austria at the invitation of FRA and our gathering's organizers, social scientists Nicole Grégoire and Michael McEachrane. FRA, *Being Black*, 8. FRA launched *Being Black in the EU* in November 2018 at the European

Parliament (EP), hosted by MEP Cécile Kyenge, MEP Malin Björk, and the European Parliament's Anti-Racism and Diversity Intergroup (ARDI). Several civil society organizations, researchers, and EP/EU representatives were present. My thanks to members of ARDI and Michael McEachrane for invitations to those meetings.

42. Anonymous email to the author, April 25, 2021.

43. Givens and Evans Case, *Legislating Equality*, 93, Kindle.

44. Patrick Simon, "The Choice of Ignorance."

45. Trica Keaton, "The Politics of Race-Blindness"; Didier Fassin, "Ni race, ni racisme. Ce que racialiser veut dire," in *Les Nouvelles frontières de la société française*, ed. Didier Fassin (Paris: La Découverte, 2012), 147–172.

46. European Parliament, *On Fundamental Rights of People of African descent in Europe* (2018/2899 [RSP]), March 29, 2018, http://www.europarl.europa.eu/doceo/document/B-8-2019-0212_EN.html.

47. European Parliament, *On Fundamental Rights*.

48. For more on antiblackness in Italy, see Jacqueline Andall, *Gender, Migration and Domestic Service: The Politics of Black Women in Italy* (Aldershot: Ashgate, 2000); Alessandra Di Maio, *Wor(L)ds In Progress: A Study Of Contemporary Migrant Writings* (Milan: Mimesis International, 2014); Donald Carter, *Navigating the African Diaspora: The Anthropology of Invisibility* (Minneapolis: University of Minnesota Press, 2010); Camilla Hawthorne, *Contesting Race and Citizenship: Youth Politics in the Black Mediterranean* (Ithaca: Cornell University Press, 2022); Heather Merrill, *Black Spaces: African Diaspora in Italy* (New York: Routledge, 2018); Maya Smith, *Senegal Abroad: linguistic Borders, Racial Formations, and Diasporic Imaginaries* (Madison: University of Wisconsin Press, 2019); Bruno Riccio, *Exploring Senegalese Translocal Spaces* (London: Routledge, 2011); and the film *Blaxploitalian: 100 Years of Black in Italian Cinema*, dir. Fred Kudjo Kuwornu (Do the Right Thing Films, 2016), https://www.dotherightfilms.nyc/blaxploitalian-documentary.

49. Anonymous, email to author, April 8, 2019.

50. European Parliament, *On Fundamental Rights*.

51. For the photo of the European Commission's "political leadership," see the European Commission, "College 2019–2024; The Commissioners," https://ec.europa.eu/commission/commissioners/2019-2024_en.

52. Rokhaya Diallo, "Marine Le Pen Is Now Part of France's Mainstream: That Should Scare Us All," W*ashington Post*, April 25, 2022, https://www.washingtonpost.com/opinions/2022/04/25/marine-le-pen-france-elections-mainstream-macron/.

53. Michel Wieviorka, *Le Front National: Entre extrémisme, populisme et démocratie* (Paris: Editions de la Maison des sciences de l'homme, 2013), 8.

54. Ann Laura Stoler, *Duress: Imperial Durabilities in Our Times* (Durham, NC: Duke University Press, 2016), Kindle; Ann Laura Stoler, "Colonial Aphasia: Race and Disabled Histories in France," *Public Culture* 1, no. 23 (January 2011): 1, 125.

55. Priscillia Ludosky, "Pour une Baisse des Prix du Carburant à la Pompe," *Change.org*, https://www.change.org/p/pour-une-baisse-des-prix-%C3%A0-la-pompe-essence-diesel.

56. France 24 News, "France Arrests 21 after Hundreds of African Migrants Occupy Pantheon," July 13, 2019, https://www.france24.com/en/20190713-undocumented-migrants-occupy-paris-pantheon-black-vests-protest?ref=fb.

57. "Elections européennes 2019 explorez les résultats du vote en France, ville par ville," *Le Monde*, May 26, 2019, https://www.lemonde.fr/les-decodeurs/article/2019/05/26/elections-europeennes-les-resultats-en-france_5467599_4355770.html.

58. Cris Beauchemin, Christelle Hamel, and Patrick Simon, *Trajectoires et origines*, 4, 37.

59. National Institute for the Study of Demographics (INED), *Descendants of Immigrants by Country of Origin in 2020*, https://www.ined.fr/en/everything_about_population/data/france/immigrants-foreigners/descendants-of-immigrants-by-country-of-origin/.

60. American Sociological Association, *The Importance of Collecting Data and Doing Social Scientific Research on Race* (Washington, DC: American Sociological Association, 2003).

61. FRA, *Equality in the EU*.

62. Beauchemin et al., *TeO*, 41; Patrick Simon, *French National Identity and Integration: Who Belongs to the National Community*, Executive Summary (Washington, DC: Migration Policy Institute, 2012), 3. Survey data are collected on the second generation (the Labor Force Survey and Housing Survey, for example), but there is an overall lack of data on this population group. Data on religion, gathered mainly in polls and opinion surveys, are even scarcer.

63. These comments derive from our written response to the draft of *Being Black in the EU*, March 2018.

64. European Parliament, *On Fundamental Rights*, point C.

65. Beauchemin et al., *TeO*, 28.

66. Abdellali Hajjat, "Reflections on the Problem of Racism in France," *Discover Society*, https://archive.discoversociety.org/2020/07/01/reflections-on-the-problem-of-racism-in-france/; or "Réflexions sur le problème raciste," *Savoir/Agir* 1, no. 55 (2021): 25–32, https://www.cairn.info/revue-savoir-agir-2021-1-page-25.htm.

67. Anonymous, email to author, August 6, 2021.

68. Annonymous, email to author, May 1, 2020.

69. Wendy D. Roth, "The Multiple Dimensions of Race," *Ethnic and Racial Studies* 39, no. 8 (2016): 1329.

70. Stuart Hall, "Minimal Selves," in *Identity: The Real Me*, ed. Homi Bhabha and Lisa Appignanesi (London: Institute of Contemporary Arts, 1987), 44–45.

71. FRA, *Being Black in the EU*.

72. Parliamentary Assembly of the Council of Europe, *Promoting the Rights of Persons Belonging to National Minorities* (Council of Europe, 2018), https://pace.coe.int/en/files/25226/html#_TOC_d19e50.

73. Parliamentary Assembly, *Promoting the Rights of Persons Belonging to National Minorities*. On this point, see section 4.2.

74. Council of Europe, "Country-Specific Monitoring of the Implementation of the Framework Convention for the Protection of National Minorities," https://www.coe.int/en/web/minorities/country-specific-monitoring. As indicated in this document, "Belgium, Greece,

Iceland, and Luxembourg have signed but not yet ratified the Framework Convention. Andorra, France, Monaco and Turkey have neither signed nor ratified the Framework Convention." Of the Council of Europe's 47 member states, the Framework Convention is in force in 39 European states.

75. Council of Europe, "Framework Convention for the Protection of Minorities," https://rm.coe.int/fcnm-leaflet-2020-en-final/1680a0bacc.

76. Simon, "French National Identity and Integration," 14.

77. Pierre Sorgue, "Ne nous libérez pas, on s'en charge: Le cri des afroféministes," *Le Monde*, June 16, 2017, https://www.lemonde.fr/m-actu/article/2017/06/16/ne-nous-liberez-pas-on-s-en -charge-le-cri-des-afrofeministes_5145330_4497186.html#Scz3BmVgMciS2Wwe.99; see also Mwasi, Collectif Afrofeministe, *Afrofem* (Paris: Editions Syllepse, 2018).

78. See Cole Stangler, "France Is Becoming More Like America. It's Terrible," *New York Times*, June, 2, 2021, https://www.nytimes.com/2021/06/02/opinion/france-cnews-americanization .html. Departing from her position with MAWSI, Audrey Pulvar defended "non-mixed meetings" during her bid for the presidential elections in 2021. See "Audrey Pulvar s'attire les foudres de la droite et de l'extrême droite en réagissant aux 'réunions non mixtes,'" *Le Monde*, March 28, 2021, https://www.lemonde.fr/politique/article/2021/03/28/audrey-pulvar -s-attire-les-foudres-de-la-droite-et-de-l-extreme-droite-en-reagissant-aux-reunions-non -mixtes_6074747_823448.html.

79. Sorgue, "Ne nous libérez pas, on s'en charge."

80. Erik Bleich, *Race Politics in Britain and France: Ideas and Policymaking since the 1960s* (Cambridge: Cambridge University Press, 2003).

81. Sibeth Ndiaye, "Nous payons aujourd'hui l'effacement de l'universalisme républicain," *Le Monde*, June 13, 2020, https://www.lemonde.fr/idees/article/2020/06/13/sibeth-ndiaye-nous -payons-aujourd-hui-l-effacement-de-l-universalisme-republicain_6042708_3232.html.

82. Irène Ahmadi, "Macron juge le 'monde universitaire coupable' d'avoir 'cassé la République en deux,'" *Les Inrockuptibles*, June, 11, 2020, https://www.lesinrocks.com/2020/06/11/actu alite/societe/macron-juge-le-monde-universitaire-coupable-davoir-casse-la-republique -en-deux/.

83. Norimitsu Onishi, "Will American Ideas Tear France Apart? Some of Its Leaders Think So," *New York Times*, February 9, 2021, https://www.nytimes.com/2021/02/09/world/europe /france-threat-american-universities.html.

84. Magali Bessone and Daniel Sabbagh, *Race, Racisme, Discriminations: Anthologie de textes fondamentaux* (Paris: Hermann Editeurs, 2015), 6. For more on antiracism laws in the post– World War II era, see Givens and Evans Case, *Legislating Equality*, and Erik Bleich, *The Freedom to Be Racist?* (Oxford: Oxford University Press, 2011).

85. Juliette Galonnier and Patrick Simon, "Le comité pour l'élimination de la discrimination raciale: Une approche pragmatique des statistiques ethniques (1970–2018)," *Critique internationale* 1, no. 86 (2020), 67–90.

86. Bessone and Sabbagh, *Race, Racisme, Discrimination*, 6. For a similar argument about an idiom of taboo terms related to race, such as multiculturalism and race relations, see Alec G. Hargreaves, *Multi-Ethnic France: Immigration, Politics, Culture and Society* (London: Routledge, 2007), 9–10.

87. Bessone and Sabbagh, *Race, Racisme, Discrimination*, 7.

88. My interventions since the early 2000s have ranged from conferences to conceptualizing and directing the first-ever film festival on "Black France" in 2010, to study-abroad courses on Black Paris and Black France, to inviting scholars and activists to my universities to address these questions.

89. "Le 'décolonialisme,' une stratégie hégémonique: L'appel de 80 intellectuels," *Le Point*, November 11, 2018, https://www.lepoint.fr/politique/le-decolonialisme-une-strategie-hegemonique-l-appel-de-80-intellectuels-28-11-2018-2275104_20.php.

90. This incident was covered widely in French media and online. Videl was denounced by many academics and a number of petitions circulated, calling for her resignation. See, for instance, "'Islamo-gauchisme': Nous, universitaires et chercheurs, demandons avec force la démission de Frédérique Vidal," *Le Monde*, February 21, 2021, https://www.lemonde.fr/idees/article/2021/02/20/islamo-gauchisme-nous-universitaires-et-chercheurs-demandons-avec-force-la-demission-de-frederique-vidal_6070663_3232.html.

91. Change.org, "Démission de Frédérique Vidal," https://www.change.org/p/emmanuel-macron-d%C3%A9mission-de-fr%C3%A9d%C3%A9rique-vidal-913c539f-d185-4ebf-bf45-3782e4aeefef?recruiter=74639307&recruited_by_id=4db6dcf7-58d2-4eda-ba44-658e33317aa5.

92. "French academics blast minister's warning on 'Islamo-leftism,'" France 24, February 17, 2021, https://www.france24.com/en/france/20210217-french-academics-blast-minister-s-warning-on-islamo-leftism; Norimitsu Onishi, "Will American Ideas Tear France Apart? Some of Its Leaders Think So," *New York Times*, February 9, 2021/updated April 7, 2021, https://www.nytimes.com/2021/02/09/world/europe/france-threat-american-universities.html.

93. Stéphane Beaud and Gérard Noiriel, "'Racisme anti-Blancs,' non à une imposture!," *Le Monde*, November 14, 2012, https://www.lemonde.fr/idees/article/2012/11/14/racisme-anti-blanc-non-a-une-imposture_1790315_3232.html; Beaud and Noiriel, "Who Do You Think You Are?," *Le monde Diplomatique*, February 2021, https://mondediplo.com/2021/02/10race; Beaud and Noiriel, *Race et sciences sociales. Essai sur les usages publics d'une catégorie* (Marseilles: Agone, 2021).

94. Abdellali Hajjat and Silyane Larcher, "Intersectionnalité: Introduction au dossier," *Mouvements*, February 12, 2019, https://mouvements.info/intersectionnalite/; see also Lila Belkacem, Lucia Direnberger, Karim Hammou, and Zacharias Zoubir, "Prendre au sérieux les recherches sur les rapports sociaux de race," *Mouvements*, February 12, 2019, https://mouvements.info/prendre-au-serieux-les-recherches-sur-les-rapports-sociaux-de-race/.

95. Hajjat and Larcher, "Intersectionnalité." See also Silyane Larcher, "Sur les ruses de la raison nationale généalogie de la question raciale et universalisme français," *Mouvements*, February 12, 2019, https://mouvements.info/sur-les-ruses-de-la-raison-nationale.

96. Didier Fassin and Éric Fassin, *De la question sociale à la question raciale? Représenter la société française* (Paris: La Découverte, 2006).

97. Ndiaye, *La Condition Noire*.

98. Charles W. Mills, *The Racial Contract* (Ithaca: Cornell University Press, 1997). Mills writes that the racial contract is "the contract between those categorized as white over the non-whites, who are thus the objects rather than subjects."

99. Robin D. G. Kelley, "A Poetics of Anticolonialism," foreword to Aimé Césaire, *Discourse on Colonialism* (New York: Monthly Review Press, 2000 [1950]), 7; Césaire, *Discourse on Colonialism*, 9.

100. Césaire, *Discourse on Colonialism*, 36–37.

101. Frantz Fanon, "Racism and Culture," in *Toward the African Revolution: Political Essays* (New York: Grove Press, 1964), 33.

102. Crystal Fleming, *Resurrecting Slavery: Racial Legacies and White Supremacy in France* (Philadelphia: Temple University Press, 2017), 17.

103. Aurelien Breeden, "France Announces New Measures to Tackle Domestic Violence," *New York Times*, November 25, 2019, https://www.nytimes.com/2019/11/25/world/europe /france-domestic-violence.html.

104. Assemblée nationale, "Répartition des députés hommes femmes 2019," accessed April 25, 2002, http://www.assemblee-nationale.fr/dyn/vos-deputes.

105. Sénat, "Liste des Sénatrices," accessed April 25, 2002, https://www.senat.fr/senateurs/femsen .html.

106. Sénat, "Vos Sénateurs," accessed April 25, 2002, https://www.senat.fr/elus.html.

107. Elsa Dorlin, *La matrice de la race. Généalogie sexuelle et coloniale de la nation française* (Paris: La Découverte, 2009).

108. Trica Keaton, "Racial Profiling and the 'French Exception,'" *French Cultural Studies* 24, no. 2 (2013): 231–242.

109. "Hollande propose de supprimer le mot "race" dans la Constitution," *Le Monde*, March 11, 2012, https://www.lemonde.fr/election-presidentielle-2012/article/2012/03/11/hollande-propose -de-supprimer-le-mot-race-dans-la-constitution_1656110_1471069.html.

#YOUKNOWYOUREBLACKINFRANCEWHEN . . . :

1. Frantz Fanon, *Black Skin, White Masks* (New York: Grove Atlantic, 2008 [1952]), 108–109.

2. Interview in the home of this couple, June 2017.

3. "Mobilisation en France contre les violences policières, des tensions à Paris," *Le Monde*, June 12, 2020, https://www.lemonde.fr/societe/article/2020/06/12/violences-policieres-nou velle-mobilisation-en-france-samedi_6042699_3224.html.

4. Philomena Essed, *Everyday Racism: Reports from Women in Two Cultures* (Claremont, CA: Hunter House, 1990), 31.

5. Leslie Houts Picca and Joe Feagin, *Two-Faced Racism: Whites in the Backstage and Frontstage* (New York: Routledge, 2007). Eduardo Bonilla-Silva makes a similar argument in *Racism without Racists: Color-Blind Racism and the Persistence of Racial Inequality in the United States* (Lanham, MD: Rowman & Littlefield, 2006).

6. Philomena Essed and Sara Louise Muhr, "Entitlement Racism and Its Intersections: An Interview with Philomena Essed, Social Justice Scholar," *Ephemera: Theory and Politics Organization* 18, no. 1 (2018): 188.

7. Naomi Murakawa, "Racial Innocence: Law, Social Science, and the Unknowing of Racism in the US Carceral State," *Annual Review of Law and Social Science* 15 (2019): 474.

8. Murakawa, "Racial Innocence," 475.

9. *Renoi* is French urban argot for *noir* made by reversing the syllables in words, as in *cimer* for *merci* or *beur* for *Arabe*.

10. This attack played heavily in the media. See, for instance, Sam Ball, "Jail Time for Ex-National Front Candidate Over 'Monkey' Jibe," France 24, July 16, 2014, https://www.france 24.com/en/20140716-christiane-taubira-monkey-jibe-ex-national-front-candidate-leclere -jail-sentence. In 2014, the courts in French Guiana, where she had been condemned, over-turned a sentence of nine months in prison, fines, and other sanctions against Leclère. In 2016, the penal court in Paris issued a symbolic ruling that was widely condemned by antiracism groups: a suspended 3,000 euro fine for essentially racism.

11. France TV, "#RacismeOrdinaire: Les mots qui font mal," https://temoignages.francetv.fr /racisme-ordinaire/les-mots-qui-font-mal_100.html.

12. When the hashtag was released in 2015, social network users in France comprised only 34% of the population, with Twitter having a 14% user commitment and the lion's share going to Facebook at 65%. Statista Research Department, "Distribution of Engagement on Social Networks in France and the United States in 2015, by Platform and Country," Sprinklr, February 2016, https://www.statista.com/statistics/766731/ventilation-commitment-sure-the -networks-social-by-platform-la-france-states-united/.

13. *Où sont les Noirs?*, dir. Rokhaya Diallo (Redstone and Les Bons Clients, 2019).

14. Ellen Jacob, "Substitutes," accessed April 25, 2022, https://ellenjacob.com/projects/sub stitutes/statement.

15. Tamara R. Mose, *Raising Brooklyn: Nannies, Childcare, and Caribbeans Creating Community* (New York: NYU Press, 2011).

16. Caroline Ibos, *Qui gardera nos enfants? Les nounous et les mères* (Paris: Flammarion, 2012), 37, 43.

17. Ibos, *Qui gardera nos enfants*, 45.

18. Ibos, *Qui gardera nos enfants*, 45, 180.

19. Chris Wilson, "uknowurblack," *The Root*, September 9, 2009, https://www.theroot.com /uknowurblack-1790870196.

20. T. E. Ford and M. A. Ferguson, "Social Consequences of Disparagement Humor: A Preju-diced Norm Theory," *Personality and Social Psychology Review* 8, no. 1 (2004): 79. See also Michael Haugh, "'Just Kidding': Teasing and Claims to Non-Serious Intent," *Journal of Prag-matics* 95 (April 2016): 120.

21. Haugh, "Just Kidding," 129.

22. Haugh, "Just Kidding," 129.

23. Both quotes from interview, café in Paris, August 2016.

24. Bénédicte Boisseron, *Afro-Dog: Blackness and the Animal Question* (New York: Columbia Uni-versity Press, 2018), Kindle.

25. Mehdi Ba, "'L'Africain' de Michel Leeb: 'Pas une once de racisme,' vraiment?," *Jeune Afrique*, November 9, 2017, https://www.jeuneafrique.com/491126/societe/lafricain-de-michel-leeb-pas-une-once-de-racisme-vraiment/.

26. Laurent Marskick, "'Dix petits nègres': Le best-seller d'Agatha Christie débaptisé," *RTL*, August 26, 2020, https://www.rtl.fr/culture/arts-spectacles/dix-petits-negres-le-best-seller-d-agatha-christie-debaptise-7800747182.

27. Raphaël Enthoven, Twitter post, August 26, 2020, 4:35 a.m., https://twitter.com/Enthoven_R/status/1298539646599782400.

28. Achille Mbembe, *Critique of Black Reason* (Durham, NC: Duke University Press, 2019), Kindle, 38; Mbembe, *Critique de la raison nègre* (Paris: La Découverte, 2019), 76.

29. For a tweeted image of the protest, see *Libération*, "Appel à témoignages: C'est quoi être noir(e) en France, au quotidien ? Racontez-nous," *Libération*, July 1, 2015, https://www.liberation.fr/societe/2015/07/01/c-est-quoi-etre-noire-en-france-au-quotidien-racontez-nous_1340838/.

30. Media coverage was widespread, and this incident went viral on social media. See Durupt Frantz, "Polémique Laurence Rossignol et les 'nègres qui étaient pour l'esclavage,'" *Libération*, March 30, 2016, https://www.liberation.fr/france/2016/03/30/laurence-rossignol-et-les-negres-qui-etaient-pour-l-esclavage_1442820/.

31. "Laurence Rossignol évoque les 'nègres' puis concède une 'faute de langage,'" *Europe 1*, March 30, 2016, https://www.europe1.fr/politique/laurence-rossignol-evoque-les-negres-puis-concede-une-faute-de-langage-2706883.

32. Gaëlle Dupont, "Les propos de Laurence Rossignol comparant le voile à l'esclavage soulèvent un tollé," *Le Monde*, March 31, 2016, https://www.lemonde.fr/societe/article/2016/03/31/laurence-rossignol-les-negres-et-le-voile_4892777_3224.html.

33. This story circulated widely in mainstream and social media. See also Isabelle Boni-Claverie, *Trop noire pour être française* (Paris: Editions Tallandier), Kindle.

34. Boni-Claverie, *Trop Noire*.

35. Boni-Claverie, *Trop Noire*.

36. Boni-Claverie, *Trop Noire*; Nicole Vulser, "Guerlain, Guerlain, le nègre vous emmerde!," *Le Monde*, October 25, https://www.lemonde.fr/economie/article/2010/10/25/guerlain-guerlain-le-negre-vous-emmerde_1430871_3234.html.

37. Marie Treps, *Maudits Mots: La fabrique des insultes racistes* (Paris: TohuBohu Editions, 2017), 243; "'Bamboula, ça reste encore à peu près convenable,' lâche un syndicaliste policier sur France 5," France Info, February 9, 2017, https://www.francetvinfo.fr/faits-divers/arrestation-violente-a-aulnay-sous-bois/video-bamboula-ca-reste-encore-a-peu-pres-convenable-dit-un-syndicaliste-policier-dans-c-a-vous_2055347.html.

38. *Négro* and *nègre* fall within French n-word idiom that has also undergone stigma reversal, as in the United States, as these words can function as intragroup terms of endearment and subjectivity. Echoing others, an interviewee in his thirties explained *négro* this way: "Yes, it's a really an affectionate word between us. //T: like nigga?// Yes, yes absolutely //T: like how Jay-Z uses it?// Yes. *Négro* is a very very exclusive term"—but as an antiblack attack its use is very violent.

39. Maboula Soumahoro, *Black Is the Journey, Africana the Name* (Cambridge: Polity, 2021), Kindle, and Soumahoro, *Le Triangle et l'Hexagone* (Paris: La Découverte, 2021).

40. Mbembe, *Critique of Black Reason*, Kindle.

41. W. de Saint Just, Twitter, August 29, 2020, 3:52 a.m., https://twitter.com/wdesaintjust/status /1299615957359493120.

42. Ariane Chemin and François Krug, "Entre Emmanuel Macron et 'Valeurs actuelles,' les secrets d'un flirt," *Le Monde*, October 31, 2019, https://www.lemonde.fr/politique/article /2019/10/31/entre-emmanuel-macron-et-valeurs-actuelles-les-secrets-d-un-flirt_6017528 _823448.html.

43. See Salomé Vincendon, "'J'ai mal à ma France:' Danièle Obono Répond à Valeurs Actuelles Après Leur 'Souillure,'" BFMTV, August 29, 2020, https://www.bfmtv.com/politique/j -ai-mal-a-ma-france-daniele-obono-repond-a-valeurs-actuelles-apres-leur-souillure_AV -202008290120.html; Outre-Mer, "Représentée en esclave par Valeurs actuelles, la députée Danièle Obono dénonce 'un racisme abject,'" France Info, August 29, 2020, https://la1ere .francetvinfo.fr/representee-esclave-valeurs-actuelles-deputee-daniele-obono-denonce -racisme-abject-866098.html.

44. Boni-Claverie, email to author, June 17, 2020.

45. Dienke Hondius, *Blackness in Western Europe: Racial Patterns of Paternalism and Exclusion* (New Brunswick: Transaction Publisher, 2014), Kindle.

46. Jordan Bardella, Twitter, July 23, 2019, 2:32 a.m., https://twitter.com/J_Bardella/status /1153553421871583232.

47. Nadine Morano, Twitter, July 16, 2019, 1:41 a.m., https://twitter.com/nadine__morano/status /1152091022320648193.

48. Annette Joseph-Gabriel, *Reimagining Liberation: How Black Women Transformed Citizenship in the French Empire* (Urbana: University of Illinois Press, 2020). See also Lorelle Semley, "Women Citizens of the French Union Unite! Jane Vialle's Post-war Crusade," in *Gender and Citizenship in Historical and Transnational Perspective: Agency, Space, Borders*, ed. Anne R. Epstein and Rachel G. Fuchs (London: Palgrave Macmillan, 2017).

49. These events were widely covered in the media, which political opponents cast as fake news until video surfaced showing the incident. See Richard Poirot, "'Taubira traitée de 'guenon': La vidéo qui le prouve," *Libération*, November 2, 2013, https://www.liberation.fr /societe/2013/11/02/taubira-traitee-de-guenon-la-video-qui-le-prouve_944083/, and "La vidéo de Christiane Taubira insultée à Angers," *Le Figaro*, November 2, 2013, https://www.lefigaro .fr/actualite-france/2013/11/02/01016-20131102ARTFIG00294-la-video-choc-de-christiane -taubira-insultee-a-angers.php.

50. Tony Cross, "Far-Right Paper Causes Storm with Racist Insult to French Justice Minister Taubira," *RFI*, November 11, 2013, https://www.rfi.fr/en/france/20131113-far-right-paper -causes-storm-racist-insult-french-justice-minister-taubira.

51. Angela Giuffrida, "Senator Convicted Over Racist Remark about Italy's First Black Minister," *Guardian*, January 14, 2019, https://www.theguardian.com/world/2019/jan/14/league -senator-convicted-for-racist-remark-about-italy-first-black-minister-roberto-calderoli-cecile -kyenge.

52. The European Parliament Anti-Racism and Diversity Intergroup (ARDI), "Letter to UEFA about Racism and Discrimination in Football," European Parliament Anti-Racism and Diversity Intergroup (ARDI), November 20, 2019, https://www.ardi-ep.eu/letter-to-uefa-about-racism-and-discrimination-in-football/.

53. *Mediapart* covered extensively this investigation and subsequent "Football Leaks" and financial scandals involving French professional football. Fabrice Arfi, Mathilde Mathieu, and Michaël Hajdenberg, "French Football Ethnic Quota Plan: The Verbatim Record of the Closed-door Discussions," *Mediapart*, May 1, 2011, https://www.mediapart.fr/en/journal/france/300411/french-football-ethnic-quota-plan-verbatim-record-closed-door-discussions?_locale=en&onglet=full.

54. Clément Guillou and Maxime Goldbaum, "'Noirs costauds' et 'Blancs intelligents': Comment le sport entretient les préjugés raciaux," *Le Monde*, November 9, 2019, https://www.lemonde.fr/sport/article/2018/11/09/noirs-costauds-et-blancs-intelligents-comment-le-sport-entretient-les-prejuges-raciaux_5381505_3242.html.

55. Guillou and Goldbaum, "'Noirs costauds' et 'Blancs intelligents.'"

56. Guillou and Goldbaum, "'Noirs costauds' et 'Blancs intelligents.'"

57. BBC News, "Chelsea Fans Guilty Over Paris Metro Racism," *BBC News*, January 3, 2017, https://www.bbc.com/news/uk-england-london-38501033.

58. "Racisme: De la prison avec sursis pour quatre supporters anglais racistes," France Info, January 3, 2017, https://www.francetvinfo.fr/sports/supporters-de-chelsea/racisme-de-la-prison-avec-sursis-pour-quatre-supporters-anglais-racistes_1999613.html.

59. Louis Chude-Sokei, *The Last "Darky": Bert Williams, Black-on-Black Minstrelsy, and the African Diaspora* (Durham, NC: Duke University Press, 2006), 54. For a fascinating history of blackface and other antiblack representations in US popular culture, see Henry Louis Gates Jr.'s PBS documentary, *Reconstruction: America After the Civil War*, part 2, hour 2, https://www.pbs.org/weta/reconstruction/.

60. Gloria Wekker, *White Innocence: Paradoxes of Colonialism and Race* (Durham, NC: Duke University Press, 2016), 140–141.

61. The outcry from antiracism associations about this "harmless fun" compelled the French Rights Defender to recommend sanctions against the officers, but the decision has had no real teeth at a societal level. "Policiers grimés en Noirs [capitalization theirs] lors d'une soirée: Le défenseur des droits demande des sanctions," *20 Minutes*, March 28, 2017, https://www.20minutes.fr/societe/2039123-20170328-policiers-grimes-noirs-lors-soiree-defenseur-droits-demande-sanctions.

62. Des Bieler, "French Soccer Star Defends Blackface Costume as a 'Tribute' before Apologizing," *Washington Post*, December 17, 2017, https://www.washingtonpost.com/news/early-lead/wp/2017/12/17/french-soccer-star-defends-blackface-costume-as-a-tribute-before-apologizing/; "Antoine Griezmann Apologises for Painting Himself Black at Party," *Guardian*, December 18, 2017, https://www.theguardian.com/football/2017/dec/18/antoine-griezmann-aplogises-painting-himself-black.

63. Conseil Représentatif des Associations Noires (CRAN), "Scandale: Blackface chez Altran," December 13, 2017, http://le-cran.fr/scandale-blackface-chez-altran/.

64. Kim Willsher, "Greek Tragedy Prompts 'Blackface' Racism Row at Sorbonne," *Guardian*, March 28, 2019, https://www.theguardian.com/world/2019/mar/28/sorbonne-at-centre-of-racism-row-after-alleged-blackface-in-theatre-show.

65. Ministre de la Culture, République Française, Communiqués de Presse, "Réaction de Frédérique VIDAL et de Franck RIESTER à la perturbation de la pièce de théâtre Les Suppliantes en Sorbonne," March 27, 2019, https://www.culture.gouv.fr/Presse/Communiques-de-presse/Reaction-de-Frederique-VIDAL-et-de-Franck-RIESTER-a-la-perturbation-de-la-piece-de-theatre-Les-Suppliantes-en-Sorbonne.

66. Laurent Carpentier, "A la Sorbonne, la guerre du 'blackface' gagne la tragédie grecque," March 27, 2019, https://www.lemonde.fr/culture/article/2019/03/27/a-la-sorbonne-la-guerre-du-blackface-gagne-la-tragedie-grecque_5441663_3246.html.

67. All quotes in this paragraph were emailed to the author, December 17, 2018.

68. Didier Reynders, Twitter, March 14, 2015, 4:45 p.m., https://twitter.com/dreynders/status/576846512992489472.

69. "Les "Noirauds" changent de maquillage pour mettre fin à la polémique," *Médias de Bruxelles*, March 1, 2019, https://bx1.be/communes/bruxelles-ville/noirauds-changent-de-maquillage-mettre-fin-a-polemique/.

70. France Info: Hauts-de-France, "Dunkerque: la justice autorise la 'Nuit des Noirs,' les associations dénoncent un 'racisme d'État,'" March 9, 2018, https://france3-regions.francetvinfo.fr/hauts-de-france/nord-o/dunkerque-justice-autorise-nuit-noirs-associations-denoncent-racisme-etat-1437763.html.

71. "Carnaval: Le maire de Dunkerque défend la 'Nuit des Noirs' et 'un droit à la caricature,'" France Info: Hauts-de-France, February 11, 2018, https://france3-regions.francetvinfo.fr/hauts-de-france/nord-o/dunkerque/carnaval-maire-dunkerque-defend-nuit-noirs-droit-caricature-1421821.html. See also "Louis-Georges Tin: 'Le blackface est l'envers grimaçant de l'esclavage,'" *Le Monde*, February 10, 2018, https://www.lemonde.fr/idees/article/2018/02/10/louis-georges-tin-le-blackface-est-l-envers-grimacant-de-l-esclavage_5254667_3232.html.

72. Lauren Michele Jackson, "The Women 'Blackfishing' on Instagram Aren't Exactly Trying to Be Black," *Slate*, November 29, 2018, https://slate.com/culture/2018/11/blackfishing-instagram-models-emma-hallberg-appropriation.html. Variations on the blackface theme over the years in European countries include the "Venus Hottentot" cake in Sweden in 2012; Spanish actress Paz Vega becoming "chocolate" in the Magnum chocolate multimedia ad campaign in 2011 in Spain; and in that same year, related to France, Beyoncé's blacking up, for the cover of the magazine *l'Officiel Paris* in a tribute to Fela Kuti, the pioneering Nigerian musician. In Germany, there was the unforgettable UNICEF ad campaign in 2007 to "help repair 350 schools and educate 100,000 African children" that featured grinning white children with mud on their face, a variation on blackface. Jennifer Brea, "Saving Africa in blackface," *Guardian*, July 25, 2007, https://www.theguardian.com/commentisfree/2007/jul/25/savingafricainblackface.

73. Jackson, "The Women 'Blackfishing' on Instagram Aren't Exactly Trying to Be Black."

74. European Parliament, *On Fundamental Rights of People of African descent in Europe* (2018/2899(RSP)), March 29, 2018, http://www.europarl.europa.eu/doceo/document/B-8-2019-0212_EN.html, section G.

1. Frantz Fanon, *Peau Noire, Masques Blancs* (Montreal: Kiyikaat Éditions, 2015), 183. I have retained the French term, *nègre*, used by Fanon in relation to the material in this chapter.

2. Fanon, *Peau Noire*, 211.

3. Anne Lafont, "How Skin Color Became a Racial Marker: Art Historical Perspectives on Race," *Eighteenth-Century Studies* 51, no. 1 (2017): 90.

4. Kimberly Juanita Brown, email to author, February 24, 2021. See also Kimberly Juanita Brown, *Mortevivum: Photography and the Politics of the Visual* (Cambridge, MA: MIT Press, forthcoming).

5. "Au nègre joyeux, 19 rue Mouffetard," *Paris Villages* (January 2003), no. 1.

6. This quote derives from documents provided by Buffon Library (Bibliothèque Buffon), "Au nègre joyeux, 19 [*sic*] rue Mouffetard" *Paris Villages* (January 2003). See also "Don de l'enseigne 'Au nègre joyeux,' no. 14 rue Mouffetard à la ville de Paris," *Paris Villages* (January 2003): 130.

7. Philomena Essed and David Theo Goldberg, "Cloning Cultures: The Social Injustices of Sameness," *Ethnic and Racial Studies* 25, no. 6 (2002): 1070.

8. Scott Akalis, Mahzarin Banaji, and Stephen Kosslyn, "Crime Alert! How Thinking about a Single Suspect Automatically Shifts Stereotypes toward an Entire Group," *DuBois Review: Social Science Essays and Research on Race* 5 (2008): 227.

9. Lewis Gordon, *What Fanon Said: A Philosophical Introduction to His Life and Thought* (New York: Fordham University Press, 2015), Kindle.

10. Phillip Goff, Jennifer Eberhardt, et al., "Not Yet Human: Implicit Knowledge, Historical Dehumanization, and Contemporary Consequences," *Journal of Personality and Social Psychology* 94 (2008): 305; Andrew Scott Baron and Mahzarin R. Banaji, "The Development of Implicit Attitudes Evidence of Race Evaluations from Ages 6 and 10 and Adulthood," *Journal of Psychological Science* 17, no. 1 (2006): 53–58; Joseph Graves and Alan Goodman, *Racism Not Race: Answers to Frequently Asked Questions* (New York: Columbia University Press, 2021), 40.

11. Marita Sturken and Lisa Cartwright, *Practices of Looking* (New York: Oxford University Press. 2018), 13.

12. Susan J. Terrio, *Crafting the Culture and History of French Chocolate* (Berkeley: University of California Press, 2000), 248, 249.

13. Fanon, *Black Skin, White Masks*, 32. In the same footnote, Fanon cites anthropologist Geoffrey Gorer who expands on the grin, writing: "Nevertheless the whites demand that the blacks be smiling, attentive and friendly in all their relationships with them" in order to demonstrate that they are not a threat.

14. Guillaume Poingt, "Un boulanger retire son gâteau 'Mamadou,' jugé raciste, et s'excuse," *Le Figaro*, February, 21, 2019, https://www.lefigaro.fr/flash-eco/un-boulanger-retire-son -gateau-mamadou-juge-raciste-et-s-excuse-20190221.

15. Christina Boyle, "Greenwich Village Bakery Owner Causes Uproar with 'Drunken Negro Face' Obama Cookies," *Daily News*, January 23, 2009, https://www.nydailynews.com/news/green wich-village-bakery-owner-uproar-drunken-negro-face-obama-cookies-article-1.424639.

16. Dana S. Hale, *Races on Display: French Representations of Colonized Peoples, 1886–1940* (Bloomington: Indiana University Press, 2008), Kindle. See also Hale's article, "French Images of Race on Product Trademarks during the Third Republic," in *The Color of Liberty*, 131–146.

17. Franck Freitas-Ekué, "Corps Black: Généalogie d'une production et d'une valorisation marchande du corps noir sous l'industrialisation capitaliste," PhD diss., Université Paris 8—Vincennes—Saint-Denis, 2021.

18. Kimberly Brown, email to author, December 20, 2021.

19. Robin Mitchell, *Vénus Noire: Black Women and Colonial Fantasies in Nineteenth-Century France* (Athens: University of Georgia Press, 2020).

20. See also Anna Radwan, *Paris 5e arrondissement* (Paris: Parimagine, 2006), 206.

21. Robert Sivard, "Painters Luck," *Time*, April 18, 1955, 75.

22. Official from City of Paris, email to author, July 1, 2014.

23. For more insights into Black associations and leadership in metropolitan France, see Abdoulaye Gueye, "The Labyrinth to Blackness: On Naming and Leadership in the Black Associative Space in France," *French Cultural Studies* 24, no. 2 (May 2013), and Vanessa Thompson's forthcoming book on antiblackness and social mobilizations in metropolitan France.

24. La B.A.N., "Bannie de la commémoration de l'abolition de l'esclavage," May 23, 2013, https://www.youtube.com/watch?v=OKXERayxiOA.

25. Trica Keaton, "Au Nègre Joyeux: Everyday Anti-Blackness on 14 Rue Mouffetard," paper presented at Black Portraiture[s]: The Black Body in the West, New York University and Harvard University, Paris, France, January 2013. Other public lectures include presentations at the annual meetings of the International Sociological Association in 2014 and Council of European Studies in 2015. See also Trica Keaton, "Au Nègre Joyeux: Everyday Antiblackness Guised as Public Art," *Nka: Journal of Contemporary African Art* 38–39 (November 2016); Vanessa Thompson, "Black Jacobins in Contemporary France: On Identities on Politics, Decolonial Critique, and the Other Blackness," *Sociological Focus* 49 (2016): 44–62.

26. Email to author from M. François Monnier, Président de la Commission des Travaux Historiques and Membre du Comite d'histoire de la ville de Paris, April 17, 2013. Tourist materials from Paris Village date the sign from 1738. See also "Don de l'enseigne 'Au nègre joyeux,'" 130. See also Kévi Donat, Le Paris Noir Afro/Black French Heritage tours, https://www.leparisnoir.com/.

27. Anne Lafont, *L'Art et la Race: L'Africain (tout) contre l'œil des Lumières* (Dijon: Les Presses du Réel, 2019), 238–239.

28. Lafont, *L'Art et la Race*, 238–239. See also Marie-Victoire Lemoine's *Portrait d'un jeune homme* (1785), which is also identified with the sign.

29. Pap Ndiaye, *Le Modèle Noir: De Géricault à Matisse, La Chronologie* (Paris: Musée d'Orsay/Flammarion, 2019), 4; Kaija Tiainen-Anttila, *The Problem of Humanity: The Blacks in the European Enlightenment* (Helsinki: Suomen Historiallinen Seura, 1984), 69.

30. Tiainen-Anttila, *The Problem of Humanity*, 69.

31. Officials at the City of Paris, email to author, July 1 and 24, 2014.

32. E. Léon Lamothe-Langon, *Memoirs of Madame Du Barri* (London: H. S. Nichols, 1896), chapter 23.

33. Lafont, "How Skin Color Became a Racial Marker," 106.

34. Lafont, "How Skin Color Became a Racial Marker," 106.

35. Adrienne L. Childs and Susan Houghton Libby, *The Black Figure in the European Imaginary* (Winter Park, FL: The Cornell Fine Arts Museum, Rollins College, 2017), 24.

36. Childs and Libby, *The Black Figure*, 26.

37. Manthia Diawara, *In Search of Africa* (Cambridge, MA: Harvard University Press, 1998), 3.

38. Official of the City of Paris, email to author, July 1, 2014.

39. On the concept of "civilizational legitimacy," see sociologist Nacira Guénif-Souilamas's observation cited in Robert Stam and Ella Shohat, *Race in Translation: Culture Wars around the Postcolonial Atlantic* (New York: NYU Press, 2012, Kindle): "the normative biopolitics that shape citizenship and subcitizenship in postcolonial France, regulat[e] the bodies and behavior of the children of immigrants of color. While the dominant discourse assumes a general freedom of self-invention for all people, the marginalized are made to feel incarcerated in their own bodies, held back by the invisible barrier that separates off those who lack "civilizational legitimacy."

40. Jean-Pierre Willesme, *Enseignes du Musée Carnavalet: Histoire de Paris* (Paris: Paris Musées, 1996).

41. Jean-Pierre Willesme, *Enseignes du Musée Carnavalet*.

42. Leora Auslander and Thomas C. Holt, "Sambo in Paris: Race and Racism in the Iconography of the Everyday," in *The Color of Liberty: Histories of Race in France*, ed. Sue Peabody and Tyler Stovall (Durham, NC: Duke University Press, 2003), 152.

43. Auslander and Holt, "Sambo in Paris," 163.

44. Auslander and Holt, "Sambo in Paris," 153–154.

45. Henry Louis Gates Jr., "Should Blacks Collect Racist Memorabilia?," PBS, accessed April 26, 2022, https://www.pbs.org/wnet/african-americans-many-rivers-to-cross/history/should-blacks-collect-racist-memorabilia/ (originally posted on *The Root*).

46. Françoise Vergès and Seumboy Vrainom, *De la violence coloniale dans l'espace public* (Paris: Shed Publishing, 2021).

47. Christian Taubira, "Introduction," in *Codes Noirs: De l'esclavage aux abolitions*, ed. André Castaldo (Paris: Editions Dalloz, 2006), ix.

48. Vergès and Vrainom, *De la violence coloniale*, 32.

49. Sihame Assbague (@s_assbague). "Franco, the activist of the Anti-Negrophobia Brigade who painted "State Negrophobia" on the statue of Colbert in front of the National Assembly, will be tried this Friday, August 14 in the Paris court." Twitter, August 13, 2020, https://twitter.com/s_assbague/status/1293902951409491969.

50. Franco Lollia and Guy Florentin, "The Black Code, Colbert, State Negrophobia, Explained to France: Time for Reparations," Facebook, June 23, 2020, https://www.facebook.com/BrigadeAntiNegrophobiePageOfficielle/.

51. Media coverage of this event was extensive. See, for instance, Morgane Bona, "French Black Activist Fined for Defacing Colonial Statue," AP News, June 28, 2021, https://apnews.com/article/french-black-activist-fined-for-defacing-colonial-statue-f9cb322307fba8c4996464bd5c7d2847.

52. Louis-Georges Tin, "Vos héros sont parfois nos bourreaux," *Libération*, August 28, 2017, https://www.liberation.fr/debats/2017/08/28/vos-heros-sont-parfois-nos-bourreaux_1592510/.

53. The "grand replacement" thesis, also known as the "white extinction" narrative, has deep roots in Europe and the United States and was repopularized in 2012 by Renaud Camus in his similarly titled book. Camus, no relation to Albert Camus, is a staunch supporter of Marine Le Pen and a darling of white nativists. See also Thomas Chatterton Williams, "The French Origins of 'You Will Not Replace Us': The European Thinkers behind the White-Nationalist Rallying Cry," *New Yorker*, November 27, 2017, https://www.newyorker.com/magazine/2017/12/04/the-french-origins-of-you-will-not-replace-us.

54. "Mobilisation en France contre les violences policières, des tensions à Paris," *Le Monde*, June 12, 2022, https://www.lemonde.fr/societe/article/2020/06/12/violences-policieres-nouvelle-mobilisation-en-france-samedi_6042699_3224.html. See also Lauren Collins, "Assa Traoré and the Fight for Black Lives in France," *New Yorker*, June 18, 2020, https://www.newyorker.com/news/letter-from-europe/assa-traore-and-the-fight-for-black-lives-in-france.

55. Gérald Darmanin, Twitter, March 3, 2021, 6:33 a.m., https://twitter.com/GDarmanin/status/1367075681067237379.

56. "Statue de Colbert taggée: Ndiaye condamne 'ceux qui veulent effacer des traits de notre histoire,'" BFMTV, June 24, 2020, https://www.bfmtv.com/politique/statue-de-colbert-tagguee-ndiaye-condamne-ceux-qui-veulent-effacer-des-traits-de-notre-histoire_AN-202006240087.html; "Top French Historian Slams Macron's Statue Stance as Another Is Attacked," France 24, June 24, 2020, https://www.france24.com/en/20200624-top-french-historian-slams-macron-s-statue-stance-as-another-is-attacked.

57. "Statue de Colbert taggée," BFMTV; "Top French Historian Slams Macron's Statue Stance," France 24.

58. Email to author, November 2, 2020.

59. Mame-Fatou Niang and Julien Suaudeau, "Banalisation du racisme à l'Assemblée nationale: Ouvrons les yeux," *L'Obs*, April 4, 2019, https://www.nouvelobs.com/bibliobs/20190404.OBS11119/banalisation-du-racisme-au-c-ur-de-la-republique-ouvrons-les-yeux.html. See also Angelique Chrisafis, "Academics Launch Petition against 'Racist' Mural in French Parliament," *Guardian*, April 12, 2019, https://www.theguardian.com/world/2019/apr/12/academics-launch-petition-against-racist-mural-in-french-parliament.

60. Niang and Suaudeau, "Banalisation du racisme à l'Assemblée nationale."

61. Thomas Hermans, "Pétition contre une fresque célébrant l'abolition de l'esclavage à l'Assemblée nationale," *Le Figaro*, April 9, 2019, https://www.lefigaro.fr/arts-expositions/petition-contre-une-fresque-celebrant-l-abolition-de-l-esclavage-a-l-assemblee-nationale-20190409.

62. Lauren Collins, "The Campaign to Remove a Shocking Painting from the French National Assembly," *New Yorker*, April 12, 2019, https://www.newyorker.com/culture/cultural-comment/the-campaign-to-remove-a-shocking-painting-from-the-french-national-assembly.

63. Collins, "The Campaign to Remove a Shocking Painting from the French National Assembly."

64. Anna Sansom, "Petition Launched to Remove 'Racist' Anti-Slavery Fresco in France's National Assembly," *The Art Newspaper*, April 11, 2019, https://www.theartnewspaper.com/2019/04/11/petition-launched-to-remove-racist-anti-slavery-fresco-in-frances-national-assembly.

65. "Accusé de racisme, l'artiste sétois Hervé di Rosa réagit vivement," France 3 Occitanie, YouTube, April 11, 2019, https://www.youtube.com/watch?v=VSmTINuUYfc.

66. Kimberly Brown, email to author, December 20, 2021.

67. "Deux universitaires condamnent une œuvre de l'artiste sétois Hervé Di Rosa," France 3 Occitanie, YouTube, April 12, 2019, https://www.youtube.com/watch?v=Qpm4jhDVteg; and https://france3-regions.francetvinfo.fr/occitanie/herault/sete/deux-universitaires-condamnent-oeuvre-artiste-setois-herve-di-rosa-qui-eux-vehicule-racisme-1654598.html.

68. Collins, "The Campaign to Remove a Shocking Painting from the French National Assembly."

69. Annette Joseph-Gabriel, *Reimagining Liberation: How Black Women Transformed Citizenship in the French Empire* (Urbana: University of Illinois Press, 2020).

70. Mame-Fatou Niang, "Des particularités françaises de la négrophobie," in *Racismes de France*, ed. Omar Slaouti and Olivier Le Cour Grandmaison (Paris: La Découverte, 2020), 190, Kindle.

71. Tina M. Campt, *A Black Gaze: Artists Changing How We See* (Cambridge, MA: MIT Press, 2021), 47.

72. Alexis Peskine, "Artist's Statement: The French Evolution: Race, Polices and the 2005 Riots," curated by Kimberli Grant (Brooklyn, NY: The Museum of Contemporary African Diasporan Art, 2007), 9.

73. Peskine, "Artist's Statement," 9.

74. Mathieu Dejean, "Le Street artist Combo accusé de 'racisme et de "sexisme' par l'extrême droite," *Les Inrockuptibles Magazine*, June 17, 2015, https://www.lesinrocks.com/arts-et-scenes/le-street-artist-combo-accuse-de-racisme-et-de-sexisme-par-lextreme-droite-94914-17-06-2015/.

75. Alyssa Buffenstein, "Art and Law French Porn Star Vandalizes Public Mural with White Supremacist, Anti-Immigration Slogans," June 23, 2015, https://news.artnet.com/art-world/racist-porn-star-vandalizes-paris-street-art-310108.

76. Vanessa Thompson, "Black Jacobins in Contemporary France: On Identities on Politics, Decolonial Critique, and the Other Blackness," *Sociological Focus* 49 (2016): 45.

77. Fanon, *Black Skin, White Masks*, 204.

78. Fanon, *Black Skin, White Masks*, 204, 205.

79. Nora Schweitzer, "Enseignes racistes. Des enseignes héritées du temps des colonies sèment la zizanie à Paris," France 24, https://www.france24.com/fr/20170929-negre-joyeux-planteur-paris-enseigne-colonisation-racisme-esclavagisme-france; "Paris Votes to Remove Chocolate Factory's 'Happy Negro' Sign," France 24, September 27, 2017, https://www.france24.com/en/20170926-paris-votes-remove-happy-negro-sign-chocolate-factory.

1. Frantz Fanon, *The Wretched of the Earth* (New York: Grove/Atlantic, 2004/1961), 3.

2. Open Society Foundations, *L'égalité trahie: l'impact des contrôles au faciès* (*Equality Betrayed: The Impact of Racial Profiling*), YouTube, September 17, 2013, https://www.youtube.com/watch?app=desktop&v=LJbhE7FLQ3c.

3. Remarks by Minister Darmanin after the passing of the 2021 comprehensive security bill that increased powers held by the police while criminalizing attempts to record and expose police violence. Social justice groups have denounced the law, in particular a redrafted provision that makes it "punishable by up to 5 years in prison and a 75,000 euro-fine ($89,800)," to "identify on-duty police officers with 'obvious' harmful intent.'" Filming police committing acts of violence could fall under that category. Amnesty International in France also decried the bill as a threat to civil liberties. See "French Lawmakers OK Security Bill Increasing Police Powers," Associated Press, April 15, 2021, https://apnews.com/article/police-paris-france-emmanuel-macron-bills-84d29f72f1f30b1d7ec5166aaf0146b5.

4. Défenseur des droits, *Enquête sur l'accès aux droits/Relations police/population: Le cas des contrôles,* vol. 1 (Paris: République Franaise, 2017), 17. See also Human Rights Watch, *"They Talk to Us Like We're Dogs": Abusive Police Stops in France,* June 2020, https://www.hrw.org/sites/default/files/media_2020/06/France0620_web_0.pdf.

5. Ivan du Roy and Ludo Simbille, "Base de données," *Basta!*, accessed April 27, 2022, https://bastamag.net/webdocs/police/. See also European Union Agency for Fundamental Rights (FRA), *Second European Union Minorities and Discrimination Survey* (*EU-MIDIS II): Being Black in the EU* (Luxembourg: Publications Office of the European Union, 2018).

6. Patricia Hill Collins, *Black Sexual Politics: African Americans, Gender, and the New Racism* (New York: Routledge, 2005).

7. Le Collectif: Vie Volés, "Qui sommes-nous ?" April 26, 2022, https://www.viesvolees.org/le-collectif/.

8. Didier Fassin, *Enforcing Order: An Ethnography of Urban Policing* (Hoboken, NJ: Wiley, 2013), 133.

9. *Dire à Lamine*, dir. Cases Rebelles (Cases Rebelles, 2018), https://www.cases-rebelles.org/dire-a-lamine/.

10. *Dire à Lamine*, 1:00–2:32.

11. Collectif Angles Morts, *Permis de Tuer: Chronique de l'Impunité Policière* (Paris: Editions Syllepse, 2014), 60, 67.

12. To be clear, I am not criticizing researchers who have interviewed Ramata or others who have suffered trauma. It didn't feel appropriate for me at the time.

13. *Dire à Lamine*, 26:24–27:03.

14. In *James Baldwin: The Price of the Ticket*, dir. Karen Thorsen (California Newsreel, 1990), Maya Angelou states that France "is not without race prejudice . . . Algerians were the niggers of France . . . they were his [Baldwin's] brother."

15. "Le point sur l'évacuation du camp de migrants à Paris: coups de matraque et 'chasse à l'homme', indignation politique et enquêtes de l'IGPN," *Le Monde*, November 24, 2020,

https://www.lemonde.fr/societe/article/2020/11/24/un-nouveau-camp-de-migrants-au-c-ur-de
-paris-aussitot-violemment-demantele_6060869_3224.html.

16. "Afghanistan: 'L'État vise à invisibiliser' les migrants installés à Paris, dénonce l'adjoint à la mairie Ian Brossat," France Info, August, 20, 2021, https://www.francetvinfo.fr/monde /afghanistan/afghanistan-letat-vise-a-invisibiliser-les-migrants-installes-a-paris-denonce -ladjoint-a-la-mairie-ian-brossat_4743659.html.

17. Mathieu Rigouste, *La Domination Policière: Une Violence Industrielle* (Paris: La Fabrique, 2012), 23.

18. Jean-Luc Einaudi, *Octobre 1961: Un massacre à Paris* (Paris: Fayard, 2001).

19. Laila Amine, *Postcolonial Paris: Fictions of Intimacy in the City of Light* (Madison: University of Wisconsin Press, 2018). Leïla Sebbar, *The Seine Was Red: Paris, October 1961* (Bloomington: Indiana University Press, 2008). My use of "racist policing with race" is informed by the concept "racism without race"; see "Framing Everyday Antiblackness in a Raceblind France" in the appendix.

20. Sue Peabody, *"There Are No Slaves in France": The Political Culture of Race and Slavery in the Ancien Régime* (New York: Oxford University Press, 1996), Kindle.

21. For post-revolutionary legislation and lawsuits, see Pierre H. Boulle and Sue Peabody, *Le droit des noirs en France au temps de l'esclavage*, Éditions Autrement Mêmes (Paris: L'Harmattan, 2014), especially chapters 6–9; Sue Peabody, "Fantaisie, a slave belonging to the Desbassayns, applying the principle of 'Free Soil' in Paris," *Musée historique de Villèle: Slavery/ Resistance to Slavery* (2021), https://www.portail-esclavage-reunion.fr/en/documen taires/slavery/resistance-to-slavery/fantaisie-a-slave-belonging-to-desbassayns-applying -the-principle-of-sol-libre-in-paris/; and Sue Peabody, "Bissette and the *Police des Noirs*: Free Soil, Mobility, and the Status of the Patroné in Early Nineteenth Century," *French Colonial History* (forthcoming).

22. "Déclaration du Roi pour la Police des noirs, donnée à Versailles le 9 août 1777," quoted in Boulle and Peabody, *Le droit des noirs en France au temps de l'esclavage*, 99. The law goes on to say that the intent is not to deprive the colonists of their "black servants" during their journey but that "said servants" would not be allowed to disembark on mainland shores, all in the interest of preserving the decorum and orderliness of the kingdom.

23. Laurent Dubois, *A Colony of Citizens: Revolution and Slave Emancipation in the French Caribbean, 1787–1804* (Chapel Hill: University of North Carolina Press, 2012), 64.

24. Fassin, *Enforcing Order*, 9.

25. Harold Garfinkel, "Conditions of Successful Degradation Ceremonies," *American Journal of Sociology* 61, no. 5 (March 1956), 420.

26. Emmanuel Blanchard, "Contrôle au faciès: Une cérémonie de dégradation," *Plein droit* 103, no. 4 (2014): 11–15.

27. Blanchard, "Contrôle au faciès," 13–14.

28. Blanchard, "Contrôle au faciès," 13–14.

29. Nikki Jones, "'The Regular Routine': Proactive Policing and Adolescent Development among Young, Poor Black Me," in *Pathways to Adulthood for Disconnected Young Men in Low-Income Communities*, ed. Kevin Roy, Nikki Jones, et al. (San Francisco: Jossey-Bass, 2014), 34;

Nikki Jones, *The Chosen Ones: Black Men and the Politics of Redemption* (Berkeley: University of California Press, 2018), 91.

30. Ronan Maël, "Des milliers de policiers s'échangent des messages racistes sur un groupe Facebook," *Street Press*, April 6, 2020, https://www.streetpress.com/sujet/1591288577-milliers-policiers-echangent-messages-racistes-groupe-facebook-racisme-violences-sexisme.

31. Human Rights Watch, *"They Talk to Us Like We're Dogs,"* 1.

32. This attack was reported widely in the media. David Perrotin, "À côté de Michel Zecler, de jeunes artistes traumatisés par leur violente interpellation," *Mediapart*, January 13, 2021, https://www.mediapart.fr/journal/france/130121/cote-de-michel-zecler-de-jeunes-artistes-traumatises-par-leur-violente-interpellation.

33. This case received wide media coverage. See especially "Les images accablantes du tir de LBD qui a mutilé Adnane Nassih," *Libération*, May 4, 2021, https://www.youtube.com/watch?v=Oo-9ELO2xiY&t=1s; and "Mutilé par un tir de LBD à 7 mètres: Des images de vidéo-surveillance accablent un policier de la BAC," *L'Obs*, May 5, 2021, https://www.nouvelobs.com/societe/20210505.OBS43666/mutile-par-un-tir-de-lbd-a-7-metres-des-images-de-video surveillance-accablent-un-agent-de-la-bac.html.

34. Tristan Goldbronn, *Sélom et Matisse: Pourquoi des jeunes courent*, *RadioParleur*, August 21, 2021, https://radioparleur.net/2021/07/03/selom-et-matisse-episode-1-enquete-podcast-2/.

35. The horrific event was widely reported in the media and video published on Facebook by journalists Nadir Dendoune and Twitter by journalist and activist Taha Bouhafs. See, for example, Service Actu, "Un bicot comme ça, ça ne nage pas': Racisme et violences policières en Seine-Saint-Denis," *Les Inrockuptibles*, April 27, 2020, https://www.lesinrocks.com/actu/un-bicot-comme-ca-ca-ne-nage-pas-racisme-et-violences-policieres-en-seine-saint-denis-151584-27-04-2020/.

36. Human Rights Watch, *"The Root of Humiliation": Abusive Identity Checks in France.* Accessed January 2012, https://www.hrw.org/sites/default/files/reports/france0112ForUpload.pdf.

37. Human Rights Watch, *"The Roots of Humiliation."*

38. Human Rights Watch, *"They Talk to Us Like We're Dogs,"* 24. As the interview was translated into English, it is unclear if the term was *nègre* or *négro*, both of which are n-words in this context.

39. Brittney Cooper, *Beyond Respectability: The Intellectual Thought of Race Women* (Urbana: University of Illinois Press, 2017), 5; Craig Calhoun, "Social Theory and the Politics of Identity," in *Social Theory and the Politics of Identity*, ed. Craig Calhoun (Malden, MA: Blackwell, 2003), 20–21.

40. Jean-Pierre Mignard and Emmanuel Tordjman, *L'Affaire Clichy: Morts pour rien* (Paris: Stock, 2006), 48–49.

41. Mignard and Tordjman, *L'Affaire Clichy*, 48–49.

42. Laila Amine, *Postcolonial Paris: Fictions of Intimacy in the City of Light* (Madison: University of Wisconsin Press, 2018), 151.

43. Amnesty International News, *France: Shootings, Killings and Alleged Ill-Treatment by Law Enforcement Officers*, October 11, 1994, https://www.amnesty.org/en/documents/eur21/002/1994/en/.

44. Amnesty International, *France*.

45. Amnesty International, *France*.

46. Amnesty International, *France*.

47. Fabien Leboucq and Sarah Boumghar, "Si, Malik Oussekine est bien mort après avoir été victime de violences policières, contrairement à ce qu'affirme un directeur du 'Figaro,'" *Libération*, August 6, 2019, https://www.liberation.fr/checknews/2019/08/06/si-malik-ous sekine-est-bien-mort-apres-avoir-ete-victime-de-violences-policieres-contrairement -a-ce-_1743995/?redirected=1.

48. University students, joined by immigrant advocate groups, had taken to the streets against proposed hikes in university fees whose intent was to create competition among public universities, among other rejected reforms (i.e., *Le projet de loi Devaquet*) and the infamous Pasqua laws of 1986, which were seen as targeting African and Muslim immigration. These laws both facilitated the deportation of the undocumented and restricted citizenship acquisition of children born of that immigration.

49. Fassin, *Enforcing Order*, 135. In citing Etienne Balibar, Fassin also writes, "power must be not only violent, powerful, brutal but also 'cruel'; that is why it must draw from itself and produce for those who exercise it an effect of 'enjoyment.'"

50. Phillip Goff, Jennifer Eberhardt, et. al., "Not Yet Human: Implicit Knowledge, Historical Dehumanization, and Contemporary Consequences," *Journal of Personality and Social Psychology* 94 (2008): 305.

51. Max Weber, "Politics as a Vocation," in *From Max Weber: Essays in Sociology*, trans. H. H. Gerth and C. Wright Mills (Oxford: Oxford University Press), 78.

52. Fassin, *Enforcing Order*, 126–127.

53. Nancy Scheper-Hughes and Philippe Bourgois, *Violence in War and Peace* (Malden, MA: Blackwell, 2005), 1.

54. Frantz Fanon, *The Wretched of the Earth* (New York: Grove Press, 1968), 8.

55. Dominic Thomas, *Africa and France: Postcolonial Cultures, Migration, and Racism* (Bloomington: Indiana University Press, 2013), 193. See also Thomas, *Black France: Colonialism, Immigration, and Transnationalism* (Bloomington: Indiana University Press, 2007).

56. Fanon, *Wretched*, 7, 16.

57. Rigouste, *La Domination Policière*, 53.

58. Fassin, *Enforcing Order*, Kindle.

59. Fassin, *Enforcing Order*, Kindle.

60. Fassin, *Enforcing Order*, Kindle.

61. All references to this class action result from a communiqué shared by a research informant involved in this case. Interviewee, email to author, January 27, 2021.

62. Insights shared during a symposium on police violence that I co-organized on April 11, 2021. See also Jérémie Gauthier, "Le contrôle au faciès devant les juges. Entretien avec Slim Ben Achour," *La Vie Volée*, February 2, 2018, https://laviedesidees.fr/Le-controle-au-facies -devant-les-juges.html.

63. "George Zimmerman Sues Trayvon Martin's Family for $100 Million in Damages," CBS News, December 4, 2019, https://www.nbcnews.com/news/us-news/george-zimmerman-sues-trayvon-martin-s-family-100-million-damages-n1095916.

64. Stop le Contrôle au Faciès (Action contre les contrôles abusifs), Facebook, https://www.bibguru.com/g/chicago-facebook-post-citation/.

65. Human Rights Watch, *"They Talk to Us Like We're Dogs"*; Open Society Justice Initiative, *Challenging Ethnic Profiling in Europe: A Guide for Campaigners and Organizers* (Paris: Open Society Foundation, 2021); Marion Guémas, *Maintien de l'ordre: A quel Prix? Enquête sur l'évolution des pratiques de maintien de l'ordre en France et leurs incidences sur les libertés* (Paris: L'ACAT, 2020).

66. See Cour de Cassation, "Contrôles d'identité discriminatoires (09.11.16)," https://www.courdecassation.fr/communiques_4309/contr_identite_discriminatoires_09.11.16_35479.html#:~:text=La%20d%C3%A9cision%20de%20la%20Cour,la%20responsabilit%C3%A9%20de%20ol'Etat.

67. Human Rights Watch, *"They Talk to Us Like We're Dogs,"* 12.

68. Open Society Justice Initiative, *Challenging Ethnic Profiling in Europe*, 6.

69. See Cour de Cassation, "Contrôles d'identité discriminatoires."

70. See Cour de Cassation, "Contrôles d'identité discriminatoires."

71. Human Rights Watch, *"They Talk to Us Like We're Dogs,"* 27–28.

72. Open Society Justice Initiative, *Challenging Ethnic Profiling in Europe*, 128.

73. Défenseur des droits, *Enquête sur l'accès au droits: relations police/population: Le cas des contrôles d'identité* (Paris: République Française, 2017), 28.

74. Fabien Jobard, "Policing the Banlieues," in *Policing in France*, ed. Jacques de Maillard and Wesley Skogan (New York: Routledge, 2021), 198, Kindle.

75. Angelique Chrisafis, "French Police Brutality in Spotlight Again after Officer Charged with Rape," *Guardian*, February 6, 2017, https://www.theguardian.com/world/2017/feb/06/french-police-brutality-in-spotlight-again-after-officer-charged-with. Cf. "'Affaire Théo L.': Le CSA épingle une chronique de Canteloup sur Europe 1," *Le Monde*, July 31, 2017, https://www.lemonde.fr/actualite-medias/article/2017/07/31/affaire-theo-l-le-csa-epingle-une-chronique-de-canteloup-sur-europe-1_5167161_3236.html.

76. William Cohen, *The French Encounter with Africans, 1530–1880* (Bloomington: Indiana University Press, 1980), 15, 20.

77. Human Rights Watch, *"They Talk to Us Like We're Dogs,"* 35–36.

78. Human Rights Watch, *"They Talk to Us Like We're Dogs,"* 13.

79. Fabien Jobard and Jacques de Maillard, "Identity Checks as a Professional Repertoire," in *Policing in France*, Kindle.

80. European Union Agency for Fundamental Rights (FRA), *Second European Union Minorities and Discrimination Survey (EU-MIDIS II): Being Black in the EU* (Luxembourg: Publications Office of the European Union, 2018), 30.

81. Jerome Karabel, "The Other Capital Punishment," *HuffPost*, December 10, 2014, https://www.huffpost.com/entry/the-other-capital-punishment_b_6301928; Frank Edwards, Michael

H. Esposito, and Hedwig Lee, "Risk of Police-Involved Death by Race/Ethnicity and Place, United States, 2012–2018," *American Journal of Public Health* 108 (2018), https://ajph.aphapublications.org/doi/abs/10.2105/AJPH.2018.304559.

82. Washington Post Police Shootings Database, *Washington Post*, https://www.washingtonpost.com/graphics/investigations/police-shootings-database/.

83. "Black Americans 2.5X More Likely Than Whites to Be Killed by Police," *Statista*, June 2, 2020, https://www.statista.com/chart/21872/map-of-police-violence-against-black-americans/.

84. Mapping Police Violence, https://mappingpoliceviolence.org/. Researchers note that in 2019 their data show that "black Americans were nearly three times more likely to die from police than white Americans. Other statistics showed that black Americans were nearly one-and-a-half times more likely to be unarmed before their death."

85. Mapping Police Violence, https://mappingpoliceviolence.org/.

86. For more on this period, including how the success of the FN in the elections "forced both the mainstream right and mainstream left to engage with exclusionary visions that had demonstrable public appeal," see Rita Chin, *The Crisis of Multiculturalism in Europe: A History* (Princeton, NJ: Princeton University Press, 2017), 166, Kindle. See also Adrian Favell, *Philosophies of Integration: Immigration and the Idea of Citizenship in France and Britain* (London: Palgrave MacMillan, 1998).

87. Roy and Simbille, "Base de données," *Basta!*, https://bastamag.net/webdocs/police/.

88. Roy and Simbille, "Base de données," *Basta!*.

89. Roy and Simbille, "Base de données," *Basta!*.

90. Roy and Simbille, "Base de données," *Basta!*.

91. *Ni Pute Ni Soumises*, "Neither Whore Nor Submissive," references both mobilizations and an association founded in 2002 in France to bring greater attention to violence against Muslim girls and women. See Fadela Amara and Sylvia Zappi, *Ni Putes Ni Soumises* (Paris: La Decouverte, 2003) and Keaton, *Muslim Girls and the Other France*. *Pute* ("whore") also addresses how abusive police refer to outer-city girls and women.

92. Loïc Wacquant, *Les Prisons de la misère* (Paris: Raison d'Agir, 1999); Wacquant, *Punishing the Poor: The Neoliberal Government of Social Insecurity* (Durham, NC: Duke University Press, 2009).

93. Jacques de Maillard and Mathieu Zagrodzki, "Community Policing Initiatives in France," in *Policing in France*.

94. Guémas, *Maintien de l'ordre*, 68.

95. "'Gilets jaunes': Quatre questions sur l'enquête réclamée par l'ONU sur l''usage excessif de la force' lors des manifestations," France Info, March 7, 2019, https://www.francetvinfo.fr/economie/transports/gilets-jaunes/gilets-jaunes-quatre-questions-sur-l-enquete-reclamee-par-l-onu-sur-l-usage-excessif-de-la-force-lors-des-manifestations_3221937.html.

96. United Nations' Human Rights Council, "A/HRC/RES/43/1," adopted by the Human Rights Council on June 19, 2020, to promote and protect "the human rights and fundamental freedoms of Africans and of people of African descent against excessive use of force and other

human rights violations by law enforcement officers," June 30, 2020, https://undocs.org/A/HRC/RES/43/1.

97. United Nations' Human Rights Council, "Human Rights Council Holds an Urgent Debate on Current Racially Inspired Human Rights Violations, Systemic Racism, Police Brutality and Violence against Peaceful Protests," June 17, 2020, https://www.ohchr.org/EN/NewsEvents/Pages/DisplayNews.aspx?NewsID=25971&LangID=E.

98. *Brut*, "Entretien exclusif: Emmanuel Macron répond à Brut," YouTube, December 4, 2020, https://www.youtube.com/watch?v=IvkewyupR_8.

99. Gérard Davet, "Mort de Lamine Dieng: L'IGS écarte la responsabilité des fonctionnaires," *Le Monde*, July 10, 2007, https://www.lemonde.fr/societe/article/2007/07/10/mort-de-lamine-dieng-l-igs-ecarte-la-responsabilite-des-fonctionnaires_933823_3224.html.

100. Collectif Angles Morts, *Permis de Tuer*, 49.

101. Dominique Day, "The Role of Race: The Practice of Pivoting to Police as Problem-Solvers in Uncertain Times," Keynote address, The Police Violence Symposium, April 5, 2021, Dartmouth College, Hanover, New Hampshire.

102. On this point, see also Fanon, *Black Skin, White Masks*, 157.

103. Vivienne Walt, "How Assa Traoré Became the Face of France's Movement for Racial Justice," *Time*, December 11, 2020, https://time.com/5919814/guardians-of-the-year-2020-assa-traore/.

104. Assa Traoré with Elsa Vigoureaux, *Lettre à Adama: Vérité et Justice* (Paris: Seuil, 2017), 16–17.

105. Lucie Soullier, "Affaire Adama Traoré: Une expertise réalisée à la demande de la famille met en cause les gendarmes," *Le Monde*, March 4, 2021, https://www.lemonde.fr/societe/article/2021/03/04/affaire-adama-traore-une-expertise-realisee-a-la-demande-de-la-famille-met-en-cause-les-gendarmes_6071972_3224.html.

106. Soullier, "Affaire Adama Traoré."

107. Michael LaForgia and Jennifer Valentino-DeVries, "How a Genetic Trait in Black People Can Give the Police Cover," *New York Times*, May 15, 2021, https://www.nytimes.com/2021/05/15/us/african-americans-sickle-cell-police.html?referringSource=articleShare.

108. Dorothy Roberts, *Fatal Invention: How Science, Politics, and Big Business Re-create Race in the Twenty-First Century* (New York: The New Press, 2011), 113.

109. Joseph Graves and Alan Goodman, *Racism Not Race: Answers to Frequently Asked Questions* (New York: Columbia University Press, 2021), 40.

110. LaForgia and Valentino-DeVries, "How a Genetic Trait in Black People Can Give the Police Cover."

111. Nicholas Shapiro and Terence Keel, "'Natural Causes?' 59 Autopsies Prove Otherwise Evaluating the Autopsies of 59 Deaths in Los Angeles County Jails, 2009–2019" (Los Angeles: The Carceral Ecologies Lab and The BioCritical Studies Lab, 2022), 2, https://www.terencekeel.com/_files/ugd/022b3a_411d290629ae455fb6323a4d80375150.pdf.

112. Laurent Bonelli, "We Can't Breathe Either," *Le Monde Diplomatique*, July 2020, https://mondediplo.com/2020/07/02police.

113. Jason Smith and David Merolla, "Black, Blue, and Blow: The Effect of Race and Criminal History on Perceptions of Police Violence," *Sociological Inquiry*, 89: 624–644, https://doi.org/10.1111/soin.12275.

114. See, for instance, "French Appeals Court Sentences Cop for Shooting Man in Back," Radio France International, March 11, 2017, https://www.rfi.fr/en/france/20170311-french-appeals-court-sentences-cop-shooting-man-back.

115. Alban Elkaïm, "Dans l'affaire Amine Bentounsi, 'comme un sentiment de toute puissance' chez le policier accusé," *Bondy Blog*, March 17, 2017, https://www.bondyblog.fr/societe/police-justice/dans-laffaire-amine-bentounsi-comme-un-sentiment-de-toute-puissance-chez-le-policier-accuse/.

116. Magda Boutros, "La police et les indésirables," *La vie des idées*, September 14, 2018, https://laviedesidees.fr/La-police-et-les-indesirables.html.

117. Jacques Toubon, "Observations devant le tribunal judiciaire de Paris présentées dans le cadre de l'article 33 de la loi n° 2011–333 du 29 mars 2011," March 29, 2011. This document, issued by the French Rights Defender about the 12th arrondissement case, was shared by an informant via email, March 11, 2021. See also Gauthier, "Le contrôle au faciès devant les juges."

118. Toubon, "Observations devant le tribunal judiciaire de Paris."

119. Press conference, attorney's offices, July 2017.

120. Press conference, attorney's offices, July 2017.

121. Nikki Jones, *The Chosen Ones: Black Men and the Politics of Redemption* (Berkeley: University of California Press, 2018), 97.

122. Boutros, "La police et les indésirables."

123. Press Conference, attorney's offices, July 2017.

124. Kyle G. Brown, "Questioning Authority: What the Evolution of policing Can Teach Us about Today's Law Enforcement," *CBC Radio-Canada*, February 8, 2021, https://www.cbc.ca/radio/ideas/questioning-authority-what-the-evolution-of-policing-can-teach-us-about-today-s-law-enforcement-1.5905428. See also Jennifer Boittin, *Undesirable: Passionate Mobility and Women's Defiance of French Colonial Policing, 1919–1952*.

125. *Police, illégitime violence*, dir. Marc Ball (Talweg Productions, 2018), 12:48–13:12.

126. Fanon, *Wretched*, 39.

127. See also "Framing Everyday Antiblackness" in the appendix for more context on my variations of "racism without race."

CODA

1. Mitchell Abidor and Miguel Lago, "France's Old Bigotry Finds a New Face," *New York Times*, December 2, 2021, https://www.nytimes.com/2021/12/02/opinion/eric-zemmour-france-jews.html.

2. See Chin, *The Crisis of Multiculturalism*, on this point.

3. Bennetta Jules-Rosette, *Josephine Baker in Art and Life: The Icon and the Image* (Urbana: University of Illinois Press, 2007).

4. Tyler Stovall, *Paris Noir: African Americans in the City of Light* (Boston: Houghton Mifflin, 1996); Kaiama L. Glover, ed., *Josephine Baker: A Century in the Spotlight*, Special Double Issue, *Scholar and Feminist Online*, 6, nos. 1–2 (Fall, 2007–Spring 2008); see also Glover's essay, "Josephine Baker," https://www.100years100women.net/participants-round2/project-one-kkt3n-eca4n; Terri Simone Francis, *Josephine Baker's Cinematic Prism* (Bloomington: Indiana University Press, 2021); Florence Ladd, *The Spirit of Josephine Baker* (Scotts Valley, CA: Create Space Independent Publishing, 2014); Matthew Pratt Guterl, *Josephine Baker and the Rainbow Tribe* (Cambridge, MA: Harvard University Press, 2014); Ayo Abiétou Coly, "Housing and Homing the Black Female Body in France: Calixthe Beyala and the Legacy of Sarah Baartman and Joseph Baker," *Black Womanhood: Images, Icons, and Ideologies of the African Body* (2008): 258–277.

5. Fanon, *Black Skin, White Masks*, 101.

6. "REPLAY: Josephine Baker Becomes First Black Woman to Enter France's Panthéon," France 24 English, YouTube, November 30, 2021, https://www.youtube.com/watch?v=CdLQsVqHiaE.

7. "REPLAY," France 24 English.

8. Brent Hayes Edwards, *The Practice of Diaspora: Literature, Translation, and the Rise of Black Internationalism* (Cambridge, MA: Harvard University Press, 2003), 119.

9. Maryse Condé, "Body and Soul: Josephine, Jane and Paulette," in *Josephine Baker: A Century in the Spotlight*, 2.

10. Camille Polloni and David Perrotin, "Dans l'Essonne, un 'harcèlement discriminatoire' par amendes interposées," *Mediapart*, December 9, 2021, https://www.mediapart.fr/journal/france/091221/dans-l-essonne-un-harcelement-discriminatoire-par-amendes-interposees.

11. Fabien Leboucq, "75 % des policiers votent-ils pour l'extrême droite?" *Libération*, June 12, 2020, https://www.liberation.fr/france/2020/06/12/75-des-policiers-votent-ils-pour-l-extreme-droite_1791112/.

12. Matti Faye, "CARTE. Résultats législatives 2022: Les députés Rassemblement National (RN) élus à l'Assemblée," *France Info*, June 19, 2022, https://france3-regions.francetvinfo.fr/grand-est/carte-resultats-legislatives-2022-les-deputes-rassemblement-national-elus-a-l-assemblee-2564092.html.

APPENDIX

1. Philomena Essed, *Understanding Everyday Racism: An Interdisciplinary Theory* (Newbery Park, CA: Sage Publications, 1991).

2. Essed, *Understanding Everyday Racism*, 145.

3. Essed, *Understanding Everyday Racism*, 147.

4. Lewis Gordon, *What Fanon Said: A Philosophical Introduction to His Life and Thought* (New York: Fordham University Press, 2015), Kindle.

5. bell hooks, *Teaching to Transgress: Education as the Practice of Freedom* (New York: Routledge, 1994), 49; cf. Gayatri Spivak, "Preface to Concerning Violence," *Film Quarterly*, October 29, 2014, https://filmquarterly.org/2014/10/29/preface-to-concerning-violence/.

6. Frantz Fanon, *Peau noire, masques blancs* (Paris: Éditions Seuil, 1952), 111.

7. Lewis Gordon, *Bad Faith and Antiblack Racism* (New York: Humanity Books, 1999).

8. Ronald T. Judy, "Fanon's Body of Black Experience," in *Fanon: A Critical Reader*, ed. Lewis R. Gordon et al. (Oxford: Blackwell, 1996), 61.

9. Paget Henry, "Africana Phenomenology: Its Philosophical Implications," *Worlds and Knowledges Otherwise* 11, no. 1 (2006): 6.

10. Michelle Wright, *Becoming Black: Creating Identity in the African Diaspora* (Durham, NC: Duke University Press, 2004), 27.

11. Frantz Fanon, *The Wretched of the Earth* (New York: Grove Press, 1968), 150.

12. Fanon, *The Wretched of the Earth*, 150, Kindle. Karim Murji and John Solomos, in their edited volume, *Racialization: Studies in Theory and Practice* (Oxford: Oxford University Press, 2005), note that Robert Miles traces the origins of his conceptualization of racialization to Fanon, 139.

13. Karim Murji and John Solomos, *Racialization: Studies in Theory and Practice*, 97, Kindle. Cf. Stephen Small, *Racialised Barriers: The Black Experience in the United States and England in the 1980s* (New York: Routledge, 1994).

14. Murji and Solomos, *Racialization*, 103–105, Kindle.

15. Gordon, *What Fanon Said*, Kindle.

16. Philomena Essed, *Understanding Everyday Racism: An Interdisciplinary Theory* (Newbury Park: Sage Publications, 1991), 2, 3, Kindle; *Everyday Racism: Reports from Women in Two Cultures* (Clarement, CA: Hunter House, 1990).

17. Essed, *Understanding Everyday Racism*, 120, 122.

18. Essed, *Everyday Racism*, 56.

19. Essed, *Everyday Racism*, 11.

20. Essed, *Understanding Everyday Racism*, 7.

21. Essed, *Understanding Everyday Racism*, 167.

22. Frantz Fanon, *Toward the African Revolution* (New York: Grove Press, 1967), 32.

23. Fanon, *Toward the African Revolution*, 32.

24. Fanon, *Toward the African Revolution*, 33.

25. Étienne Balibar, "Is There a 'Neo-Racism'?" in *Race, Nation, Class: Ambiguous Identities*, ed. Étienne Balibar and Immanuel Wallerstein (New York: Verso, 1991), 21.

26. Bonilla-Silva, *Racism without Racists*, 56, Kindle.

27. Trica Keaton, *Muslim Girls and the Other France: Race, Identity Politics, and Social Exclusion* (Bloomington: Indiana University Press, 2006).

28. For a succinct distillation of the theory, see "Everyday Racism," in *Encyclopedia of Race and Racism*, ed. John Hartwell Moore (New York: Macmillan, 2007), 448.

29. Gordon, *What Fanon Said*, Kindle.

30. Essed, *Everyday Racism*, 31.

31. Essed, *Everyday Racism*, 146.

32. Essed, *Everyday Racism*, 147.

33. Essed, *Everyday Racism*, 146, 147.

34. Essed, *Understanding Everyday Racism*, 5.

35. Essed, *Understanding Everyday Racism*, 160.

36. Essed, *Understanding Everyday Racism*, 161; Fanon, *Black Skin, White Masks*, 101, Kindle.

37. Essed, *Understanding Everyday Racism*, 34, Kindle.

38. Juliette Sméralda, "Foreword," *Peau noire, masques blancs* (Montreal: Kiyikaat Editions, 2015), 9.

39. For similar encounters, see Fleming, "On the Illegibility of French Antiblackness."

40. Essed, *Understanding Everyday Racism*.

41. France Winddance Twine, *A White Side of Black Britain* (Durham, NC: Duke University Press, 2010), 8, Kindle.

INDEX

Page numbers in italics indicate images.